About Island Press

Since 1984, the nonprofit organization Island Press has been stimulating, shaping, and communicating ideas that are essential for solving environmental problems worldwide. With more than 800 titles in print and some 40 new releases each year, we are the nation's leading publisher on environmental issues. We identify innovative thinkers and emerging trends in the environmental field. We work with world-renowned experts and authors to develop cross-disciplinary solutions to environmental challenges.

Island Press designs and executes educational campaigns in conjunction with our authors to communicate their critical messages in print, in person, and online using the latest technologies, innovative programs, and the media. Our goal is to reach targeted audiences—scientists, policymakers, environmental advocates, urban planners, the media, and concerned citizens—with information that can be used to create the framework for long-term ecological health and human well-being.

Island Press gratefully acknowledges major support of our work by The Agua Fund, The Andrew W. Mellon Foundation, Betsy & Jesse Fink Foundation, The Bobolink Foundation, The Curtis and Edith Munson Foundation, Forrest C. and Frances H. Lattner Foundation, G.O. Forward Fund of the Saint Paul Foundation, Gordon and Betty Moore Foundation, The Kresge Foundation, The Margaret A. Cargill Foundation, The Overbrook Foundation, The S.D. Bechtel, Jr. Foundation, The Summit Charitable Foundation, Inc., V. Kann Rasmussen Foundation, The Wallace Alexander Gerbode Foundation, and other generous supporters.

The opinions expressed in this book are those of the author(s) and do not necessarily reflect the views of our supporters.

HOW TO STUDY PUBLIC LIFE

HOW TO STUDY PUBLIC LIFE

Jan Gehl and Birgitte Svarre

Translation by Karen Ann Steenhard

ISLANDPRESS | Washington | Covelo | London

Island Press is a trademark of Island Press The Center for Resource Economics.

Gehl, Jan, 1936-
    [Bylivsstudier. English]
    How to study public life / by Jan Gehl and Birgitte Svarre ; translation by Karen Ann Steenhard.
        p. cm.
    Translation of the author's Bylivsstudier.
    Includes bibliographical references.
    ISBN-13: 978-1-61091-423-9 (cloth : alk. paper)
    ISBN-10: 1-61091-423-6 (cloth : alk. paper) 1. City planning.
        2. Public spaces—Social aspects. I. Svarre, Birgitte. II. Title.
    HT166.G43713 2013
    307.1'216—dc23
                        2013023649

Printed on recycled, acid-free paper

Manufactured in the United States of America
10 9 8 7 6 5

Project team
Camilla Richter-Friis van Deurs, graphic layout and cover
Annie Matan, project assistant
Kristian Skaarup, project assistant
Emmy Laura Perez Fjalland, student assistant
Johan Stoustrup, student assistant
Janne Bjørsted, student assistant

English translation
Karen Ann Steenhard

This project was conducted as a research project under the auspices of Gehl Architects Urban Quality Consultants, Copenhagen.

The project was made possible with the financial support of Realdania, Copenhagen.

Keywords: Action research, area studies, behavioral mapping, diary method, GPS, modernism, pedestrian activity, pedestrian realm, photo documentation, shadowing, social responsibility, stationary activity, simulation laboratory, sustainability, time-lapse photography, tracking, urban policy

Shinjuku Station, Tokyo, Japan. Approximately 1990.

Contents

Foreword by George Ferguson

Jan Gehl has devoted a lifetime to the field of public life studies, which has developed since the sixties when, as a young student of architecture, I first became aware of his work. Gehl's vision is one of making cities fit for people. He and his colleagues, including Birgitte Svarre, have written about it and advised cities, developers, NGOs and governments.

This book goes behind the scenes and reveals the variety of tools in the public life studies toolbox. A proper understanding of its application is vital to all those involved in city planning and others responsible for the quality of life in our cities.

As more of us move to the city, the quality of urban life moves higher on both the local and global political agendas. Cities are the platform where urgent matters such as environmental and climate questions, a growing urban population, demographic changes, and social and health challenges must be addressed.

Cities compete to attract citizens and investment. Should that competition not be focused on the quality of life, on the experience of living in, working in, and visiting cities rather than on those superficial aspects represented by the tallest building, the biggest spaces or the most spectacular monuments?

This fascinating book's examples from Melbourne, Copenhagen, New York and elsewhere illustrate how, by understanding people's behaviour and systematically surveying and documenting public life, our emphasis can change.

Major changes can take place by using public life studies as one of the political tools. Think back five years; nobody would have dreamt of turning Times Square into a people place rather than a traffic space. Public life study was a key part of the process that enabled it to be realized so successfully.

'Look and learn' is the underlying motto of this book: get out in the city, see how it works, use your common sense, use all senses, and then ask whether this is the city we want in the 21st century? City life is complex, but with simple tools and systematic research it becomes more understandable.

When we get a clearer image of the status of life in cities, or even just start to focus on life, not on individual buildings or technicalities, then we can also ask more qualified questions about what it is we want – and then public life studies can become a political tool for change.

The study of public life represents a cross-disciplinary approach to planning and building cities, where the work is never finished, where you always take a second look, learn, and adjust – always putting people first. It is the essence of good urbanism.

George Ferguson CBE, PPRIBA
Mayor of City of Bristol, United Kingdom

Preface

Public life studies are straightforward. The basic idea is for observers to walk around while taking a good look. Observation is the key, and the means are simple and cheap. Tweaking observations into a system provides interesting information about the interaction of public life and public space.

This book is about how to study the interaction between public life and public space. This type of systematic study began in earnest in the 1960s, when several researchers and journalists on different continents criticized the urban planning of the time for having forgotten life in the city. Transport engineers concentrated on traffic; landscape architects dealt with parks and green areas; architects designed buildings; and urban planners looked at the big picture. Design and structure got serious attention, but public life and the interaction between life and space was neglected. Was that because it wasn't needed? Did people really just want housing and cities that worked like machines? Criticism that newly built residential areas lacked vitality did not come only from professionals. The public at large strongly criticized modern, newly built residential areas whose main features were light, air and convenience.

The academic field encompassing public life studies, which is described in this book, tries to provide knowledge about human behavior in the built environment on an equal footing with knowledge about buildings and transport systems, for example. The original goal is the same goal today: to recapture public life as an important planning dimension.

Although the concept of public life may seem banal compared to complex transport systems, reinvigorating it is no simple task. This is true in cities where public life has been squeezed almost into nonexistence, as well as in cities that have an abundance of pedestrian life, but a depressed economy that prevents establishing the basic conditions for a decent walking and biking environment.

It takes political will and leadership to address the public life issue. Public life studies can serve as an important tool for improving urban spaces by qualifying the goal of having more people-friendly cities. Studies can be used as input in the decision-making process, as part of overall planning, or in designing individual projects such as streets, squares or parks.

Life is unpredictable, complex and ephemeral, so how on Earth can anyone plan how life might play out in cities? Well, of course, it is not possible to pre-program the interaction between public life and space in detail, but targeted studies can provide a basic understanding of what works and what does not, and thus suggest qualified solutions.

The book is anchored in Jan Gehl's almost 50 years of work examining the interplay between public life and public space. He honed his interest in the subject as a researcher and teacher at the School of Architecture, The Royal Danish Academy of Fine Arts in Copenhagen, and in practice at Gehl Architects, where he is a founding partner. Thus many of the examples in the book come from Jan Gehl's work. The book's second author, Birgitte Svarre, received her research education at the Center for Public Space Research at

The Royal Danish Academy of Fine Arts, School of Architecture. The center was established in 2003 under Jan Gehl's leadership. Birgitte Svarre has a master's degree in modern culture and cultural communication and thus carries on the interdisciplinary tradition that is characteristic of the field of public life studies.

Our goal with this book is twofold: we want to inspire people generally to take public life seriously in all planning and building phases, and we want to provide tools and inspiration from specific examples of how public life can be studied simply and cheaply.

Our hope is that the book will inspire readers to go into the city and study the interaction between city space and city life in order to acquire more knowledge and to qualify the work regarding living conditions in cities. The book focuses on tools and process, not results. In this context, these tools – or methods, if you prefer – should not be seen as anything other than different ways of studying the interaction between city life and city space. They are offered as an inspiration as well as a challenge to develop them further, always adjusted to local conditions.

The first chapter gives a general introduction to public life study. Chapter 2 presents a number of basic questions in this field of studies. Chapter 3 provides an overview of tools used to study the interaction of public space and public life. Chapter 4 summarizes the social history and academic background for public life studies. Key people and ongoing themes tie the field together. Chapter 5 contains several reports from research frontlines with various views on public life studies. Early studies are emphasized, because the methods were developed in order to describe the considerations about their use and further development. Chapter 6 reviews examples from practice, the so-called public space-public life studies developed by Jan Gehl, and later Gehl Architects, and used systematically since the end of the 1960s in many different cities: large, medium, small, located north, south, east and west. Therefore, today there is a large body of material from which to draw conclusions. Chapter 7 recounts the history of the use of public life studies in Copenhagen as a political tool. In conclusion, public life studies are put into a historic, social and academic perspective – in relation to research as well as practice.

Although the book is a collaborative effort between two authors, it would not have been possible without the rest of the team: Camilla Richter-Friis van Deurs, responsible for layout and graphics; Annie Matan, Kristian Skaarup, Emmy Laura Perez Fjalland, Johan Stoustrup and Janne Bjørsted for their various types of motivated and qualified input and effort. Once again, it was a pleasure to work with Karen Steenhard on the English translation of the book.

Our heartfelt thanks go to Gehl Architects for workspace, assistance and an inspiring environment – and a particular thanks to the many colleagues, partners and other friends of the firm who helped with photographs and as sparring partners. Special thanks to Lars Gemzøe, to Tom Nielsen for his constructive reading of draft texts and to Island Press, Heather Boyer in particular, as well as the Danish publisher Bogværket.

We thank Realdania for their support of the project idea and the financial assistance to help make it happen.

Jan Gehl and Birgitte Svarre
Copenhagen, May 2013

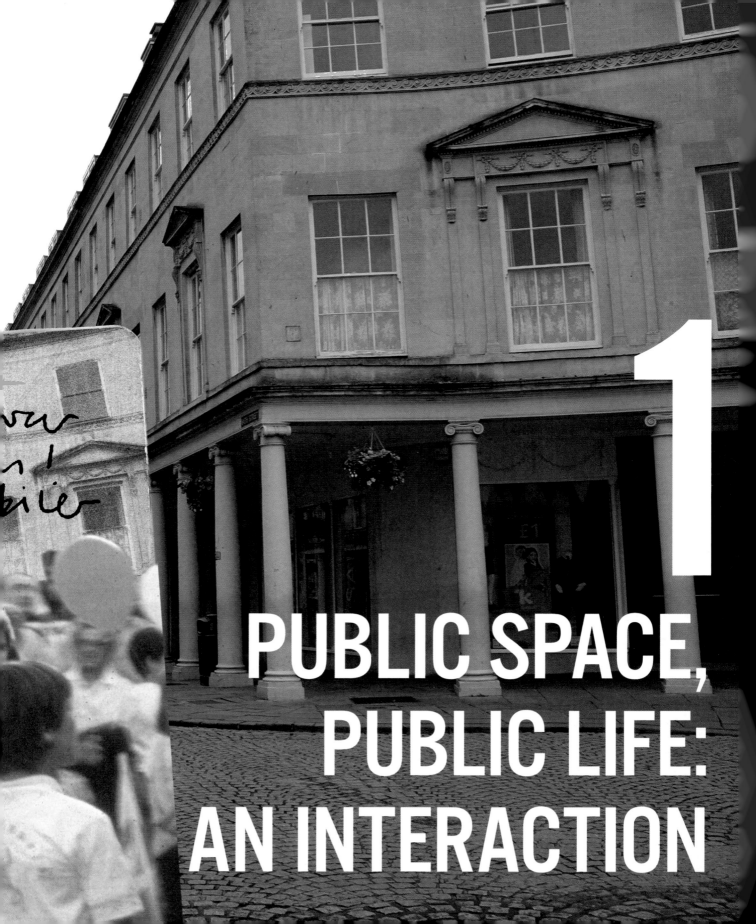

PUBLIC SPACE, PUBLIC LIFE: AN INTERACTION

1

Like the weather, life is difficult to predict. None-theless, meteorologists have developed methods enabling them to predict the weather, and over the years their methods have become so refined that they can make forecasts with greater accuracy and reach. The methods described in this book also deal with foreseeing phenomena in constant flux, but the focus here is how life unfolds in city space. Just as with weather forecasting, this doesn't mean that anyone can develop a sure-fire method to predict how people will use a particular city space. Masses of data have been gathered over the years concerning the interaction of life and space in cities, and just like meteorologists' knowledge about the weather, this data can provide greater understanding of city life and predict how it will presumably unfold in the given framework.

This book describes the methods that have been developed over the past 50 years to study the interaction between public life and space. They are tools to help us understand how we use public space so that we can make it better and more functional. Observation is the key for most of the studies presented in the book.

It has been necessary to develop, almost from scratch, special tools for looking at people because people's use of cities has been overlooked, while abstract concepts, large structures, traffic challenges and other amorphous issues have dominated urban planning.

Public Space and Public Life – on Speaking Terms

Good architecture ensures good interaction between public space and public life. But while architects and urban planners have been dealing with space, the other side of the coin – life – has often been forgotten. Perhaps this is because it is considerably easier to work with and communicate about form and space, while life is ephemeral and therefore difficult to describe.

Public life changes constantly in the course of a day, week, or month, and over the years. In addition, design, gender, age, financial resources, culture and many other factors determine how we use or do not use public space. There are many excellent reasons why it is difficult to incorporate the diverse nature of public life into architecture and urban planning. Nonetheless, it is essential if we are to create worthy surroundings for the billions of people who daily make their way between buildings in cities around the world.

In this context, public space is understood as streets, alleys, buildings, squares, bollards: everything that can be considered part of the built environment. Public life should also be understood in the broadest sense as everything that takes place between buildings, to and from school, on balconies, seated, standing, walking, biking, etc. It is everything we can go out and observe happening – far more than just street theatre and café life. However, we do not mean city life to be understood as the city's psychological well-being. Rather it is the complex and versatile life that unfolds in public space. It makes no difference whether our point of departure is Copenhagen, Dhaka, Mexico City, or a small city in Western Australia. The nub is the interplay between life and space in all its guises.

The Missing Tools

At the beginning of the 1960s, critical voices began to point out that something was very wrong in many of the new districts being built, in record numbers, during this period of rapid urban growth. Something was missing, something that was difficult to define, but was expressed in concepts like 'bedroom communities' and 'cultural impoverishment.' Life between buildings had been forgotten, pushed aside by cars, large-scale thinking, and overly rationalized, specialized processes. Among the critics of the time were Jane Jacobs and William H. Whyte in New York City, Christopher Alexander in Berkeley, and one of the authors of this book, Jan Gehl in Copenhagen.

Public life and public space were historically treated as a cohesive unit. Medieval cities grew little by little in accordance with changing needs, in contrast to the rapid tempo of modernism's large-scale planning.

Cities have grown gradually for hundreds of years, rooted in many years of experience and an intuitive feeling for human senses and scale. The organic growth of medieval cities encompassed a building tradition based on generations of experience in how to create cities with well-functioning interaction between life and space. But this knowledge was lost somewhere in the process of industrialization and modernization, which led to dysfunctional city environments for the important and yet ignored segment of city life on foot. Of course, society has changed since the Middle Ages. The solution is not to recreate pre-modern cities, but to develop contemporary tools that can be applied analytically to once again forge an alliance between life and space in cities.

The Contours of an Academic Field
The environmental design pioneers of the 1960s took the basic steps needed to better understand the ephemeral concept of public life and its interaction with public space and buildings. Their method was to study existing, and as a rule pre-industrial, cities and public space to gain basic knowledge about how we use and get around in cities.

Several books published from 1960 to the mid-1980s are still considered the basic textbooks for public life studies.[1] Although the methods described were later refined and new agendas and technologies emerged, the basic principles and methods were developed in that period.

Up to the mid-1980s, this work was carried out primarily at academic institutions. However, by the end of that decade, it was clear that the analyses and principles regarding public life and public space should be converted into tools that could be used directly in urban planning practice. City planners and politicians wanted to make conditions better for people in order to have an edge in inter-city competition. It became a strategic goal to create attractive cities for people in order to attract residents, tourists, investments and employees to fill new jobs in the knowledge society. Meeting this goal required understanding people's needs and behavior in cities.

From about the year 2000, it increasingly became taken for granted in the fields of architecture and urban planning practice generally that working with life in cities was crucial. Much bitter experience had shown that vibrant city life does not happen by itself. This is particularly noticeable in cities that are highly developed economically, because apart from commuters, people are no longer on the street by necessity to work, sell trinkets, do errands, and so on.

However, less economically viable cities are also impacted, because the rapidly growing volume of motorized traffic and related infrastructure provides obstacles for pedestrians and produces noise and air pollution for many people in their daily lives. The core of the matter is to get the large volumes of life in public spaces to function in a way that allows daily life to take place under decent conditions and partner with the physical framework instead of fighting against it.

Observations in the City
Direct observation is the primary tool of the type of public life studies described in this book. As a general rule, users are not actively involved in the sense of being questioned, rather they are observed, their activities and behavior mapped in order to better understand the needs of users and how city spaces are used. The direct observations help to understand why some spaces are used and others are not.

"...Please look closely at real cities. While you are looking, you might as well also listen, linger and think about what you see."[2]

Jane Jacobs

Studying people's behavior in public space can be compared to studying and structuring other forms of living organisms. They could be animals or cells: counting how many there are in total, how quickly they move under various conditions, and generally describing how they behave on the basis of systematic observation. People's behavior is documented, analyzed, and interpreted, but this is not done under the microscope. The observations are conducted with the naked eye and occasionally using cameras or other aids to zoom in on situations or fast-freeze the moment in order to analyze the situation more closely. The point is to sharpen the gaze of the observer.

A literary author who made a virtue out of describing ordinary life as it unfolds in public space was Frenchman Georges Perec (1936-82).[3] In *Species of Spaces and Other Pieces* (1974), Perec instructed his readers in how to see what is overlooked in the city.[4] He encouraged them to practice by occasionally taking notes of what they see, preferably using some type of system.

Perec wrote that if you don't notice anything, it is because you have not learned to observe. "You must try more slowly, almost foolishly. Force yourself to write down what is not of interest, the most banal, ordinary, colorless."[5] Life in the city can seem banal and fleeting, and therefore, according to Perec, the observer must look and take the time needed to really see the ordinariness unfolding in public space.

In *The Death and Life of Great American Cities* (1961), Jane Jacobs wrote in the preface to her descriptions of public life, primarily gathered from her own neighborhood of Greenwich Village in Manhattan: "The scenes that illustrate this book are all about us. For illustrations, please look closely at real cities. While you are looking, you might as well also listen, linger and think about what you see."[6] According to Jacobs, when you are in the city you should take the time to reflect over what you are sensing – note: using all your senses. Certainly the sense of sight is key to observation, but this does not mean closing down our other senses; on the contrary. It means focusing our attention and noticing the surroundings we move through quite unconsciously every day.

According to the *Macmillan* online dictionary, to observe means "to watch or study someone or something with care and attention in order to discover something".[7] And watching with care and attention is precisely what it takes to wrest useful knowledge from ordinary scenes. Anyone who decides to observe life in the city will quickly realize that you have to be systematic in order to get useful knowledge from the complex confusion of life in public space. Perhaps the person being observed is actually running an errand, but takes time to look at other people along the way, or catches sight of a protest march in the street that becomes all engrossing.

In general, the observer must be as neutral as the proverbial 'fly on the wall' – the party's benchwarmer rather than its lion, an invisible non-participant who takes in the big picture without taking part in the event. An observer can play various roles depending on the character of the study. The role of registrar, for example, counting units, where precision is the most important function. The registrar can also have an assessment role, categorizing people by age group, for example. Here the ability to evaluate is the most important function. Or the registrar's role can be analytical, keeping a detailed diary with a feeling for nuance, a trained eye and experienced sense of what type of information is relevant.

It is possible to train your eye in the art of observation. Naturally, there is a difference between the eye of a professional and a lay person, but in principle, anyone can observe city life. Beginners will need to hone their skills, see the world through new eyes and use tools advisedly, while the trained, professional eye can perceive new connections. However, there are great differences in the degree to which observers will understand the form aspects. If observers are also expected to interpret, they will need spatial training.

Man or Machine

In their revolt against modernism's abstract planning, city-life study pioneers such as Jane Jacobs, William H. Whyte and Jan Gehl encouraged people to see the interaction of city life and space with their own eyes, because it provides greater understanding. We believe this is still the critical starting point for going into the city to observe, using one's senses, common sense and simple registration techniques with pen and paper, which is why we emphasize these manual methods.

In using these manual methods, the observer is the human factor for good and ill. Technical solutions such as video surveillance cameras or GPS (Global Positioning System) tracking devices can sometimes serve as more objective solutions. The decision must be made as to the degree of precision needed and the form of knowledge wanted. The key difference is that human registration always brings more than cold facts to the table. When people are doing the counting, for example, they can add information from the site that can have decisive influence on interpretation. Observers often bring extra material home by using their senses and common sense. An automatic bicycle counter is set up on a bike path to count passing bikers. One day almost no bicyclists are registered. What the human registrar can see is that a van is parked on the bike path a few feet ahead of the automatic counter, so on that day the bicyclists veer around the counter. Naturally, the human registrar counts the bicycles anyway, noting the conditions and taking a picture, while the automatic counter simply registers a low number of bicyclists.

Ethical Considerations

When gathering data on human behavior, it is always important to weigh how and where ethical considerations should be made. Data should be anonymized. Legislation varies from country to country.

Observations are often accompanied by photo documentation. In Denmark, it is legal to photograph as long as the photos are taken from places that are 'freely accessible'. In other words, you are not allowed to enter private property without permission, but you can take a picture of someone standing in his own front yard, if that person can be seen with the naked eye from a public street. The rules serve a double purpose: to protect individuals from invasion of privacy and to protect the freedom of journalists and others to freely gather information.[8]

Photo series from Strøget, Copenhagen's main pedestrian street, illustrating what Jane Jacobs calls "sidewalk ballet."[9] The ballet is rendered in brief scenes in which life unfolds like a dance in public space. The example opposite shows a little ballet involving a bench in inner Copenhagen. The study of the nuances of bench use originate from an article by Jan Gehl, "People on Foot", from 1968.[10] The running dialog under the photographs was originally written in Danish by Jan Gehl together with Mark von Wodtke, who was part of the study group that conducted Copenhagen's first large public life study in 1968.

How is a bench used?

Jan Gehl, "People on Foot", Arkitekten no. 20/1968[11]
- Mark Von Vodtke

There's a bench.

A+B: "Great, let's sit..."

A+B: "... so I can puff on my pipe"
(The man in the background is still waiting.)

C: "Ah, an empty seat on the end: I'll grab that."

A+B: "Well, time to move on."

C: "This is a good place to sit."

C: "Here come two apprentices with paint all over their pants. I think I've been here long enough."

D+E: "Wow, did you get a look at her?"

There's an empty bench.

F: "Ah, an empty bench. I wonder if there are any red ones left?"

G: "This is a nice place. I'll sit at the opposite end. What on Earth is that white stuff? Fresh paint! – well, I'm not going to sit there"

F: "So he didn't really want to sit down. I guess I'll manage with my own company"... (The little guy is still waiting patiently in his stroller.)

H. 7.5 m

2 WHO, WHAT, WHERE?

It is necessary to ask questions systematically and divide the variety of activities and people into subcategories in order to get specific and useful knowledge about the complex interaction of life and form in public space. This chapter outlines several general study questions: how many, who, where, what, how long? An example is given showing how each basic question has been studied in various contexts.

The list of questions that can be asked about the interaction between life and form is essentially endless. The questions listed in the paragraph at left are the most basic, and, naturally, can be combined in any way. When asking where people stay, it is usually relevant to ask who they are, how long they are staying or some other combination of questions.

It is not possible to draw up a list of fixed questions that can be investigated in all areas or cities. Every city is unique, and observers must use their eyes, other senses and good common sense. Most important is that the context and site determine the methods and tools, and on the whole, how and when the study should be conducted.

However, common to all sites and situations is that at the very moment observers fasten their gaze on a group of people or types of activities or otherwise fix their attention on the diversity of activities, groupings, tendencies, etc., it becomes patently clear that the prospect is complex, overlapping and not easy to study. Different types of activities are interwoven: recreation and purposeful activities take place side by side. We can speak of chains of events – and of continuous change. Precisely because the interaction between life and space is so complex and difficult to pin down, it can be useful to ask basic questions in an insistent, journalistic manner, and to ask them again and again.

To focus attention on who, what, where and other basic questions can provide general knowledge about behavior in public space and special knowledge of a specific issue in practice. Studying these key questions can provide documentation and understanding of a given pattern of activity or concrete knowledge about who goes where or not in a given place. Thus these elementary questions can be used in practice as well as for more basic research purposes.

Once we begin observing city life and its interaction with physical surroundings, even the most ordinary street corner can provide interesting knowledge about the interplay of city life and form - anywhere in the world. We can systematize our observations by asking basic question like who, what and where.

Left: Cordoba, Argentina, where architect Miguel Angel Roca formulated a holistic strategy for an architectural and social urban policy in 1979-80.[1]

New Road, Brighton, England

How many people are walking and how many are stationary? In Brighton New Road, a public life study helped to determine use before and after improvements were made. The number of pedestrians rose by 62% after the street was converted into a pedestrian-priority street in 2006. The number of stationary activities increased by 600%.[2]

This type of before-and-after headcount quantifies the extent to which the initiative is used. In Brighton, the numbers document that New Road has shifted status from a transit street to a destination. Statistics like these can be used as a good argument for prioritizing other pedestrian projects, both local and general.

Before

After

Question 1. How Many?

Making a qualitative assessment by counting *how many* people do something makes it possible to measure what might otherwise seem ephemeral: city life. Almost all cities have a traffic department and precise data on how many cars drive through major arteries while departments for 'pedestrians and public life' are almost unknown, as are headcounts of people.

Counting provides quantitative data, which can be used to qualify projects and as arguments one way or the other in decision-making processes. Indisputable measurements can often serve as convincing arguments.

Starting with the question of *how many* is basic to public life studies. In principle, everything can be counted, but what is often registered is *how many* people are moving (pedestrian flow) and *how many* are staying in one place (stationary activity).

The question of *how many* or *how few* comes in several varieties in public life studies, such as before and after urban improvement projects. If we know *how many* people are staying in a square, and we then improve the square and count the number of people again, we can evaluate the success of the renewal project. If the objective was for more people to stay at the square, counting *how many* using the same methodology on comparable days will quickly reveal the degree of success or failure. Usually quite a number of counts have to be made in order to be able to compare different times of day, different days and different seasons.

A number on its own is seldom of interest. It is important that results can be compared. Therefore, it is essential to register precisely and comparably. Factual conditions like weather and time of day must also be noted consistently and precisely so that similar studies can be conducted at a later date.

Question 2. Who?

We see gathering knowledge about people's behavior in public space as the cornerstone of a public life study. When we say 'people', we mean widely different groups of people measured by various parameters. It is often relevant to be more specific about precisely *who* uses various public spaces. While registration can be done on the individual level, it is often more meaningful to investigate more general categories such as gender or age.

Basic knowledge about the behavior of various groups of people can be used to plan more precise ways of accommodating the needs of women, children, the elderly and disabled, for example. We emphasize these groups here because they are often overlooked.[3]

The general question of gender and age can be registered by observation, naturally allowing for a certain degree of inaccuracy in making a subjective evaluation of age group. It is difficult or impossible to categorize people with respect to job or economic situation, for example, on the basis of observation alone.

Bryant Park, New York City

Bryant Park is in the middle of Manhattan between Times Square and Grand Central Terminal. One possible indicator for whether a park is safe is the presence of a sufficient number of women. Every day at 1:00 and 6:00 p.m., the park officer walks systematically through Bryant Park and clicks on two counters to record the number of men and women, respectively. The park officer also notes weather conditions and temperature.[4]

In Bryant Park the ideal gender division is on the order of 52% women and 48% men. If the percentage of women falls, it could be a sign that park safety is on the wane. Weather conditions do play a role, however, as Bryant Park's data show that the number of women in the park increases in warmer weather.[5]

52% women

Question 3. Where?

Planners and architects can design public space on the basis of *where* people are expected to go and to stay. However, many trampled footpaths across otherwise pristine lawns attest to the fact that people do not always act as intended. In order to encourage crowds of pedestrians to flow smoothly and still create the best conditions for inviting people to use public space, it is vital to have basic and specific knowledge of *where* people move and stay in individual spaces. Studies of movement and staying can help uncover barriers and pinpoint where pedestrian paths and places to stay can be laid out.

If the study area is a delimited city space, it is often relevant to study where people stay: on the edges, in the middle or evenly distributed in the space? In public, semi-public or private zones? The *where* question allows observers to zoom in on positioning relevant to function or elements such as furniture, garden gates, entrances, doors, bollards, etc.

If the study area is a neighborhood or quarter, it can be relevant to determine *where* people and activities are gathered or dispersed to a greater or lesser degree. On the city level this can mean registering or localizing numerous functions, activities, direction of pedestrian flow and preferred places to stay.

Gråbrødre Torv, Copenhagen

Microclimate, the local climate of a specific site, can heavily impact whether people stay there. If people are walking from point A to point B, they can usually live with suboptimal wind, sun or shadow conditions, but for staying activites a place needs a higher level of climate quality.

This springtime photo from Grey Friars' Square in Copenhagen clearly shows the significance of climate on whether people stay in a given space. In cold Northern European climes, people want a place in the sun. The photo also illustrates how trees serve as a focal point, how many people use benches, and the fact that people keep a certain social distance between themselves. That people attract more people is also exemplified.

The *where* question can relate to where people situate themselves relative to other people, buildings and city spaces or to the climatic conditions. If we try to picture the same place on a gloomy overcast day or at night, where people stay will most probably be very different.

Sun

Shadow

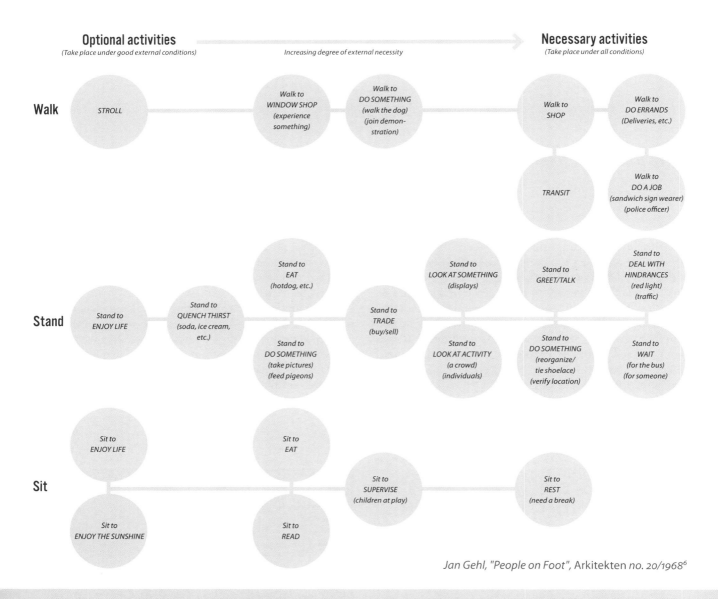

Optional activities
(Take place under good external conditions)

Increasing degree of external necessity

Necessary activities
(Take place under all conditions)

Walk

STROLL

Walk to
WINDOW SHOP
*(experience
something)*

Walk to
DO SOMETHING
*(walk the dog)
(join demon-
stration)*

Walk to
SHOP

Walk to
DO ERRANDS
(Deliveries, etc.)

TRANSIT

Walk to
DO A JOB
*(sandwich sign wearer)
(police officer)*

Stand

Stand to
ENJOY LIFE

Stand to
QUENCH THIRST
*(soda, ice cream,
etc.)*

Stand to
EAT
(hotdog, etc.)

Stand to
DO SOMETHING
*(take pictures)
(feed pigeons)*

Stand to
TRADE
(buy/sell)

Stand to
LOOK AT SOMETHING
(displays)

Stand to
LOOK AT ACTIVITY
*(a crowd)
(individuals)*

Stand to
GREET/TALK

Stand to
DO SOMETHING
*(reorganize/
tie shoelace)
(verify location)*

Stand to
DEAL WITH
HINDRANCES
*(red light)
(traffic)*

Stand to
WAIT
*(for the bus)
(for someone)*

Sit

Sit to
ENJOY LIFE

Sit to
ENJOY THE SUNSHINE

Sit to
EAT

Sit to
READ

Sit to
SUPERVISE
(children at play)

Sit to
REST
(need a break)

Jan Gehl, "People on Foot", Arkitekten no. 20/1968[6]

Necessary and Optional Activities

This illustration of necessary and optional activities comes from "People on Foot" by Jan Gehl in the architectural journal *Arkitekten* in 1968. It was part of the first large study of the correlation between public space and public life.

This early categorization of activities is part of Gehl's basic work to describe life in city spaces. Later, the general categories of necessary and optional activities were described in a historical perspective in the book *New City Life.*[7]

In the course of the 20th century, fewer necessary activities took place in public space. If this illustration of activities had been made in 2012, it would include new activities such as talking on cell phones – while walking, standing and seated – smoking in public space due to changes in smoking legislation and many types of exercise. And the type of activities would vary widely from place to place.

Question 4. What?

Mapping *what* happens in city space can provide specific knowledge of the types of activities in an area, such as staying, commercial or physical activities, and the requirements these various activities make on the physical environment. This can be relevant for shop owners, for city planners with regard to designing city space, and more generally or politically, in relation to a given theme such as health or safety.

Broadly speaking, the primary activities in public space are walking, standing, sitting and playing. The list of activities that can be registered is almost endless. It is often most meaningful to note several types of activities at the same time. However, it is important to find the categories that best cover registering the various events. While activities can also be noted less categorically, being systematic will sharpen your general awareness.

In general, public space activities can be divided into two categories: necessary and optional. Necessary activities could include shopping, walking to and from a bus stop, or working as a parking enforcement attendant, police officer or postman. Optional activities comprise strolling or jogging, sitting on a stair step, chair or bench to rest, reading the newspaper, or simply enjoying life while walking around or seated. Activities that are necessary for some people may be freely chosen by others.

In a historical perspective, the use of public space has gradually evolved from activities primarily motivated by necessity to those more optional in nature.[8]

Social activities can be developed around either necessary or optional activities and are conditional on the presence of others: people in the same space, passing each other or looking at each other in connection with other activities. Examples include children playing, greetings and conversations, common activities, or the most widespread social activity of all: passive contact in the form of just watching and listening to other people.[9]

It is important for public life studies to define and record social activities in order to support the function of public space as meeting place. Here is where people meet others who live in the quarter, community and city. Meeting others can be stimulating and interesting and, in a broader sense, heavily impact the individual's understanding of the social context of life.

One can differentiate between social activities with people who know each other and encounters with strangers on the street. While it is less common to talk to strangers, it is easier to strike up a conversation with people standing nearby, even strangers, if you experience something together in common space. William H. Whyte uses the term *triangulation* to define the scenario where two people who don't know each other start talking due to an external event. The catalyst could be a street artist or physical object like a sculpture. Or it could be an unusual condition such as hail in summer, power failure, fire in a neighboring building or anything else that spurs people who do not know each other to start talking.[10]

Sunday morning on Swanston Street, Melbourne, Australia.

The average speed it took randomly selected pedestrians to cover 100 meters. Four registrations were made on Strøget, Copenhagen's pedestrian street, in January, March, May and July, respectively.

The photographs and captions are from an article by Jan Gehl entitled "People on Foot" in Arkitekten, 1968.[11]

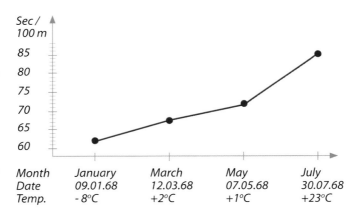

Month	January	March	May	July
Date	09.01.68	12.03.68	07.05.68	30.07.68
Temp.	- 8°C	+2°C	+1°C	+23°C

Fastest man: 100 m in 48 seconds.

A convoy has to follow its slowest member.

Slowest man: 100 m in 137 seconds.

How Fast People Walk?

The 1968 study above comprises four registrations of the average speed of pedestrians covering a 100-meter stretch along the walking street in Copenhagen. The entire 1.1 km-long street can be walked in 12 minutes, but in practice, speed is influenced by weather, age, mobility, errands and whether the pedestrian is alone or part of a group.

A representative segment of pedestrians was shadowed through a 100-meter stretch and their speed registered in seconds per 100 meters. The graph clearly shows the tendency to walk slower in warmer weather. Shown at bottom is how different people walk at different speeds: "... individual pedestrians walk faster than people in groups. Individual men walk fastest (record: 48 seconds/100 meters), with teenagers and women slightly slower. Then come people in groups, and just like in any other convoy, they are forced to follow the speed of the slowest participant. The slowest time (137 seconds/100 meters) was clocked by a police officer on patrol."[12]

Question 5. How long?

Walking speed and the amount of time spent staying can provide information about the quality of physical frameworks. It is often the case that people walk slower and stay longer in places relative to the qualities and pleasures offered.

Registering human activity in relation to the physical environment presents a number of special problems, first and foremost because the question involves processes – chains of events – undergoing continuous change. One moment is not like the previous or the one to follow. In contrast to measuring buildings, for example, time is an important factor in activity studies.

The time dimension is essential to understanding life in public spaces, which makes *how long* a key question. In addition to the passing of days, weeks and months, the individual study also concerns *how long* it takes people to cover a certain distance, *how long* they stay in a certain place, and how long the activity lasts.

The answers to these questions are relevant for finding out *how long* we are willing to walk in order to use public transport, or to determine which activities contribute to the whole activity level, for example.

Basic knowledge about *how long* various activities last can qualify the work of orienting selected public spaces toward inviting people for longer periods of staying while allowing other spaces to have a transient character. In some places, it is desirable for people to hurry by as quickly as possible in order to make room for others.

Studies of the duration of various activities can illustrate more precisely how much time is spent on specific activities. For example, it doesn't take long to walk to and from a parked car on a residential street, and only slightly longer to empty the mailbox, while activities such as gardening or children's play can take considerably longer.[13] Obviously, establishing numbers for the relationship between activities of short and long duration can provide new insights.

In addition, the time spent by individuals is often easy to influence through careful planning and design.

As a rule, it does not take a major expensive initiative to invite people to stay longer. However, if they do stay longer, an invitation can significantly influence their perception of whether or not a place is vibrant and worth a stay, or if they would rather move on as quickly as possible to something better.

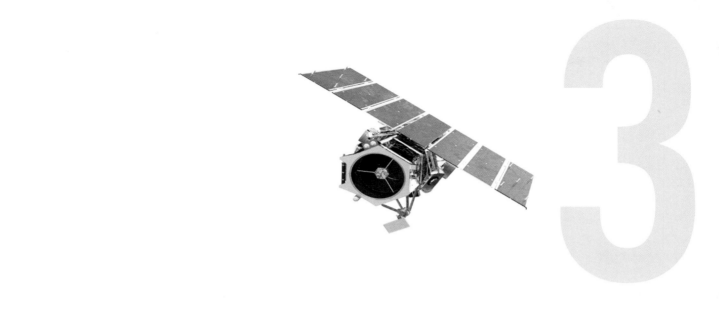

3

COUNTING, MAPPING, TRACKING AND OTHER TOOLS

This chapter describes various tools for system-atizing and registering direct observations of the interaction between public space and public life. A few cases of indirect observations are mentioned, such as using cameras or other technical devices to register or look for traces of human activity.

Regardless of the tools selected, it is always necessary to consider the purpose and timing of the study. General questions of this type are dealt with briefly in this chapter, and the key registration tools described. Other tools exist, of course, but we present those that the authors of the books consider the most important, based on their own experiences.

Purpose of Study and Tool Selection

Purpose, budget, time and local conditions determine the tools selected for a study. Will the results be used as the basis for making a political decision, or are some quick before-and-after statistics needed to measure the effect of a project? Are you gathering specific background information as part of a design process, or is your study part of a more general research project to gather basic information over time and across geographic lines?

The choice of tools is dependent on whether the area studied is a delimited public space, a street, a quarter or an entire city. Even for a delimited area, it is necessary to consider the context of the study holistically, including the local physical, cultural and climate aspects. A single tool is rarely sufficient. It is usually necessary to combine various types of investigation.

Choosing Days – Wind and Weather

The purpose of the study and local conditions determine which points in time are relevant for registration. If the study area has a booming night life, the hours right up to and after midnight are important. If the area is residential, perhaps it is only relevant to register data until early evening. Registration at a playground can be wrapped up in the afternoon. There is a big difference between weekdays and weekends, and in general, patterns change on days leading up to holidays.

Since good weather provides the best conditions for outdoor public life, registrations are usually made on days with good weather for the time of year. Naturally, regional differences are dramatic, but for public life studies, the criterion is the kind of weather that provides the best conditions for outdoor life, especially staying. The weather is particularly sensitive for registering stays, because even if inclement weather clears up, people do not sit on wet benches, and if it feels like rain, most people are reluctant to find a seat. If the weather no longer lends itself to staying in public space in the course of a registration day, it can be necessary to postpone the rest of an investigation to another day with better weather. It is usually not a problem to combine registrations from two half days into one useful full-day study.

Registration can be interrupted by factors other than weather. A large crowd of fans on their way to a game or a demonstration would significantly change an ordinary pattern of movement.

The results of registrations will always be a kind of modified truth because, hopefully, nothing is entirely predictable. Unpredictability is what makes cities places where we can spend hours looking at other people, and unpredictability is what makes it so difficult to quite capture the city's wonderfully variable daily rhythm. The impulsiveness of cities heightens the need for the observer to personally experience and notice the factors that influence the urban life. Herein lies one of the principal differences between using man as registrar rather than automated tools and machines.

Manual or Automated Registration Methods

The observation tools described are primarily manual, which by and large can be replaced by automated registration methods. In the 1960s, 70s and 80s, most studies were conducted manually, but newer technological solutions can register numbers and movements remotely. Automated registration makes it possible to process large amounts of data. It does not require the same manpower to conduct observations, but does require investments in equipment as well as in manpower to process the data collected. Therefore, the choice of manual or automated method is often dependent on the size of the study and the price of the equipment. Much of the technical equipment is either not very common or in an early stage of development, which makes it even more relevant to consider the advantages and disadvantages. However, it is likely that automated registration will play a more prominent role in public life studies in future.

In addition, automated registration must often be supplemented by a careful evaluation of the data collected, which can end up being as time-consuming as direct observation.

Simple Tools Almost for Free

All the tools in the public life toolbox were developed for a pragmatic reason: to improve conditions for people in cities by making people visible and to provide information to qualify the work of creating cities for people. It is also important for the tools to function in practice. The tools can be adapted to fit a specific task, and are usually developed to meet the general professional, societal and technological development.

Generally, the tools are simple and immediate, and the studies can be conducted on a very modest budget. Most studies only require a pen, a piece of paper, and perhaps a counter and stopwatch. This means that non-experts can conduct the studies without a large expenditure for tools. The same tools can be used for large or small studies.

Key for all studies are observation and the use of good common sense. The tools are aids for collecting and systematizing information. The choice of one tool over another is not as important as choosing relevant tools and adapting them to the purpose of the study.

In order to compare the results within a study or compare with later studies in the same or some other place, it is essential to make precise and comparable registrations. It is also important to carefully note weather conditions and time of day, day of the week and month in order to conduct similar studies later.

Counting

Counting is a widely used tool in public life studies. In principle, everything can be counted, which provides numbers for making comparisons before and after, between different geographic areas or over time.

Mapping

Activities, people, places for staying and much more can be plotted in, that is, drawn as symbols on a plan of an area being studied to mark the number and type of activities and where they take place. This is also called *behavioral mapping*.

Tracing

People's movements inside or crossing a limited space can be drawn as lines of movement on a plan of the area being studied.

Tracking

In order to observe people's movements over a large area or for a longer time, observers can discreetly follow people without their knowing it or follow someone who knows and agrees to be followed and observed. This is also called *shadowing*.

Looking for traces

Human activity often leaves traces such as litter in the streets, dirt patches on grass etc., which gives the observer information about the city life. These traces can be registered through counting, photographing or mapping.

Photographing

Photographing is an essential part of public life studies to document situations where urban life and form either interact or fail to interact after initiatives have been taken.

Keeping a diary

Keeping a diary can register details and nuances about the interaction between public life and space, noting observations that can later be categorized and/or quantified.

Test walks

Taking a walk while observing the surrounding life can be more or less systematic, but the aim is that the observer has a chance to notice problems and potentials for city life on a given route.

Counting

Counting is basic to public life studies. In principle, everything can be counted: number of people, gender division, how many people are talking to each other, how many are smiling, how many are walking alone or in groups, how many are active, how many are talking on their cell phones, how many shop windows have metal bars after closing, how many banks there are, and so on.

What is often registered is how many people are moving (pedestrian flow) and how many are staying (stationary activities). Counting provides quantitative data that can be used to qualify projects and as arguments in making decisions.

Numbers can be registered using a handheld counter or by simply making marks on a piece of paper when people walk past an imaginary line. If the goal is to count people staying, the observer typically walks around the space and does a headcount.

Counting for ten minutes, once an hour, provides a rather precise picture of the daily rhythm. City life has shown to be quite rhythmic and uniform from one day to the next, rather like a lung that breathes. Yesterday is very much like tomorrow.[1]

Naturally, it is crucial to conduct the count for exactly ten minutes, because this is a random sample that will later have to be repeated in order to calculate pedestrian traffic per hour. All of the individual hours will then be compiled in order to get an overview of the day. Therefore, even small inaccuracies can invalidate the results. If the site is thinly populated, counting must be continued for a longer interval in order to reduce uncertainly. If anything unexpected happens, it must be noted: for example, a demonstration involving lots of people, road work or anything else that might influence the number of people present.

By conducting headcounts before and after initiatives in city space, planners can quickly and simply evaluate whether the initiative resulted in more life in the city, broader representation of age groups, etc. Counting is typically conducted over a longer period in order to compare different times of day, week or year.

Headcounts in Chongqing, China.[2]
Registering all the pedestrians who walk by.
If there are many pedestrians, a counter is
invaluable (right).

Mapping

1.

2.

Mapping behavior is simply mapping what happens on a plan of the space or area being investigated. This technique is typically used to indicate stays, that is, where people are standing and sitting. The locations of where people stay are drawn at different times of day or over longer periods. The maps can also be combined layer on layer, which gradually provides a clearer picture of the general pattern of staying activities.

In order to envision activities throughout the day, it is essential to register several samples in the form of momentary 'pictures' in the course of a day. This can be done by mapping stays on a plan of the area being investigated at selected points in time throughout the day. Thus mapping shows where the stays are made, and the observer can use a symbol (an X, a circle, a square) to represent the different types of stationary activities – what is going on, in other words. One registration answers several questions, and the qualitative aspects about where and what supplement the quantitative nature of the counting.

This method provides a picture of a moment in a given place. It is like an aerial photo that fast-freezes a situation. If the entire space is visible to the observer, he or she can plot all the activities on the plan from one vantage point. If the space is large, the observer must walk through it, mapping stays and putting the many pieces together to get the total picture. When walking through a space, it is important for observers not to be distracted by what is going on behind them, but rather to focus on what is happening abreast. The point is to capture one single picture of the moment rather than several.

Original captions from "People in Cities", Arkitekten no. 20, 1968:

1. "Winter day. Tuesday, 2.27.68 (...) Plan B1, which indicates standing and seated people in the area at 11.45 a.m., shows that all the seating in the sun is occupied, while none of the other benches in the area are being used. The largest concentration of people standing is near the hotdog stand on Amagertorv. The plan also shows that people standing to talk and standing to wait are either in the middle of the street or along the façades."

2. "Spring day. Tuesday, 05.21.68 (...) As in February, about 100 people on average are standing in front of shop windows, but all other forms of activity have increased. Most marked is the growth in the number of people standing and looking at what is going on. It is warmer now, and more is happening, therefore more to look at."

3. "Summer day. Wednesday, 07.24.68 (...) The number of pedestrians, about 30%, standing in front of shop windows is unchanged. This would appear to be a constant. (...) In general it can be observed that the center of gravity in the area has shifted from the commercial street Vimmelskaftet to the more recreational square Amagertorv."[3]

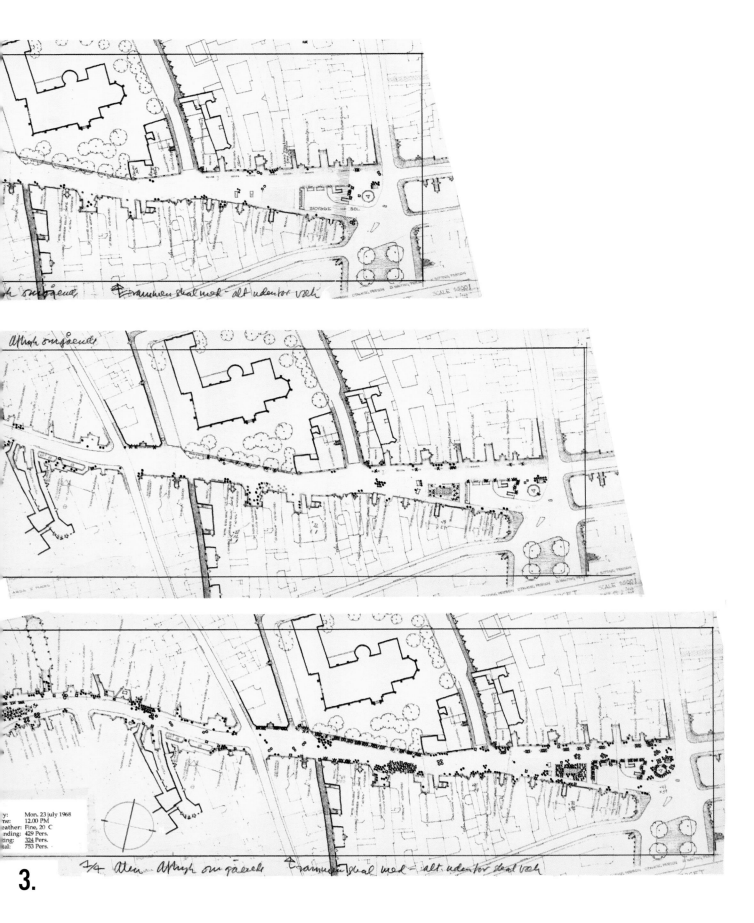

a ou gaend, ↟ rammen skal med - alt udenfor vol

Afhush ou gaende

y: Mon. 23 July 1968
ne: 12.00 PM
eather: Fine, 20 C
nding: 429 Pers.
ting: 324 Pers.
tal: 753 Pers.

3/4 Aten Afhugh ou gaende ↟ rammen skal med - alt udenfor skal vol

3.

Tracing

Registering movement can provide basic knowledge about movement patterns as well as concrete knowledge about movements in a specific site. The goal can be to gather information such as walking sequence, choice of direction, flow, which entrances are used most, which least, and so on.

Tracing means drawing lines of movement on a plan. People's movements are watched in a given space in full view of the observer. The observer draws the movements as lines on a plan of the area during a specific time period, such as 10 minutes or half an hour.

Tracing is not exact, as it can be difficult to represent lines of movement if there are many people moving through a given space. It may be necessary to divide the space into smaller segments. Tracing movements on a plan provides a clear picture of dominant and subordinate lines of flow as well as areas that are less trafficked. GPS equipment can be used to register movements in a large area such as an entire city center or over a long period.

Registration, hand-drawn sketch: Movements on a plan made in the courtyard of the Emaljehaven housing complex in Copenhagen, by Gehl Architects in 2008. Every line represents one person's movements in the space. Lines were drawn every 10 minutes on tracing paper, which was then layered to provide an overall picture of the movement patterns.

Rentemestervej
Saturday the 13th of September from 12-3 p.m.
Walking patterns at noon, 1, 2, and 3 o'clock

NEDGANG

SKRALD

Tracking

In addition to standing in one place to register movement, observers can also follow selected people in order to register their movements, which is called *shadowing* or *tracking*. This method is useful for measuring walking speed, or where, when and to what extent certain activities take place along a route. Activities could be actual stays or more subtle acts such as turning the head, stopping, making unexpected detours, etc. The method could also be used, for example, to map the route to and from a school in order to make it safer.

Speed observations can be made with the naked eye and a stop watch by following the person whose speed you want to measure. Observers must keep a reasonable distance so that the person being observed does not get the feeling that he or she is being followed. Another option is to observe speed over a measured distance from a window or other site above street level.

If the goal is to get a total picture of an individual's movements over a period of time, a pedometer is useful. GPS registration is also useful for measuring speeds on given routes. A variation of shadowing is to follow someone who knows and agrees to being followed and observed. GPS registration can be used for remote shadowing of selected people.

Photo from the tracking registrations on Strøget, Copenhagen's main pedestrian street, in December 2011.[4] The observer follows randomly selected pedestrians (every third), using a stop-watch to time how long it takes the person to walk 100 meters. When the person being shadowed passes the imaginary 100-meter line, the watch is stopped. If the pedestrian does not follow the pre-measured route, tracking that particular person is abandoned.

Looking for Traces

Human activity can also be observed indirectly by looking for traces. Indirect observation requires observers to sharpen their senses just like detectives on the trail of human activity or the lack hereof.

A core tenet of public life studies is to test the actual conditions in the city by observing and experiencing them firsthand and then considering which elements interact and which do not. What is relevant for testing differs from place to place.

Looking for traces could mean recording footprints in the snow, which attest to the lines people follow when they cross a square, for example. Traces might also be found in trampled paths over grass or gravel, or as evidence of children's play in the form of temporarily abandoned toys. Traces could be tables, chairs and potted plans left outside in the evening, which indicate a quarter where residents confidently move their living room into public space and leave it there. Traces could show just the opposite: hermetically sealed shutters and bare porches can indicate a quarter with no signs of life. Traces can be things left behind or things used in ways not originally intended, such as traces of skateboarding on park benches.

Left: Tracks left in the snow at Town Hall Square, Copenhagen, Denmark
Right: Like everyone else, architecture students take the most direct route: The Royal Danish Academy of Fine Arts, School of Architecture, Copenhagen, Denmark.

Photographing

Photographs are frequently used in the field of public life studies to illustrate situations. Photographs and film can describe situations showing the interaction or lack thereof between urban form and life. They can also be used to document the character of a site before and after an initiative.

While the human eye can observe and register, photographs and film are good aids for communication. Photographing and filming can also be a good tool for fast-freezing situations for later documentation and analysis. By later studying photographs or film, it is possible to discover new connections or to go into detail with otherwise complex city situations that are difficult to fully comprehend with the naked eye.

Photographs often illustrate and enliven data. In the field of public life studies, photographs of public life scenes are not subjected to the usual aesthetic principles so dear to the hearts of architects generally. Here the emphasis is not on design but rather on situations that occur in the interaction between public life and public space.

Photographs can be used generally as well as in specific projects to document life and conditions for life in public space. And even though it is a bit of a cliché, one picture can be worth 1000 words, particularly because the viewer can identify with the people in the pictures, which are often snapped at eye level.

Variations include time-lapse photography or video sequences to show situations over time, with or without the presence of the observer. The angle and size of the lens is relevant if either film or photograph is to correspond to the human field of vision.

Good observation post, good company and good study objects: Piazza Navona, Rome, Italy.

Keeping a Diary

All of the tools described above provide only random samples of the interaction of public life and public space. These samples of what is taking place can rarely provide all the details. However, details can be vital additions to our understanding of how life in public space develops as sequences and processes. One way to add detail is to keep a diary.

Noting details and nuances can increase knowledge about human behavior in public space for individual projects as well as to add to our more basic understanding in order to develop the field. The method is often used as a qualitative supplement to more quantitative material in order to explain and elucidate hard data.

Keeping a diary is a method of noting observations in real time and systematically, with more detail than in quantitative 'sample' studies. The observer can note everything of relevance. Explanations can be added to general categories such as standing or sitting, or brief narratives can aid our understanding of where, why and how life plays out in

an event that is not exclusively purpose-driven. Examples could include someone mowing a front-yard lawn at several times during the day, or an older woman who empties her mailbox several times on a Sunday.[6]

Keeping a diary can also be used as a supplementary activity, with the observer adding explanations and descriptions to facts and figures.

Keeping a diary can register events that cannot easily be documented using more traditional methods. This example shows notes from a study of residential streets in Melbourne, Australia. Shown at right is a page from a diary for the Melbourne study.[5]

The two-page spread below depicts Y Street, Prahran, Melbourne, Australia. The physical framework is described on the left-hand page – the dimensions and form of the street. The right-hand page describes the activities taking place on the street during one Sunday.

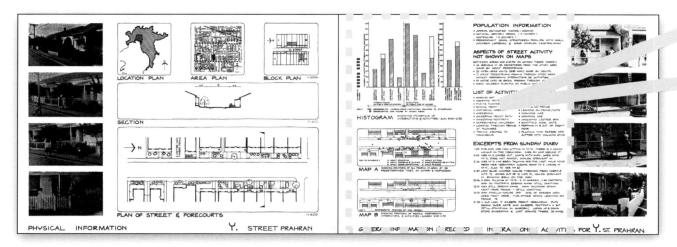

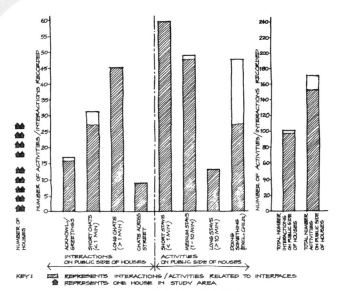

HISTOGRAM · SHOWING INCIDENCE OF INTERACTIONS & ACTIVITIES - SUN. 8·00-6·30

KEY: ▨ REPRESENTS INTERACTIONS/ACTIVITIES RELATED TO INTERFACES
🏠 REPRESENTS ONE HOUSE IN STUDY AREA

(Histogram axis labels) NUMBER OF ACTIVITIES/INTERACTIONS RECORDED · NUMBER OF HOUSES

INTERACTIONS ON PUBLIC SIDE OF HOUSES: ACKNOWL./GREETINGS · SHORT CHATS (< 1 MIN) · LONG CHATS (> 1 MIN) · CHATS ACROSS STREET

ACTIVITIES ON PUBLIC SIDE OF HOUSES: SHORT STAYS (< 1 MIN) · MEDIUM STAYS (1-10 MIN) · LONG STAYS (> 10 MIN) · DOING SOMETHING (EXCL. CHILD.)

TOTAL NUMBER INTERACTIONS ON PUBLIC SIDE OF HOUSES · TOTAL NUMBER ACTIVITIES ON PUBLIC SIDE OF HOUSES

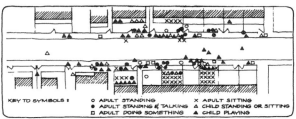

MAP A · SHOWING POSITIONS OF ALL PEOPLE IN AREA AT 38 PREDETERMINED TIMES ON SUNDAY & WEDNESDAY

KEY TO SYMBOLS: ○ ADULT STANDING · ● ADULT STANDING & TALKING · □ ADULT DOING SOMETHING · ✕ ADULT SITTING · △ CHILD STANDING OR SITTING · ◇ CHILD PLAYING

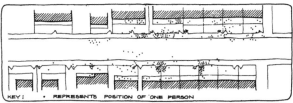

MAP B · SHOWING POSITIONS OF PEOPLE PERFORMING INTERACTIONS & ACTIVITIES - SUNDAY 8·00-6·30

KEY: · REPRESENTS POSITION OF ONE PERSON

POPULATION INFORMATION

- APPROX. ESTIMATED INCOME: MEDIUM
- NATIONAL GROUPS: GREEK (9 HOUSES), AUSTRALIAN (9 HOUSES).
- PREDOMINANT SOCIAL STRUCTURES: FAMILIES WITH SMALL CHILDREN (GREEKS) & SOME COUPLES (AUSTRALIANS)

ASPECTS OF STREET ACTIVITY NOT SHOWN ON MAPS

BETWEEN 8·30AM AND 6·30PM ON SUNDAY THERE WERE:
- 92 ARRIVALS IN OR DEPARTURES FROM THE STUDY AREA MADE BY ADULT PEDESTRIANS
- 29 INTRA-AREA VISITS (ONE WAY) MADE BY ADULTS
- 71 ADULT PEDESTRIANS PASSING THROUGH STUDY AREA WITHOUT PERFORMING INTERACTIONS OR ACTIVITIES
- 191 MOTOR CARS OR BIKES PASSING THROUGH STUDY AREA
- MANY CHILDREN PLAYING ON PUBLIC SIDE OF HOUSES

LIST OF ACTIVITIES ON SUNDAY

- SHAKING MAT
- CARRYING POTPLANTS
- PICKING FLOWERS
- RAKING FRONT GRASS
- WATERING GARDEN
- GARDENING
- SWEEPING FRONT PATH
- SWEEPING FOOTPATH
- SUPERVISING CHILDREN
- LOOKING THROUGH FENCE AT FLOWERS
- TAKING GRAPES TO NEIGHBOUR
- WALKING DOGS
- SITTING ON VERANDAH SEATS
- SITTING IN GATEWAY
- SITTING ON FENCE
- LEANING ON FENCE/GATE
- WASHING CAR
- MENDING CAR
- CHECKING LETTER BOX
- SHUTTING SIDE GATE
- POPPING IN & OUT OF FRONT DOOR
- FLICKING TINY PAPERS INTO GUTTER WITH WALKING STICK

EXCERPTS FROM SUNDAY DIARY

1·59 FIVE KIDS ARE NOW SITTING IN № 12; THERE IS A CHAISE LONGUE ON THE VERANDAH. KIDS ON AND AROUND IT.

2·06 MRS № 12 COMES OUT, CHATS WITH KIDS, GOES INTO № 10, DOES NOT KNOCK, WALKS STRAIGHT IN.

2·26 MRS № 16 HAS BEEN TALKING FOR THE LAST HALF HOUR FROM HER VERANDAH ACROSS ROAD TO 2 LADIES IN № 13, ALSO TO MRS № 20

2·47 LADY IN BLUE JUMPER WALKS THROUGH FROM NORTH & INTO 12. COMES OUT OF 12 INTO 10, WALKS STRAIGHT IN, RINGING BELL ON THE WAY.

12·06 3 MEN TALKING AT № 13. 2 IN GARDEN, 1 ON FOOTPATH. MAN ON FOOTPATH EDGING AWAY STILL CHATTING.

12·10 MAN STILL EDGING AWAY. MAN HALFWAY DOWN NEXT-DOOR FENCE — STILL CHATTING

12·13 MAN FINALLY WALKS OFF. ONE OF GARDEN MEN GOES NEXT DOOR; THE OTHER STAYS LEANING ON FENCE 13

2·34 V. OLD LADY 17 SWEEPS FRONT VERANDAH. PUTS BROOM OVER GATE AND SWEEPS FOOTPATH A BIT (STILL STANDING IN GARDEN) LOOKS UP & DOWN. STOPS SWEEPING & JUST STANDS THERE (10 MINS)

Test Walks

To make test walks, the observer walks selected important routes, noting waiting times, possible hindrances and/or diversions on the way.

There can be great differences in walking a distance measured in sight lines and a theoretical idea about how long it takes to walk from point A to point B, and the time it actually takes to walk that distance. The actual walk can be slowed by having to wait at stoplights or by other hindrances that not only slow the pedestrian but make the walk frustrating or even unpleasant. Test walks are a good tool for discovering this type of information.

Test walks were carried out as an important element in the public life studies conducted in Perth and Sydney, Australia (1994 and 2007, respectively). In both cities, pedestrians spent a significant amount of their time waiting at the many traffic lights prioritizing car traffic.[7] The test walks proved to be a strong political tool in efforts to provide better conditions for pedestrian traffic.

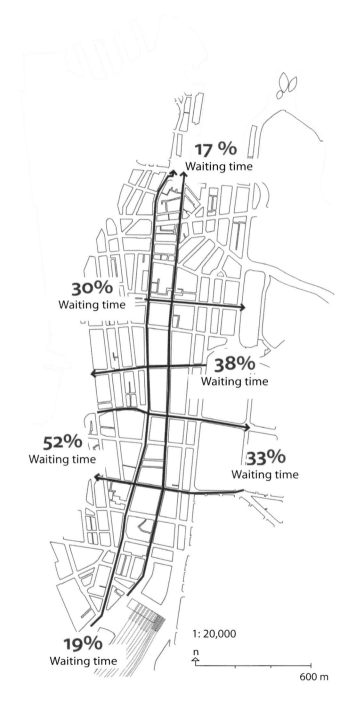

17 % Waiting time

30% Waiting time

38% Waiting time

52% Waiting time

33% Waiting time

19% Waiting time

1: 20,000

n

600 m

Test walks in Sydney showed that up to 52% of total walking time was spent waiting at traffic lights.[8]

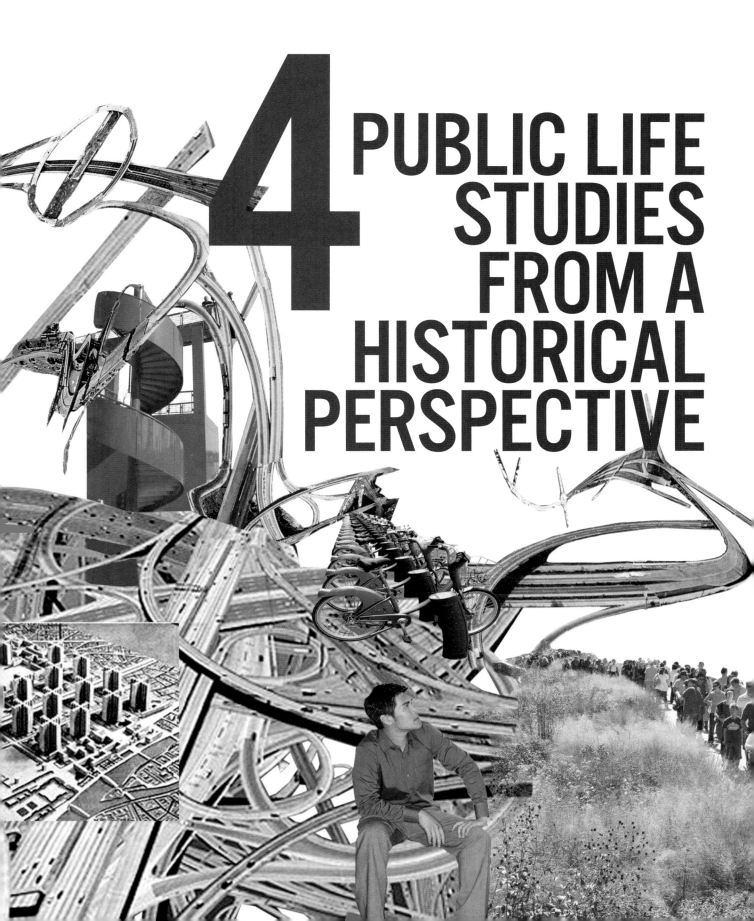

4 PUBLIC LIFE STUDIES FROM A HISTORICAL PERSPECTIVE

The Concise
TOWNSCAPE
Gordon Cullen

This chapter provides a historical overview of some of the societal and structural factors in the disciplines of architecture and city planning that fueled the establishment of public life studies as a special field.

The first period starts with the dawning of industrialization in 1850, and continues to the height of economic growth and booming construction in 1960. The next segment covers the origin and establishment of an academic environment for public life studies from the 1960s to the middle of the 1980s. Next is a description of how, in the mid-1980s, planners and politicians began to take an interest in city life and thus in public life studies in order to perform better in inter-city competition. Last is the period from about 2000 to the present, when consideration for public life has been increasingly taken for granted.

In 1961, Gordon Cullen (1914-1994) published The Concise Townscape, *which became one of the most influential books in the field of urban design.[1]*

We chose Cullen's cover to open this historical chapter, because it sums up the history of public life studies. At the beginning of the 1960s, several researchers with different backgrounds living in various parts of the world sent out the rallying cry that there was something wrong with modern urban planning. Certainly, cities had more light and more air, but public life had disappeared. On this cover of his Townscape *book, Gordon Cullen illustrates the dream of the multifaceted city, inspired by the way cities have traditionally been built.*

From Traditional Urban Building to Rational Planning (1850-1960)

Industrialization began in earnest in the middle of the 19th century. Many people moved from rural to urban areas, and the clear demarcation of city boundaries dissolved. The steadily increasing number of new urban inhabitants put pressure on old cities, which fell short of meeting the requirements of industrial society. New building materials, more effective building methods and a more specialized building process that could build larger, higher and faster challenged the traditional city that was low and dense.

The meandering streets of traditional medieval cities were under strain as early as the Renaissance, which had a penchant for straight lines and symmetry. But not until modernism and the introduction of cars as the dominant form of traffic in the 20th century was there a definite break with traditional city structures based on streets and squares.

Camillo Sitte: Reinterpreting the Traditional City

The movement of people from country to city hastened an urbanization process following on the heels of 19th-century industrialization. The increased urban population was an encumbrance on the cities, which were unable to accommodate all of the newcomers and led to slum conditions. More systematic planning became the response to population growth.[2]

At the beginning of the 20th century, there were basically two responses to the challenges of overpopulated cities. The first model, which dominated urban planning in the 1920s, was based on the classic urban forms and construction typologies of traditional city design. This movement was exemplified by the Amsterdam School and Dutch architect Hendrik Berlage. The second was Modernism's radical break with the building tradition of the past, which made a show of strength in the 1960s after a more modest start in the years between the two world wars.

Before public life studies became an academic field

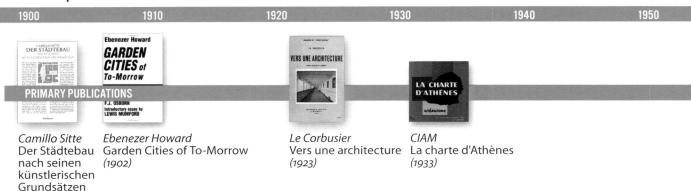

Camillo Sitte
Der Städtebau
nach seinen
künstlerischen
Grundsätzen
(1889)

Ebenezer Howard
Garden Cities of To-Morrow
(1902)

Le Corbusier
Vers une architecture
(1923)

CIAM
La charte d'Athènes
(1933)

Public life studies from a historical perspective

The history of public life studies is illustrated here by selected publications. The timeline above features seminal works, starting in 1889 with the publication of Camillo Sitte's book on the art of building cities written from an intuitive and aesthetic viewpoint. In 1923, Le Corbusier published a modernist manifesto of the city from a functionalist perspective. Between these two extremes is Ebenezer Howard's *Garden Cities of To-Morrow*, published in 1902. Modernism's position as the leading 20th-century ideology in planning and architecture was sealed by the Athens Charter in 1933.

In 1966, Aldo Rossi promoted the rediscovery of the qualities of traditional cities, while *Learning from Las Vegas* (1972) put everyday life on the agenda. Together with his earlier writings, Koolhaas' book *S,M,L,XL* signaled a reinterpretation of modernism on a city scale, as well as renewed interest in books about urban development.

Richard Florida emphasized the status of cities as a framework for creativity. His book *The Rise of the Creative Class* (2002) ranked cities in terms of popularity, marking the increasing competition between cities as well as numerous attempts to rank them. In 2007, the number of urban dwellers surpassed the number of people living in rural areas. Increasing urbanization is also the theme for *The Endless City*, a compilation of the London School of Economics' The Urban Age project.

The works on the top line have been defining for the planning field in general – including the field of public life studies. The inspiration timeline shows several works that are closely related to, but not directly part of, the field of public life studies. These books have had direct influence on the formation of the field as a source of inspiration through several academic approaches: anthropologist Edward T. Hall, sociologist Erving Goffman, environmental psychologist Robert Sommer and architects Kevin Lynch, Gordon Cullen and Oscar Newman. Interdisciplinary approaches played a special role in the development of public life studies as an academic field. At the beginning of the 1990s, Sorkin's anthology *Variations on a Theme Park* dealt with the preoccupation of American cities with public space as a crucial element in a democratic society now threatened by privatization. At the end of the 1990s, an exhibition in Barcelona heralded renewed interest in public space with examples of how the city had been reconquered. The tribute to Jane Jacobs, *What We See* (2010), shows the continued interest in Jane Jacobs and in public life studies in general, across the numerous disciplines that have contributed to the anthology of public space and public life study books.

The bottom line features the most important works in the field of public life studies. They are described in more detail in this chapter.

The first public life studies

Public life studies as a strategic tool

Public life studies become mainstream

Jane Jacobs
Death and Life of Great American Cities *(1961)*

Aldo Rossi
L'architettura della città *(1966)*

Robert Venturi, Steven Izenour and Denise Scott Brown
Learning from Las Vegas *(1972)*

Rem Koolhaas and Bruce Mau
S,M,L,XL *(1995)*

Richard Florida
The Rise of the Creative Class *(2002)*

Ricky Burdett and Deyan Sudjic
The Endless City *(2008)*

INSPIRATION

William H. Whyte
The Exploding Metropolis *(1958)*

Kevin Lynch
The Image of the City *(1960)*

Gordon Cullen
The Concise Townscape *(1961)*

Edward T. Hall
The Silent Language *(1959)*

Oscar Newman
Defensible Space *(1972)*

red. Michael Sorkin
Variations on a Theme Park *(1992)*

Barcelona
Den genero-brede by *(exhibition 1999)*

red. Goldsmith, Elizabeth and Goldbard.
What We See. Advancing the Observations of Jane Jacobs *(2010)*

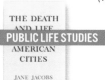

Erving Goffman
Behavior in Public Places *(1963)*

Edward T. Hall
The Hidden Dimension *(1966)*

Robert Sommer
Personal Space *(1969)*

PUBLIC LIFE STUDIES

Jane Jacobs
The Death and Life of Great American Cities *(1961)*

Jan Gehl
Life between buildings *(1971)*

William H. Whyte
The Social Life of Small Urban Spaces *(1980)*

Clare C. Marcus and Carolyn Francis
People Places *(1990)*

Peter Bosselmann
Representation of Places *(1998)*

Urbanism on Track *(2008)*

Christopher Alexander, Sara Ishikawa and Murray Silverstein
A Pattern Language *(1977)*

Donald Appleyard
Livable Streets *(1980)*

Allan Jacobs
Looking at Cities *(1985)*

Allan Jacobs
Great Streets *(1995)*

PPS
How to Turn a Place Around *(2000)*

Jan Gehl
Cities for People *(2010)*

The Austrian historian and architect Camillo Sitte represents a reinterpretation of the qualities of the traditional city. His book *Städtebau nach seinen künstlerischen Grundsätzen* from 1889 is not about aesthetics in relation to individual works or the usual art-historical focus on style. Instead, Sitte writes about the art of building cities and seeing the whole city as an artwork in which buildings and public space interact.[3]

Sitte did not carry out public life studies as such, but he did criticize much of the rational urban planning of his time for being overly rigid in comparison with the labyrinthine and diverse expression of medieval cities. Sitte stressed the importance of creating space for people rather than focusing on straight lines and technical solutions, and he used the qualities of traditional medieval cities as a good example.

Le Corbusier: Breaking with the Traditional City

Seeing these same medieval qualities as the problem confronting cities, rather than the solution, Le Corbusier criticized Sitte. He argued for a break with the dense, traditional city, replacing it with a planned, functional city to give people corresponding physical frameworks for life in the 20th century, with room for cars and other modern conveniences.[4]

For Sitte the dense traditional city was not a barrier to a comfortable modern life. He was not asking people to return to the lifestyle of the past, but argued that life could still be lived well in physical surroundings with the spatial and architectural qualities of traditional cities.

However, with Le Corbusier in the forefront, modernists turned their backs on old urban patterns, although they too wanted to create better conditions for people. They had grand plans for an open urban structure that departed from traditional cities, which were often complex, overpopulated and rife with disease.

In 1923, Le Corbusier published a collection of essays under the title *Towards a New Architecture*, which argued for rational modern buildings and functional cities with straight lines, tall buildings, highways and large green areas. Many of Le Corbusier's ideals were incorporated in the Athens Charter, the manifesto for modernistic urban planning, drawn up at the Congrès International d'Architecture Moderne (CIAM) in Athens in 1933.[5]

Modernism's radical break with old, dense cities became the dominant ideology of the mid-1900s, with increasing focus on enabling rapid urban growth while helping cities to function in ways that were healthy, safe and effective.

Industrialization's focus on efficiency resulted in more rational and specialized approaches to urban building.

Despite the humane visions for people's lives and the slogan about form following function, there was considerably more form than life in the great majority of modernism's projects.

More Space and More Cars Challenge City Life

At the beginning of the 20th century, overpopulated, unhealthy cities with run-down housing, stinking alleys and insufficient sanitation invited bacterial diseases such as tuberculosis, diphtheria and cholera. The arguments for modernizing housing stock were largely centered on health and hygienic conditions.

Modern medical breakthroughs such as penicillin, coupled with massive efforts to raise the health standards of cities and housing, resulted in the dramatic decline of bacterial disease in the middle of the 20th century.

Industrialization and economic growth made it possible to realize ambitious plans using pre-fabricated elements for both single-family dwellings and apartment buildings. Although the number of people per unit of housing shrank over the years, the size of dwellings grew. There was more light and more air – inside and outside, where green areas were established as urban oases. As more space was created, the challenges of making city life vibrant grew apace.

Coupled with the financial ability to realize the dream of home ownership, the desire for light, air and modern housing as an alternative to old-fashioned apartments and tenements in the dense inner city caused a great number of people to move from old urban neighborhoods to the suburbs. Spreading the city over a larger area to encompass the suburbs also diluted the vibrancy of the city, as there were simply fewer people.

Although today it is hard to imagine, 100 years ago, there were few cars in cities. In the course of the 20th century – particularly from 1950 – cars became an integral part of daily life and the street scene. The economic upswing and new and effective, yet cheaper, forms of production meant that more and more people could afford to buy a car. The conquest of cars in the city was at odds with the prerequisites for pedestrian life.

Cities grew markedly in the middle of the 20th century, with rapid economic development driving explosive urban expansion and vehicular traffic, breaking with the dense structure of traditional medieval cities. Fewer dwellings and larger physical frameworks for housing, workplaces and recreation, together with new opportunities for

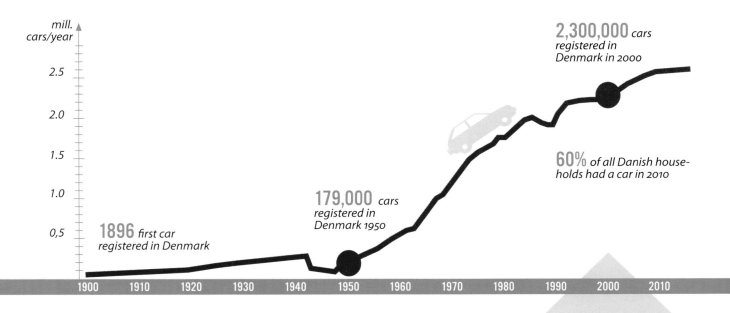

4.5 *persons per housing unit in 1900*

10 m² *per person in 1900*

2.9 *persons per housing unit in 1950*

30 m² *per person in 1950*

2.0 *persons per housing unit in 2010*

54 m² *per person in 2010*

Cars invaded cities in the course of the 20ᵗʰ century. The first car was registered in Denmark in 1896, and by 2010, 60% of all Danish households owned one.[6] The influx of vehicles led to conflicts over room in public space for moving and parked cars, pedestrians and bicyclists. The influence of traffic planners in cities increased along with the conquest of cars. While all cities have a traffic department, few have a department with resources earmarked for safeguarding the conditions of pedestrians and public life.

It was not only the increase in the number of cars that posed a challenge to public life. In the same period, urban density decreased because there were fewer people per housing unit, and people had more individual space. That, too, was a challenge to creating lively cities.[7]

The focus gradually shifted from 5-km/h (3 mph) architecture to 60-km/h (36 mph) architecture, exploding the scale of public space, and traditional knowledge about good human scale was lost or forgotten.

Two different approaches to light and air from the 20th century:
Top: Den Sønderjyske By, Frederiksberg, Denmark, built in 1921
and influenced by the English garden movement.
Bottom: Langhuset, Værløse, Denmark, built in the 1960s.
Then Denmark's longest building, influenced by the principles of
modernism.

mobility created by cars, meant a more open structure and more space between buildings and people in new urban neighborhoods. In this period, cities began in earnest to grow beyond the old city boundaries to the new extended suburban areas.

Many new urban areas had been established by the middle of the 20th century, but city life had not followed them. Although the space and life of the city have played a prominent role throughout the history of settlement, it was clear from the 1960s that public space and public life do not happen automatically: they are heavily influenced by conditions such as population density and physical frameworks. Perhaps this relationship had always been taken for granted, because until only a few decades ago, it was the way things were.

Starting in the 1960s, public life and the interaction with public space were pinpointed as a field to be studied more carefully. Knowledge needed to be gathered, tools for working with the synergy of life and space needed to be developed. This was the start of establishing public life studies as a specialized field.

From Traditional Craftsmanship to Rational Mechanized Profession

For centuries, cities were built on the traditions of craftsmanship. City space was designed more or less intuitively, with ongoing adjustments made in step with changing needs. However, the mass production that came with industrialization eclipsed the tradition of craftsmanship based on experience.

Increased specialization and rationalization mitigated the concern for public space and public life. No one was charged with responsibility for life between buildings, and traditional know-how about the interaction of urban life and space were lost during this rapid transition. This does not mean that 20th-century planners and architects were indifferent to public life – on the contrary. At the beginning and middle of the 20th century, there was intense focus on improving living conditions for people, often in the form of new urban districts intended to solve the housing problem for the many that did not have decent accommodations in rapidly growing cities. However, it can be difficult to see the individual's daily life at eye level in these often abstract, large-scale projects.

Industrialization's need for specialization divided responsibility for various aspects of urban development among various fields and professions. Planners and engineers handled large-scale infrastructure and function, focused on their various specialties such as traffic, water and sewage. Mid-scale responsibility fell to architects to make site plans and building designs and to engineers to build them. The small scale was undertaken by landscape architects, usually with emphasis on design, green elements and specific recreational requirements.

What was lost in this specialization process was concern for the space between buildings not clearly defined as park, playing field, playground or the like. Bridging the gap, landscape architecture achieved the status of an independent field in about 1860, and about a century later urban design was recognized as an antidote to the lack of focus on public space. The profession of architect became less craftsmanship and more art. The architect as artist built individual, conceptual works. The edifices of some architects could be recognized by a design signature, independent of site.

In general, the work of building cities moved from the hands of traditional craftsmen to the desks of specialized professionals. Experts counted cars in order to ensure an optimal flow of traffic, while pedestrians and bicyclists remained largely invisible in the statistics of most cities. Modernism's penchant for innovation meant a definite break with traditional forms of public space.

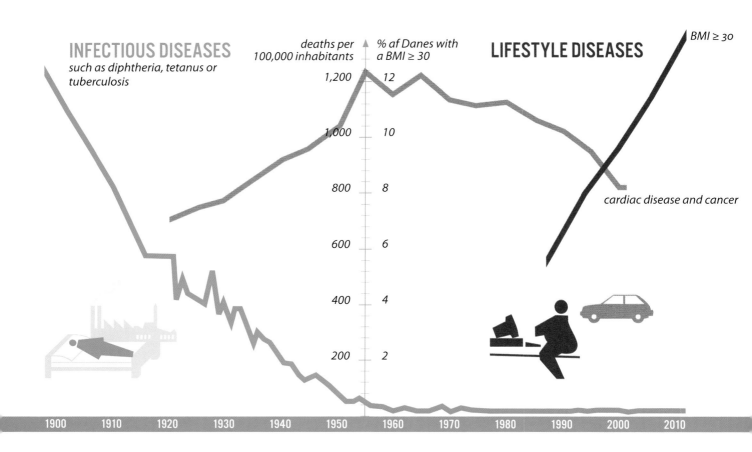

INFECTIOUS DISEASES
such as diphtheria, tetanus or tuberculosis

deaths per 100,000 inhabitants

1,200
1,000
800
600
400
200

% af Danes with a BMI ≥ 30

12
10
8
6
4
2

LIFESTYLE DISEASES

BMI ≥ 30

cardiac disease and cancer

1900 1910 1920 1930 1940 1950 1960 1970 1980 1990 2000 2010

Throughout the 20th century, architects and planners proposed urban building solutions to help offset the health-related challenges of society. At the beginning of the century, building housing in green areas with light and air helped reduce the magnitude of infectious diseases, which were rampant in dense, outdated cities. Once infectious diseases were essentially eliminated in Denmark by the middle of the 20th century, the number of lifestyle diseases began to encroach.[8] Put simply, one of the solutions to the challenge of lifestyle diseases is to build with a mixture of functions so that people can walk or bike on a daily basis instead of taking the car.

While streets had formerly been shared by vehicles, pedestrians and bicyclists, the Radburn Principle separated the various forms of transport, with paths for bicycles and pedestrians and streets for cars – not side by side, but independent of each other. Indeed, the modern solution to the motorized invasion of cities was to segregate the forms of traffic to increase road capacity and pedestrian safety.[9]

What these changes meant was that traditional, spatially well-defined public space with social urban functions was replaced by large, open, green areas intended for recreation between free-standing buildings.

Generally, modern urban planning did not pay attention to interconnections, that is, to the spaces between buildings. Increased specialization separated place and construction from life and intuitive understanding, which were quickly downplayed. However, after 1960 a number of researchers and journalists began to focus on public life and its interaction with public space.

Rallying Cry and the First Public Life Studies (1960-1985)

Although modernism gradually became the up-and-coming planning paradigm in the years between the two world wars, it had no great impact because not much was built. However, its ideals about light, air and free-standing buildings were utilized on a large scale. Buildings were meant to accommodate the large increase in urban populations and eliminate the subsequent shortage of housing, in particular providing housing that was technically up-to-date. Despite good intentions, the plans realized in the name of modernism were quickly criticized for having been built on an inhuman scale and without the qualities found in older urban environments, which had been built layer-by-layer over time. Life had been largely designed and constructed out of the cities, and people like Jane Jacobs, Jan Gehl, Christopher Alexander and William H. Whyte asked how life could be brought back in again. Their conclusion was that life had been forgotten in the planning process and would have to be rethought from the ground up.

Independent of each other, pioneering journalists and researchers in various parts of the world began studying life in cities and developing methods to investigate the interaction between life and space. Method development got its start at the beginning of the 1960s, primarily at universities, while city planners and politicians were still slow to recognize that something had to be done to strengthen public life.

Marshall Aid and the Oil Crisis

Marshall Aid was a prerequisite for the economic growth that characterized the post-war years in many European countries. Rebuilding was massive, particularly in the suburbs, after the Depression and World War II. However, in the autumn of 1973, the oil crisis paralyzed the Western economies, which put a damper on what had been a building boom of unprecedented dimensions.

The oil crisis led to increased awareness about the use of resources. Environmental awareness grew through the 1960s, drawing attention to the pollution from particles, noise and other irritants that can make cities unhealthy – or certainly unattractive – places to be. Although the English garden city movement had already drawn attention to the potential physical and psychological risk of cities in about 1900, it was not until the middle of the century that people increasingly began to demand that something be done about the sources of the problems.[10] Problems had grown in step with the use of more energy, which discharged more polluting and environmentally damaging waste products from new types of production into the atmosphere, coupled with the coming of more cars, all together providing a significant increase in the number of polluting and noise sources.

Health and Social Aspects

The hectic building activity of the 1960s was the culmination of the attempt to overcome the health challenges of cities in the first half of the 20th century: overpopulated cities with their subsequent pool of bacterial diseases such as tuberculosis, diphtheria and cholera. Almost simultaneously with the reduction in the number of bacterial diseases after the development and wide use of penicillin by the 1960s, came the increase in the number of diseases related to modern lifestyles: desk work, stressful working conditions, travel by car and increased access to large amounts and new types of food. Lifestyle diseases such as stress, diabetes and cardiac disease affected more and more people in the second half of the 20th century, making it relevant to study how and where we move about, and, perhaps even more crucial, why we do not move about on a daily basis.

In general, the social and psychological dimensions are important aspects of public life studies. While they are not psychological, sociological or even anthropological studies, public life studies do incorporate some of the angles of inquiry of these fields. In the 1960s and 1970s, the psychological and social dimensions of planning and public life studies were also a reaction to what has been described as 'the poverty of experience' in the new housing areas.[11]

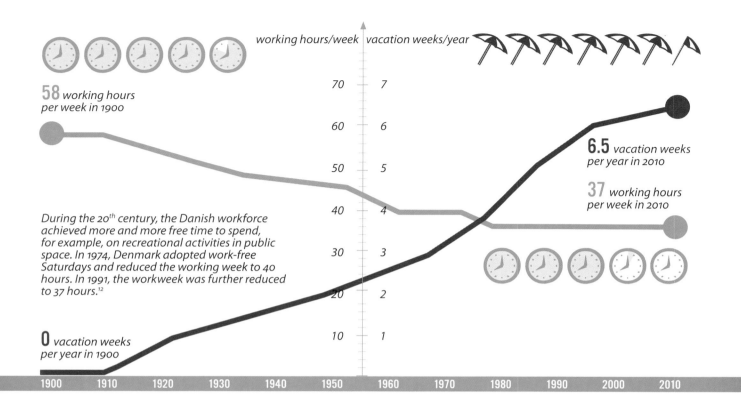

working hours/week | vacation weeks/year

58 *working hours per week in 1900*

During the 20th century, the Danish workforce achieved more and more free time to spend, for example, on recreational activities in public space. In 1974, Denmark adopted work-free Saturdays and reduced the working week to 40 hours. In 1991, the workweek was further reduced to 37 hours.[12]

0 *vacation weeks per year in 1900*

6.5 *vacation weeks per year in 2010*

37 *working hours per week in 2010*

70 | 7
60 | 6
50 | 5
40 | 4
30 | 3
20 | 2
10 | 1

1900 1910 1920 1930 1940 1950 1960 1970 1980 1990 2000 2010

The Suburbs in the Recreation Society

Starting in the 1950s, the workweek was shortened considerably and the number of vacation days increased. The concept of 'the leisure society' appeared in the 1960s, becoming a popular subject for debate in the 1970s and 1980s. The increase in free time meant more time for social and recreational activities, for example, in public space.

Urban migration to the suburbs produced a new retail structure. The car culture and suburban growth inspired malls, which attracted trade away from city centers. A good deal of the retail trade left in existing city neighborhoods moved inside large supermarkets and department stores, which to varying degrees replaced the many small specialty shops that had once lined streets.

Revolution in and about Public Space

The 1960s and 1970s were marked by challenges to authority on many levels. While the strict demarcation of disciplines was questioned at universities, citizen groups increasingly protested urban redevelopment plans. The battle over public space was fought in connection with the youth revolution, anti-war demonstrations, protests against nuclear power plants, campaigns for women's rights and much more. Challenges to authority often took place in public space, and were just as often quelled there; for example, the end of Prague Spring in Czechoslovakia in 1968, and the building of the Berlin Wall in 1961, a political manifestation that would have great impact on the daily lives of many Germans as well as a symbolic meaning for much of the rest of the world. Then as now, public space has an important political dimension: protests are made in and about public space.

More educational opportunity and the struggles for gender equality in the 1960s and 1970s increasingly brought women into the workplace and children into daycare centers. This change greatly determined the extent to which and when women and children, in particular, could be found in residential areas. Many suburban communities found themselves dominated by large residential blocks for single family dwellings and few other functions. During the day, many of the residents of these new housing areas were at work or in school or daycare centers, which led to the coining of the term 'bedroom communities'.

Prizing human values and wanting to give a voice to the people who lived in the large, newly built complexes was in keeping with the challenge to authority of the time and the struggle for rights to the city. In architectural and planning circles, it led to increased focus on the user in a more general sense.

Bicycle demonstration, Copenhagen, Denmark, 1981. The city later became known internationally for its many bicycle commuters. In 2010, almost four out of ten commuters biked daily to work or school, a far cry from the numbers in the 1970s and 80s.[13] The high percentage of bicycle commuters is due to public pressure followed by major municipal campaigns and investments in a cohesive bicycle infrastructure.

Jane Jacobs on the porch of her home on Albany Avenue in Toronto on September 2, 2001 (photographed by Jan Gehl).

The Death and Life of Great American Cities (1961)

Jane Jacobs's book *The Death and Life of Great American Cities* from 1961 is her main work, and has become a classic in the field of city planning. Jacobs wrote about what she observed in her quarter, the streets of Greenwich Village in New York City, and what it takes to make a lively, safe and multifaceted neighborhood. The book is a wake-up call to planners, politicians and people generally, with the message that something is wrong with modern urban planning. The first sentence of the book reads: "This book is an attack on current city planning and rebuilding."[14]

To avoid choking public life with freeways, large building units and the division of functions into zones, we have to learn from the way existing cities operate. Jacobs supplied an ideological foundation with her observation around town as the key to learning from the interaction of public space and buildings with public life. She left to others the development of the tools to do this.

William H. Whyte, Jacobs's mentor, wrote: "One of the most remarkable books ever written about the city... a primary work. The research apparatus is not pretentious – it is the eye and heart – but it has given us a magnificent study of what gives life and spirit to the city."[15]

Public Life Studies in New York City, Berkeley and Copenhagen

While architects and city planners were working on the basis of modernistic ideologies introduced primarily by Le Corbusier, traditional concerns about town and city building continued to influence architectural writing, design and construction. One example is the Townscape Movement, which followed up on Sitte's ideas and criticized the barren, inhuman aspect of many new modernistic districts.[16]

A countermovement against modernism began in the 1980s when Aldo Rossi and brothers Rob and Leon Krier, among others, turned to the traditional city under the banner of 'The Renaissance of European Cities'.[17] However, this happened primarily with focus on architecture and design in a typological revolt. Public life was not given much treatment in the 20th century's dominant planning ideology, modernism, or its counterparts in the form of post-modernism or new rationalism

Particularly in new building, the neglect of public life increasingly represented a challenge that invited debate and research. In the 1960s, the faint outlines of an interdisciplinary public life study environment could be glimpsed across geographic boundaries. In the course of the 1970s, a number of research environments crystallized, and methods for studying the interaction between people and their surroundings were systematized and further developed in New York, at the University of California in Berkeley and in Copenhagen at the The Royal Danish Academy of Fine Arts, School of Architecture.

In the City – Jane Jacobs

Already by the end of the 1950s and start of the 1960s, the voice of Jane Jacobs (1916-2006) could be heard from Greenwich Village in Manhattan. She criticized the planning at the time for being abstract and humanly distant, while automobile traffic was allowed to dominate cities more and more. The framework for Jacobs's life and the source of her inspiration for many years, Greenwich Village was the site of her observations and writing about the conditions for public life in public space. During this period, the area was under increasing pressure from cars and modernistic planning, which she describes with concern and empathy in her book *The Death and Life of Great American Cities* (1961).[18] The book has become a classic for city planning and related fields the world over. Jacobs warned that what had once been known as 'great cities' could become 'dead cities' if the planning ideals of modernism and traffic planners were allowed to dominate urban development.

Jacobs criticized dividing the city into residential, recreational and commercial areas, modernistic divisions that in her view destroyed social life and the city's complex connective strength.[19]

At the beginning of the 1960s, she led a group of local activists in protest against clearing large areas of south Manhattan to build the Lower Manhattan Expressway. Robert Moses, then the dominant city planner in New York City, fought to build the expressway, but Jacobs and other activists managed to ensure that the project was never realized.[20]

In order to get people to understand the interaction between public life and public space in the city, Jacobs dealt with social, economic, physical and design parameters. Her holistic approach helps explain her continued relevance today.

Jacobs objected to standard solutions invented at the drawing board. She believed in going out on the street and studying life in order to learn what works and what does not work in cities. As Jacobs wrote: "There is no logic that can be superimposed on the city; people make it, and it is to them, not buildings, that we must fit our plans. This does not mean accepting the present; downtown does need an overhaul, it is dirty, it is congested. But there are things that are right about it too, and by simple old-fashioned observation we can see what they are. We can see what people like."[21] Jacobs points out problems but does not provide tools for systematizing observations. Others do, however, including William H. Whyte, who served as a mentor for Jane Jacobs.

"A Prophet of Common Sense"[22] – William H. Whyte

Like Jane Jacobs, William H. Whyte (1917-99) also worked in and with New York City. He mainly gathered data by observing with his own eyes or with the aid of a camera that could take time-lapse photographs (i.e., with intervals between the individual picture frames).

At the end of the 1960s, efforts were made to establish more squares and parks in New York City. Developers established many new public spaces at ground level in return for being allowed to build higher buildings on the individual sites. No quality standards were set for the new semi-public space that resulted from this horse-trading. Nor were there any studies of the usefulness of the new city space, which spurred Whyte to start his pioneering project, The Street Life Project,[23] in 1971. Whyte's studies of the use of New York's new city spaces are described in his book, *The Social Life of Small Urban Spaces* (1980), which became a textbook for public life studies.[24] The book was the basis for the 1988 documentary film with the same title, which helped to fulfill Whyte's desire to reach a wide audience.[25]

Neither William H. Whyte nor Jane Jacobs had research careers in the traditional sense. Journalism is their common point of departure. They studied the interaction between public life and public space and communicated their findings in print to a wide target group rather than channeling them through special-interest books or academic journals. Nevertheless, Whyte and Jacobs are central to the development of the academic public life research environment that arose in that period.

The Social Life of Small Urban Spaces (1980)

William H. Whyte's *The Social Life of Small Urban Spaces* set out the author's methodology.[26] He compiled numerous studies deriving from The Street Life Project, a research project he started in 1971.

The book presents basic observational studies of people's social activities in small public spaces. Whyte did not call the work a book, but rather a manual, a by-product of the studies of public space. The studies are instructively explained in the book and the later documentary that illustrates vividly how some places are attractive to people and others absolutely are not. Explanations in the form of text, graphs and narrative pictures deal with climate, the design of spaces and buildings, and human behavior generally and specifically.

Whyte confronted all the basic questions of where we position ourselves in public space, and how we position ourselves relative to others. He studied public life during the day, sometimes using time-lapse photography as in this photo. There is an index at the end of the book with a manual on using a time-lapse camera.

Kevin Lynch (1918-1984) was another central figure based in 1960s New York who drew attention to the interaction between public life and public space. He had a more traditional academic career and taught for many years at MIT, the Massachusetts Institute of Technology. Although Lynch's focus was more on space than life and he does not play a prominent role in this book, he deserves to be mentioned as a source of inspiration for public life pioneers, in particular for his book *The Image of the City* (1960), which remains required reading at many universities.[27] The book deals with how users read, navigate in and experience the city.

Cities are both Space and Life – Christopher Alexander

An academic environment rooted in public life studies emerged around 1970 at the University of California in Berkeley. UC Berkeley's pioneers include Christopher Alexander, Donald Appleyard, Clare Cooper Marcus, Allan Jacobs and Peter Bosselmann.

Christopher Alexander is an architect who founded the Center for Environmental Structure at UC Berkeley in 1967. Alexander's most significant work in the field is collected in his book *A Pattern Language* (1977), which provided an important source of inspiration to followers of public life studies.[28]

Alexander was not content to simply learn from the behavior of people in public space. He wanted users themselves to design everything from furniture to housing to cities. He argued that users know more about buildings and cities than do architects and planners. His book is a 1,000-page survey of 253 qualities that should allow anyone to design regions, cities, quarters, gardens, buildings, rooms, furniture and door handles.

Alexander's critique of his contemporary functionalistic and modernistic planners is that they lack the understanding of and abilities to capture the complexities of city life. According to Alexander, this complexity is actually what creates life, beauty and site-based/place-specific harmony. In his subsequent book, *The Timeless Way of Building* (1979), Alexander argues that there is a timeless way of building cities so that people can once again feel alive. What is needed is a shift from abstract, overly intellectualized design to an approach based on people's immediate daily needs.[29]

A Pattern Language (1977)

While modernism rejected the classic way of building cities and buildings, in the 1960s Christopher Alexander presented what he considered timeless – if forgotten – principles for how to design everything from bookcases to bus stops to entire urban regions while considering human needs. He compiled his studies in his primary work, *A Pattern Language* (1977).

Alexander wanted to reinterpret earlier ways of building cities and buildings by learning from the interaction between public life and public space.[30] Among other things, he stressed the importance of the edges of buildings for well-functioning cities and public space, with reference to Jan Gehl's pool of knowledge about the powerful attraction of edges. Alexander illustrated with two different edges: one with no details or opportunities for staying by a modernist building that he called machine-like, and one that Alexander described as a lively edge with variation, details and several possibilities for staying: "The machine-like building is cut off from its surroundings, isolated, an island. The building with a lively building edge is connected, part of the social fabric, part of the town, part of the lives of all the people who live and move around it..."[31] Edges also influence the way in which buildings invite passersby to share in public life. As Alexander put it: "If the edge fails, then the space never becomes lively."[32]

"Minding small children is made much easier when they can move safely out from home into a courtyard or play area shared by a small group of neighbors."[33]
(*Caption from* Housing As If People Mattered.)

Housing as if People Mattered (1986)

Clare Cooper Marcus's first major book was *Housing As If People Mattered*, written with Wendy Sarkissian. The book's polemic title already suggested that residential planning rarely considered people. The book opens with the two authors stating their values about what constitutes a good city, interspersed with technical input and stories from their childhood and how they later lived. Cooper Marcus wrote: "I recall the strongly powerful sense of enclosure and of group territory in that cobbled courtyard. We children knew it was 'our space', and when they told us to stay there, our parents knew where we were."[34] The personal narrative style written from a value-laden standpoint was characteristic of the pioneers of public life studies.

The book summarizes 100 post-occupancy evaluations in which people who have moved into newly built housing areas tell what they like and do not like about their new neighborhood.

Concern for Women, Children and the Elderly – Clare Cooper Marcus

Clare Cooper Marcus studied history and culture as well as city and regional planning. She is one of the early pioneers who began working in the 1960s to create better public spaces by mapping their use. She began teaching at UC Berkeley in 1969, with special focus on the social and psychological dimensions of the interaction between public life and public space.

Marcus was very much on the lookout for groups otherwise overlooked in public space. With her colleague Carolyn Francis, she wrote the book *People Places* (1990) as a reaction to the lack of attention paid to women, children and the elderly: "Most of the design literature we have reviewed – if it refers to users at all – assumes that they all are able-bodied, relatively young, and male," was their criticism.[35]

From the 1990s, Marcus shifted focus from public space to the city's green elements, such as parks and flora. She studied the possible influence of green elements on health and thus continued to focus on human needs.[36]

Streets for People – Donald Appleyard

Donald Appleyard (1928-82) started his work on public life studies with Kevin Lynch on the American East Coast.[37] In 1967, he began teaching at UC Berkeley and became a professor of urban design. Together with Peter Bosselmann, he built a simulation laboratory that could simulate people's moving or stationary experiences in public space.

In 1980, Appleyard wrote in his book *Livable Streets*: "Streets have become dangerous, unlivable environments, yet most people live on them. Streets need to be redefined as sanctuaries; as livable places; as communities; as resident territory; as places for play, greenery, and local history. Neighborhoods should be protected, though not to the point of being exclusionary."[38] Appleyard's cry is an echo of Jane Jacobs's defense of the street as a space with important social dimensions, but he is more concerned with traffic than she is.

Appleyard's best known contribution to the field is a comparative study of three parallel residential streets in San Francisco with heavy, medium and light traffic, respectively. The street plans illustrate the study's conclusion with strong graphic clarity: the more traffic, the less life and sense of community.[39] Appleyard subsequently conducted more studies in streets with a socio-economic mix of residents. These studies support the conclusions of pilot studies that the amount of traffic has a great influence on life in individual streets and the number of social relationships that develop.

Livable Streets (1981)

Modernists turned their backs on the typologies of traditional cities, including the street. Public life studies brought back the street as perhaps the most important public space. In *The Death and Life of Great American Cities*, Jane Jacobs defended the street as a social space, not just a space for the transport of people and cars.[40] In 1981, the book *Livable Streets* by Donald Appleyard was published featuring studies showing that social life can unfold on the streets, if conditions invite it and public life is not discouraged by traffic, for example.[41]

The reason that *Livable Streets* is Appleyard's most prominent book may be that his studies were able to show a connection between the amount of traffic and the amount of social life that blossomed on the streets. While the conclusions were relevant to technical experts, they were also important to politicians and activists because they clearly showed the consequences of traffic on residential streets and helped generate debate about designing new types of streets with light or no traffic.

Experiencing the City – Peter Bosselmann

Architect Peter Bosselmann[42] wanted to depict the experience of the city from a user perspective, which is often in direct contrast to the one that professionals provide: "Professionals rarely represent the way people move through urban places, looking down streets or standing in a square alone or with others – actual conditions that people imagine."[43]

Because the interaction between life and space takes place in time, it is necessary to study processes, and here registering human activity in relation to physical environment presents a number of special problems. No one second is like the one before or the next, so in contrast to surveying buildings, for example, time is a crucial factor in activity studies. Peter Bosselmann is heavily committed to registering and disseminating information about these processes.

Bosselmann is one of the prime movers behind UC Berkeley's environmental simulation laboratory. Along with other architects, specialists from the film industry and an optical engineer, he builds models of city environments that make it possible to study the impact a planned building might have on how its surroundings are experienced. Models and film cameras can simulate walking, driving or flying to illustrate how a given environment can be experienced, not just as a momentary picture, but from the eye of a moving pedestrian and over time.

It took many years to develop a technique that could give a relatively realistic picture of how people experience the city. The laboratory has worked together with the city of San Francisco and other cities since 1979. San Francisco's skyscrapers, in particular, have been studied in order to show their impact on local climate and the quality of public space.[44]

For Bosselmann, like for Jane Jacobs and others, it is paramount to be in the city to learn, and he encourages his students to go out and study streets and neighborhoods first-hand.[45] He has endeavored to find methods that can show the city experienced in movement – in the simulation laboratory as well as on the street in the form of four-minute walks along various routes, comparing the experiences.

Sun, Wind, and Comfort (1984)

In 1984, Peter Bosselmann and several colleagues published *Sun, Wind, and Comfort: A Study of Open Spaces and Sidewalks in Four Downtown Areas*.[46] The report is in focus here because it represents bridge-building between the academic world and the political practice of cities. It was here in the mid-1980s that public life studies increasingly became a strategic tool for city planning.

The report documents the consequences of several planned skyscrapers for the microclimate and comfort experience of the city of San Francisco. It became a significant contribution to public debate, which ended with plans for the high-rise buildings to be either shelved or adapted to consider how they affected sunlight and wind conditions for pedestrians at street level. The study had specific significance for the guidelines adopted in local plans. Thus the study became part of public life study tradition, with the aim of improving conditions for the people who use the city.

The environmental simulation laboratory was also built on the basis of observations of the interaction of life and space.

In the middle of the 1980s, the simulation laboratory did a study to determine the kind of negative influence several planned skyscrapers would have on climate and experiences in San Francisco. The results of the study led to the adoption of legislation to ensure a better microclimate on the pedestrian level without shadowing and unnecessary wind from skyscrapers.[47] The environmental simulation laboratory continues to hold a central position in research at UC Berkeley.[48]

Bosselmann's contribution to the field stresses the experience of the city in movement, and how the city can be designed so that the physical frameworks support local climate conditions instead of working against them. By working with the experience of public space in time and how to represent it, Bosselmann reaches the heart of understanding life in the city and the interactions with the city's space. A number of his studies are featured in his book *Urban Transformation* (2008).[49]

The environmental simulation laboratory at the University of California, Berkeley, in about 1981-82: Donald Appleyard (right) explaining the strategies of the San Francisco Downtown Plan to William H. Whyte (seated third from right). Lesley Gould is standing in the middle, with Peter Bosselmann seated left.

Great Streets (1993)

Allan Jacobs gathered numerous examples from streets all over the world in his book *Great Streets* (1993). Like other public life study pioneers, he began in the realm of the personal and everyday by describing the street he and his family once lived on in Pittsburgh.

While the examples in *Great Streets* stress physical factors, there is an understanding of how other conditions such as climate support social life. This is illustrated by this description of Roslyn Place in Pittsburgh under the heading, "The great street we once lived on":

"Roslyn Place is a well-defined, intimately scaled street of solidly built structures similar in appearance. But it is more than that. It is physically comfortable. The best images are of the spring, summer, and fall when the full-leaved sycamores give shade and are dappled with sun. The street is so cool when you most want it to be. In winter, if sun is to be had, it will get to the street for at least part of every day, through the leafless branches."[50]

"We Like Cities"[51] – Allan Jacobs

At the beginning of the 1990s, architect and city planner Allan Jacobs helped start a master's program in urban design at UC Berkeley. Before he began teaching in 1975 and later became a professor, he was the head of city planning in San Francisco (1967-1975). In 1972, he spearheaded the work to create one of the first urban design plans for a city. Since 2001, Allan Jacobs has been an independent city planning consultant in the urban design field.

Jacobs accused city planners of focusing exclusively on streets as traffic space rather than places for people.[52] For Jacobs, streets are places that should be able to tolerate people with many different social backgrounds. In *Toward an Urban Design Manifesto* (1987), Jacobs along with Donald Appleyard criticized CIAM and the Garden City movement for neglecting the social significance of the street.[53] They listed values and goals for good city life: "Livability, identity and control, access to opportunity, imagination, and joy, authenticity and meaning, community and public life, urban self-reliance, an environment for all."[54] To promote reaching these goals, they formulated several planning principles that drew on the qualities of traditional cities such as density, mixed function and public space and streets.[55]

Jacobs and Appleyard wrote: "Our urban vision is rooted partly in the realities of earlier, older urban places that many people, including many utopian designers, have rejected, often for good reasons. So our utopia will not satisfy all people. That's all right. We like cities."[56] The quote is included here because it represents the recurrent norms of the pioneers of public life studies. They emphasize the pre-modern city qualities rejected by modernism. Not only the qualities of space such as density and mixed functions, and traditional public spaces like streets and squares, but also the social and psychological dimensions: public space for all, authenticity, the meaning of city and public space, delight in participating in city life and other less tangible values.

In his book *Looking at Cities* (1985), Jacobs argued for the use of systematic observation as an analytical research method and decision-making tool.[57] He believed that observing the interaction between public space and public life rather than simply looking at static drawings or maps would prevent many of the unfortunate decisions and actions that influence people's lives. He provided many examples in his book *Great Streets* (1995) – those that function well and others that are less successful.[58]

Jacobs helped define the field of urban design by making a concrete urban design plan for a city, drawing up a manifesto and establishing the field at UC Berkeley.

From Great Streets *by Allan Jacobs:*
"All fake, all stage set, yet it represents an idealized dream-memory of what made a great street, with stage set physical qualities that exist on the best streets: buildings lining the street, architectural details over which light constantly moves, transparently at ground level, pedestrian comfort, a hint of housing and habitation, a beginning and an ending.
Many doorways, one every 18 feet, but some aren't real and what appears as different stores outside is the same store inside. An appearance of many buildings, one every 22 feet on average. Many windows and signs. Upper floors are proportioned correctly but are smaller in actual dimensions than real buildings: a less than full-scale model. Cleanliness. Despite the artfulness of concept and high quality of execution, there is a sense of physical thinness, as if the walls aren't really walls, as if it's all being held up with props.
An example of how little area it takes to create a sense of urbanity. Central trolley tracks reveal ambivalence as to what this is – main street in a small town or main street in a city. All in all an exercise in gigantism made to look like populism."[59]

Main Street, Disneyland, California. Drawing by Allan Jacobs from his book Great Streets *(1993).*

Life Between Buildings[60] – Jan Gehl

Architect Jan Gehl graduated from The Royal Danish Academy of Fine Arts, School of Architecture in 1960. His schooling in modernism's paradigm meant that at the beginning of his career, he too prioritized buildings over surroundings.

One day, a client challenged his modernist thinking. The client owned a large property and wanted to build housing that was 'good for people'. He was not concerned with what the dwellings looked like, but that they would provide a good place for people to live. The year was 1962, and the project was under the auspices of the architectural firm of Inger and Johannes Exner in Copenhagen, where Jan Gehl worked at the time. The client's desire to build 'something good for people' presented a serious challenge in 1962. There was no ready-made architectural solution to his request.

The concrete result of the challenge was a proposal for a low-rise building complex with houses clustered around small squares, inspired by Italian villages. In the early 1960s, a design with low-rise dwellings around common squares was considered too avant-garde, and the plan was never realized. However, the project did have an influence because it was published and because it had grown from basic assumptions about the importance of space between buildings – a topic that was to become the hub of Gehl's work.

Central to the project were the common squares and the way the houses were oriented to the squares. While classic city squares were the inspiration, the scale was adapted to the housing complex. The character was intimate and urban, a bold contrast to the suburban gardens and open lawns popular at the time.[61]

Another person who challenged Gehl's modernist architect's thinking at the time was his wife, Ingrid Gehl, a psychologist. She had often puzzled over the fact that architects did not seem to be particularly interested in people. From the middle of the 1960s, Ingrid Gehl worked at the Danish Building Research Institute as of the first psychologist in Denmark to focus on urban and housing environments. She studied people's behavior and conditions in cities, particularly in terms of housing.

For Jan Gehl, his client's request for a good place for people to live, coupled with Ingrid Gehl's psychological insight and encouragement to think about people and not just design, was the springboard to his research on the interaction between public space and life in the city.

In the 1960s and 1970s, both Jan and Ingrid Gehl featured often in the media, their voices critical of the poverty of sensory experience and lack of human scale in the modernist housing complexes being built in that period.[62]

Although the criticism was justified, it was necessary to find the underlying reasons for what works and what doesn't work in order to offer alternatives. It quickly became obvious that new tools were needed to study public life and amass basic knowledge about the interaction between public life and public space. Initially, Jan and Ingrid Gehl conducted several seminal studies in Italy.

In 1965, Gehl was awarded a travel scholarship from The New Carlsberg Foundation, which made it possible for him to study classical public space and cities in Italy. The Italian tour resulted in three articles published by Jan and Ingrid Gehl in 1966 in the Danish architectural journal *Arkitekten*.[63] The articles laid the methodological cornerstone for Jan Gehl's continued studies of public space and public life. He mapped not only how the Italian piazzas worked in general terms, but also numerous specific details, such as where and how people stay in a square at a given point in time, by marking the places occupied and whether people were seated or standing.[64]

At another piazza, the number of people present was counted in the course of a day from morning to night, while the number of pedestrians was registered on a certain street. The studies were repeated in winter and summer in order to compare the number of people staying and walking in two different seasons.[65] During their six-month stay in Italy, Jan and Ingrid Gehl gathered basic knowledge that was later tested in other cities and outside Italy.

The articles from 1966 drew parallels to Danish conditions and more generally: "The opportunities to walk about in the city are utilized wherever they can be found, because they are necessary."[66]

A corresponding activity appears also to exist in Denmark, with urban activities culminating in three or four cities where city planning has provided reasonable conditions for mentally-healthy urban functions. As in Italy, a close connection between design and usage can be traced. The opportunities to walk about in the city are utilized wherever they are found, because they are there."

The studies in Italy confirmed the connection between design and usage. The articles detailed how to describe who goes where and what they do. One of the conclusions is a warning not to observe the character of city life too narrowly. For example, characterizing the activities along a shopping street exclusively as 'shopping' only scratches the 'surface structure' of the activity.[67] Beneath the tip of the iceberg of rational, functional activities are the social aspects: the need to see other people or simply to be in the same space as others, the need for social affirmation, to see what is going on, for exercise, for light and air, and so on.[68] Therefore, observational studies add a dimension that interviews with people about the reason for their being in the city could never capture.

The articles from 1966 documented the connection between public life and public space with narrative photographs, a signature for Jan Gehl, who became a popular spokesman through his books and lectures. His narrative photos are unlike traditional architectural photography, which accentuates space and form. Gehl uses familiar scenes from daily urban life to emphasize how space is used, examples of what works and doesn't work.

The studies from Italy provided more than examples of well-functioning city space. Gehl included an analysis of a small town, Sabbioeneta, which had failed to provide a decent connection between the town square and the main street. As a result, the square was almost deserted, which was backed up by Gehl's statistics.[69]

At The Royal Danish Academy of Fine Arts, School of Architecture, Sven-Ingvar Anderson, professor of landscape architecture, saw potential in Gehl's focus on the human dimension. Starting in 1966, Gehl's studies were developed as a research theme at the School of Architecture and resulted in Gehl's seminal work *Life Between Buildings* published in 1971.[70]

Life Between Buildings became a textbook for public life studies and more generally wherever human access to planning is the starting point. The book has been translated into more than 22 languages and continues to be reprinted.[71] The same year that *Life Between Buildings* was published, Ingrid Gehl published a book entitled *Bo-miljø* (*Living Environment*. In Danish) dealing with the psychological aspects of housing based on her work at the Danish Building Research Institute.[72]

From 1968-1971, the School of Architecture in Copenhagen developed interdisciplinary studies under the acronym SPAS, which stood for Studies for Psychologists, Architects and Sociologists, and attracted participants from many disciplines.

In 1972-1973, Jan Gehl was a guest professor at the University of Toronto, where he and Ingrid Gehl presented their people-oriented studies in a series of – for the time – quite sensational lectures about the social dimension in architecture and urban planning. Gehl's international career continued with guest professorships at numerous universities throughout the world, including Melbourne,

Life Between Buildings (1971)

Jan Gehl's book *Life Between Buildings* became a classic not restricted to the field of public life studies, but extending more generally to urban planning and strategic thinking about cities.

When the book was published in Danish in 1971, it made a notable contribution to Scandinavian debate on the direction in which architecture and more general urban planning should take. By the time the book was published in English in 1987, the idea of considering life between buildings had matured. Ralph Erskine made this point in his foreword to the first English edition: "In 1971, the year of the first edition, Jan Gehl was one of those lone protagonists for the humane values...More than a decade later we can discern an increased interest among architects and others in these values."[74]

While over time numerous books have been published on the style history of architecture, individual architects, buildings or more philosophically directed topics, few books have addressed the coupling of public life and public space. *Life Between Buildings* is still listed on many a syllabus, side by side with other publications by the pioneers in the field of public life studies.

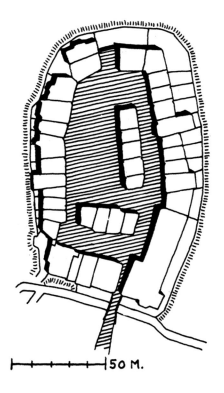

├─┼─┼─┼─┼─┤50 M.

Australia in 1976. Gehl's collaboration with the city of Melbourne started with a series of public life studies of smaller neighbourhoods in the mid-1970s and later expanded to the entire city. Jan Gehl continues his collaboration with the city of Melbourne today through Gehl Architects, which he founded in 2001 with business partner Helle Søholt. Helle has her architectural training from the The Royal Danish Academy of Fine Arts, School of Architecture, and the University of Washington, Seattle.

The early studies contributed to the pool of basic knowledge, from which the methods for studying the interaction between public space and public life continue to be developed.[73]

Left: Plan of San Vittorino Romano, Italy.[75]
Below: Amtsstuegården, Exner Architects, 1962 (not realized).
In 1962, Jan Gehl helped design a proposal for a low-rise housing complex called Amtsstuegården while he was employed by the architectural firm of Inger and Johannes Exner. The complex, a section of which is shown below, was never realized, but the design was published in journals and influenced thinking about how to organize housing.

The design was inspired by the key role of classic squares and plazas in supporting lively public space, in places like San Vittorino Romano, Italy (plan left). The buildings are not freestanding, but rather placed to form an intimate delimited space on a human scale.

An International Interdisciplinary Forum for Public Life Studies

In addition to the researchers already mentioned, many other people conducted public life studies starting in the 1960s. Three prominent examples: in 1963, Claes Göran Guinchard documented life in playgrounds with photos taken at 30-minute intervals; in Holland in the same decade, Derk de Jonge studied people's preference for edges indoors and out; later in the 1970s, Rolf Monheim conducted comprehensive studies of pedestrian areas in Germany.[76] Many other researchers have since joined the field, but the key figures mentioned in this chapter continue to be considered the pioneers of public life studies.

These pioneers laid the ideological and methodological cornerstone for public life studies as a discipline combining architecture, landscape architecture and large-scale planning. While the studies can be considered part of urban design,[77] it is characteristic for the discipline not to have design as its ultimate goal. Rather, the goal is to use observations to amass data in order to understand more about the interaction between public space and public life. It is an analytical tool that can qualify design and other urban planning and construction processes. This analytical rather than artistic approach has occasionally put the proponents of public life studies on a collision course with more artistically oriented architects.

During this early period, the various disciplines worked closely to establish public life studies as a field. While the pioneers mentioned were tied to universities in the fields of architecture and city planning, their educational backgrounds were broader, and they collaborated with people from other disciplines. Their writings and approaches have also been used in many different professional contexts. The interdisciplinary approach continues, but public life studies have gradually become anchored in various architecture and city planning programs.

It is interesting that researchers from so many different parts of the world began developing methods to study the connection between public space and public life in cities during the same period. All of them reacted to the fact that people had become overlooked and invisible in city planning. Cars had invaded cities, and traffic planners had taken over the job of planning the space between buildings that had formerly been designed to accommodate pedestrians and urban life.

The writings of this group of people are known for their communicative enthusiasm – which is not restricted to other professionals, but reaches out to lay people as well.

The public life pioneers want to spread their knowledge widely through books, film and popular magazines. This should not be interpreted to mean that their writing is free and non-analytical. On the contrary, public life studies are characterized by an analytical approach. In general, however, the writings do not include large passages of polemical discussion, nor do they contain extensive footnotes, as in traditional academic writing. Rather the writings call on 'reality' in the form of field studies and examples from practice.

The field of public life studies arises in the dialectic between research and practice. Material is gathered from the city – the city provides the fuel – and writing is often rooted in the local environment of, say, New York City, San Francisco or Copenhagen. The cities become laboratories for developing methods to study the interaction between the public life and public space of the city. It is a basic premise to go out into the city and observe in order to understand how the city's space and buildings support – or fail to support – public life. Direct observations are made, and in a number of cases, mechanical aids are also used.

With the formation of professional organizations such as the Environmental Design Research Association (EDRA), founded 1968, and general anchoring of the field at universities and other institutions of higher education, public life studies have gradually become established in academic circles. In time many more conventional academic articles have also been published, moving the field closer to the more traditional academic approaches.[78]

While the pioneers may have gone their own separate ways, they were part of a fellowship of inspiration with other professionals and, gradually, part of an international interdisciplinary forum for public life studies.

The basic books on the subject were published in the period from the start of the 1960s until the middle of the 1980s. Still today, the tools developed in that same period are the foundation for research, teaching and the practice of public life studies. In the following period from the mid-1980s to the turn of the century, this knowledge and approach were increasingly converted into practice. This happened as urban planners and local politicians became steadily more critical of the new planned environments and thus more interested in understanding the interaction between public space and public life in order to meet the challenges of creating attractive cities at a time of increasing inter-city competition.

Public Life Studies as Strategic Tools (1985-2000)

At the end of the 1980s, competition increased between cities and regions in step with the dwindling influence of the nation-state. This change was the result of increasing globalization and significant political and geographic changes symbolized by the fall of the Berlin Wall in 1989. Some of the burgeoning economic growth of the 1990s was invested in cities – in branding through iconic architecture, to be sure, but also in city environments and quality in the larger sense.

This period harbored built-in ambiguity. In part as a reaction to the consequences of globalization in the form of uniform cities with ever larger building projects, there was now increased focus on the human values of the city, public space, mixed functions, local perspective and a more human scale.

However, at the same time, architects were celebrated as artists and individual buildings as iconographic works of art. This practice culminated at the end of the 20th century, when cities all over the world hired a 'starchitect' to erect a piece of monumental architecture to brand their city with its special signature.

The reinforced orientation towards individual architectural works impoverished the conditions for people more concerned with the value of the space between buildings. Fortunately, there were still cities that emphasized holism and public life; Barcelona, Lyon and Copenhagen, for example, all worked strategically with public space planning. It is public space that makes these cities special, public space that is photographed in trade journals and tourist brochures.

Sustainability and Social Responsibility

From the end of the 1980s, several cities became interested in making life in the city visible – analyzing and discussing it – because the ability to create well functioning, livable cities was crucial in the increasing inter-city competition. It was no longer enough to be able to transport people quickly from point A to point B, cities needed to be attrac-

tive places where people want to live, work, visit. This development highlighted the political advantages of studying and documenting the conditions of public life in order to follow developments over time and measure the effects of the initiatives taken to make cities more attractive.

The city environment ideas that had been launched in the 1960s and 1970s began to win support from 1985-2000. The basic tenets of the public life study pioneers about diversity, prioritizing pedestrians over cars and increasing focus on people's conditions in public space generally were in keeping with the dominant agendas of the period. Awareness of sustainability and social responsibility increased from the end of the 1980s. In addition, the end of the decade and beginning of the 1990s saw debate about the increasing privatization and commercialization of public space. The anthology *Variations on a Theme Park: Scenes from the New American City and the End of Public Space* (1992) makes the point that urban space is privatized and commercialized at the expense of open, accessible public space.[79]

Sustainability and Experiences

The Brundtland Report from 1987 marks the arrival of the concept of sustainability as a significant, defined problem area – also in urban planning, where, in particular, the massive CO_2 emissions from vehicles support arguments to consider sustainable forms of transport. The interdisciplinary, holistic approach of public life studies, which supports prioritizing environment-friendly forms of transport, is certainly directed to solving these problems. The approach is also in keeping with the transition from a specialized industrial society with mass production and standard solutions to a more complex, and in some ways more holistic, knowledge and network-oriented society.[80]

All the talk about the 'leisure society' from the 1960s to the 1980s was silenced; satisfying recreational needs by establishing a sufficient number of green areas was no longer enough. Starting in the 1990s, the 'experience society' became the hot topic. Now people had to be provided with

The Reconquest of Europe – Urban Public Spaces 1980-1999 *was the title of an exhibition arranged by Centre de Cultura Contemporània de Barcelona (CCCB) in 1999. The concept of "the reconquered city" was launched here, illustrated by numerous examples of public spaces established in Europe in the 1980s and 1990s.*

The exhibition gave the overall impression that cities had decided to focus on public space as an important urban planning element. The city had been reconquered by people, so to say, who could now use the squares and plazas that had formerly been occupied by parked cars. Photo: Barcelona, Spain.

experiences, which increased demands for the selection of activities in public space and required increased specialization for special target groups or types of activities. It was no longer sufficient to build a standardized playground: theme playgrounds, skate parks, jogging paths and parkour training were also needed. Specialization and the demand for experiences generally gave rise to the need to test whether special target groups were being reached, and whether public space was being used for the intended purpose, or for something else, or for nothing at all.

The Reconquered City – Barcelona

In the 1980s and 1990s, planners and politicians in many cities became steadily more critical about the pressure from cars and functionalist city planning. Public space and the public life that plays out between buildings enjoyed increased attention. In 2000, Jan Gehl and Lars Gemzøe published the book *New City Spaces,* with 39 examples of new or restored streets and squares from all over the world. The authors pointed out in the introduction to the book that public space began to be taken seriously in the 1980s. In this connection Barcelona's policy stood like a beacon: "In the course of 50 years, all city space had been conquered by cars. Now the city was fighting back, both physically and culturally. It was also in Barcelona that the concept of 'the reconquered city' was born." The term is used in the sense of freeing the city from traffic dominance and returning it to the people.[81]

Starting in 1979, in the wake of the first free election in Spain since the end of Franco's dictatorship, the city government in Barcelona made public space a priority. After many years where the freedom of assembly was banned, the return to democracy was celebrated by creating new meeting places in all parts of the city.

The first public space projects were carried out at the end of the 1970s and start of the 1980s, primarily in the old part of the city. Work spread later to public space in the suburbs, and a profusion of public spaces with many different and often innovative designs was established. Barcelona became an example for inspiration in public space architecture, which in this period began to stand as an independent discipline.[82]

The inspiration from Barcelona and other cities led to increased awareness of public space as a strategic tool, for both planners and politicians. Recognition of the importance of quality in the interaction between public space and public life reinforced the need for studying life in the new city spaces.

From University to City-Driven Studies

From the mid-1980s, many city governments wanted advice about the interaction between public space and public life. Studies were often conducted in collaboration with academic institutions until around the year 2000, when a gradual shift to private consulting began.[83] The desire to put theories and ideas into practice encouraged public life researchers to combine their academic careers with private consulting practice.[84]

Numerous cities conducted what began to be termed 'public space-public life studies'. The studies were first made in a form of collaboration between cities and researchers at the The Royal Danish Academy of Fine Arts, School of Architecture in Copenhagen, and later with Gehl Architects, established in 2000.

Copenhagen has been the living laboratory for developing the methodology for public space-public life studies from 1968 up to today. Copenhagen is the first city in the world to have conducted recurring public life studies – in 1968, 1986, 1996 and 2006.[85]

A major public life study was conducted in 1986 and compared with the study made in 1968. The 18-year span allowed interesting conclusions to be drawn, both local and general. It was possible to read a change in the character of Copenhagen's public life. While the number of people on the main pedestrian street Strøget had remained largely the same, the number staying rather than just walking had increased markedly from 1968 to 1986. The selection of cultural offerings in city space had notably expanded as well in the same period. The public life study from 1986 showed the outlines of a rise in recreational and cultural use of public space.[86]

These major studies serve as an extensive check-up about once a decade, when the health of city life is carefully examined. Smaller scale studies are conducted in the years between the major studies. For several decades, Melbourne and Perth, Australia; Oslo, Norway; Stockholm, Sweden; and a provincial Danish city, Odense, have also conducted public space-public life studies, making it possible to see initiatives, policies and concrete projects in a larger perspective.[87]

The local knowledge needed to document development is gathered by conducting identical studies at recurring intervals. In addition, using comparable methods in different cities and at different points in time allows more general conclusions to be drawn about the interaction between public life and public space. The methods provide grounds for comparison that make it possible to conclude more generally about prioritizing public space and people's behavior, as well as with regard to developments in society.

Numerous cities all over the world now use public space-public life studies to establish the status of their own city life. Their starting point might be to pinpoint areas that need a special city-space initiative, or to evaluate the effect of such an initiative, or another aspect of qualifying the interaction of public space with public life.

"The Community is the Expert" – PPS[88]

Rooted in the work of William H. Whyte, the Project for Public Spaces (PPS) advises cities across North America as well as abroad, with special emphasis on citizen participation and transformation processes. Projects typically involve a defined, somewhat limited area.

The founder and head of PPS is Fred Kent, who assisted Whyte on The Street Life Project in the 1970s. With a bachelor's degree in economics and a master's degree in urban geography, Kent's approach is unmistakably interdisciplinary.

PPS was founded in 1975, but the company first became widely known through several projects starting in the mid-1990s. User involvement in projects reflects the agenda on social responsibility in the same period. Although PPS's methods feature dialogue-based tools such as interviews and workshops involving users, the company also relies on direct observations in city space as a basis for their work.

The first of the 11 PPS principles for creating 'good places' is that the community is the expert. The principles are detailed in their handbook, *How to Turn a Place Around* (2000).[89] In addition to working with concrete projects, PPS runs extensive workshops in order to give participants insight into the issue of life in public space and the tools to change conditions in their local environment.

Although many of the other methods and people mentioned in the book primarily involve observing people, one of PPS's central tenets is to ask people questions and bring them together in a dialogue. PPS uses the term 'placemaking' about their processes, which relatively quickly and preferably cheaply can make small-scale improvements in public space, such as a square, a street or a neighborhood. *The Great Neighborhood Book* (2007) contains numerous examples of PPS's work.[90]

Cities Discover Public Life Studies as a Tool

Cities became an active part of method development in the years 1985-2000. Public life studies become more integrated into city planning practice and thus incorporated in a new political framework. Many factors other than the purely technical and research-related now influenced the form of the studies, particularly how and whether they were used.

Roughly speaking, the basic books in the field of public life studies were published in the years 1960-1985. Books continued to be published after 1985, but fewer in number. As public life studies became established at academic institutions, specialization followed and specific aspects could

How to Turn a Place Around (2000)

Under the leadership of Fred Kent, the Project for Public Spaces (PPS) encourages citizen participation. The project has published books with examples of their work to serve as inspiration to others, as well as handbooks setting out the tools citizens can use to create better places in cities. One important aspect of PPS's activities is teaching in order to provide planners and citizens with the tools for conversion processes. PPS continues the activism inherited from Jane Jacobs and others who helped shape the field of public life studies.

How to Turn a Place Around from 2000 is a handbook that details PPS's approach and tools.[97] It can be used directly as a template with checklists and actual tools such as registration sheets for copying at the back of the book. PPS's books do not delineate basic knowledge about the interaction of public space and public life, but rather provide practical recommendations on how to change conditions. The focus is citizen participation and transformation processes.

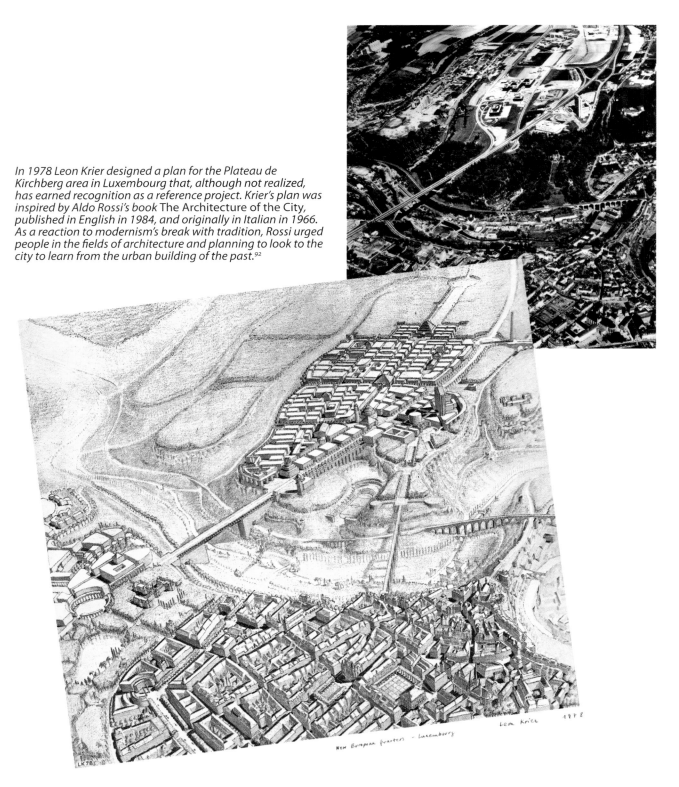

In 1978 Leon Krier designed a plan for the Plateau de Kirchberg area in Luxembourg that, although not realized, has earned recognition as a reference project. Krier's plan was inspired by Aldo Rossi's book The Architecture of the City, published in English in 1984, and originally in Italian in 1966. As a reaction to modernism's break with tradition, Rossi urged people in the fields of architecture and planning to look to the city to learn from the urban building of the past.[92]

be studied. This trend was supported by the publication of books such as *Livable Streets* (1981), *Housing as if People Mattered* (housing, children, seniors, 1988), *Sun, Wind, and Comfort* (about working with local climate conditions, 1984), *Looking at Cities* (about observations, 1985) and *Representations of Places* (about experience and communication, 1998).[93]

The Field of Architecture Turns to the City

In the same period, the field of architecture rediscovered traditional urban qualities. While the ideals of Modernism had been the dominant paradigm, particularly in the second half of the 20th century, there was a shift back to the city in the 1980s, with Aldo Rossi and the Krier brothers as the main actors in this post-modernistic revolt.[94]

Now the compact city and traditional public space typologies were discussed and written about, with focus on form and the broader context of sustainability. Richard Rogers, among others, made an important contribution in his book *Cities for a Small Planet*, published in 1997.[95]

The New Urbanism movement was founded in 1993.[96] The New Urbanists too broke with modernism, just like the pioneers before them in public life studies. One important difference was that the New Urbanists generally had a heavy focus on design, while the focus of the public life studies was primarily on people's activities. The public life study authors could certainly be as normative and idealistic as the New Urbanists, and hold their own in the talk about 'the good city.' However, the public life study pioneers placed greater emphasis on general principles, typically formulated on the basis of many studies: for example, Jan Gehl's principles in *Life Between Buildings* (1971) and Clare Cooper Marcus' principles in *Housing as if People Mattered* (1988).[97] These authors offer general principles rather than specific design guidelines.

Key concepts in *Life Between Buildings* are to assemble rather than disperse, to integrate rather than segregate, to invite rather than repel and to open up rather than close in.[98] In *Housing as if People Mattered*, Clare Cooper Marcus outlines the principles to be considered in designing outdoor space in residential areas, particularly to meet the needs of children.[99] While the principles delineated by Gehl, Cooper Marcus and others in the field of public life studies can certainly be considered normative, they are not focused on design in detail. The way design is expressed is considered subordinate; it is the fixation on design that the public life studies pioneers rebel against. Their focus is public life in interaction with design rather than design in itself.

In the 1980s and 1990s, consideration for the interaction between public life and public space gained acceptance in more and more cities. As social agendas began to demand healthier, safer and more sustainable cities, the importance of the interaction gradually became increasingly accepted.

Place des Terreaux in Lyon, France. Lyon was one of the first European cities to work strategically with public space starting at the end of the 1980s.[100]

Public Life Studies become Mainstream (2000)

In 2007, for the first time, more than half the world population was living in cities rather than rural areas. This shift makes it even more relevant to study the way life and space interact in cities, and not only in the so-called developed part of the world. Cities in developing countries are growing explosively, and here too public space studies are slowly making headway.[101]

Sustainability, health and safety are some of the items that put working with public life solidly on the agenda. After the year 2000 the concept of 'livability' often crops up.[102] The concept was used earlier in the field of public life studies by Donald Appleyard, for example, who wrote about 'livable streets' already at the end of the 1960s. However, his book by the same name, which compiled the studies made, was not published until 1981.[103]

The popular media use the concept to measure the 'livability' of various cities, publishing annual lists of the most 'livable' cities in the world.[104] While the value and credibility of the lists can be discussed, in this context it is important that they manifest the broad media's orientation about soft values as a competitive parameter in inter-city competition.

While other parts of the world use terms such as sustainability and life quality, in the USA, livability is a working concept at city and national level.[105] The US Secretary of Transportation, Ray LaHood, defined livability as follows: "Livability means being able to take your kids to school, go to work, see a doctor, drop by the grocery or post office, go out to dinner and a movie, and play with your kids at the park – all without having to get in your car."[106] Thus the American government is indicating the desire to work toward the goal of freeing people from dependence on the automobile, which has been an almost sacred symbol in the 20th century, particularly in the USA. In Copenhagen, the vision was called *Metropolis for People* in 2009.[107]

While incorporating public life in policies and projects has become increasingly widespread in the 21st century, this does not mean that the studies or similar forms of systematic planning are carried out before projects are launched.

Countless projects are realized without having had the benefit of sufficient consideration of the interaction of public life and public space, despite the fact that it has been shown over and over again that city life heavily depends on conducive physical environments. However, public life studies have become an integral part of planning in an increasing number of cities.

Public Life Pioneers are Finally Heard

Although the early pioneers had influence, it was limited. Nonetheless, they were able to plant many seeds that germinated in the 1960s and flowered through the early part of the 21st century, where their ideas were finally more generally accepted in step with changes in community values. At the turn of the century, several arguments were added to the list of why it is important to learn about people's interaction with public space.

In the 1980s and 1990s when inhabitants, investors and visitors demanded attractive, livable cities, planners and politicians saw the wisdom of incorporating public life in order to meet inter-city competition.

In the new millennium, the desire to find solutions to the challenges posed by the environment, health and safety was added to the list.

Jane Jacobs died in 2006, but continues to be recognized for her pioneering efforts to draw attention to why public space and public life must be made part of planning. In 2010 the book *What We See* was published as a tribute to Jacobs, with contributions from numerous prominent practitioners and theoreticians.[108] Despite new issues, Jane Jacobs remains relevant – perhaps even more relevant considering the kinds of problems that the world and the world's cities face in the 21st century.

Also in 2010, Jan Gehl published *Cities for People*, which looks back on 4 years of work to create better conditions for people in cities.[109] The book contains numerous examples showing that many cities want to meet people's needs and that studying and learning from the interaction between space and life is an important tool for doing so. This is rel-

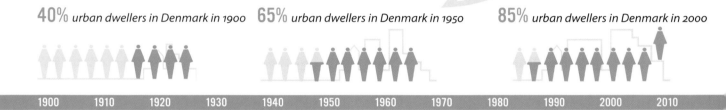

40% *urban dwellers in Denmark in 1900*   **65%** *urban dwellers in Denmark in 1950*   **85%** *urban dwellers in Denmark in 2000*

The bubble shows some of the dominant social themes that fueled the focus on public life. In 1986 sociologist Ulrich Beck introduced the concept of the risk society, while the concept of sustainability was cemented in 1987 in the Brundtland report and has since become an integral part of largely all urban development plans. Health in relation to cities earned a place on the urban agenda at the start of the new millennium, and the concept of livability was introduced at about the same time. Increasing urbanization is a recurring topic, and cities are seen as the place where future challenges must be met.[110]

evant regardless of economics and geography. "Core issues are respect for people, dignity, zest for life and the city as meeting place. In these areas, the differences between the dreams and desires of people in various parts of the world do not vary dramatically. The methods for dealing with the issues are also surprisingly similar, because it all comes down to people, who have the same basic point of departure. All people have walking, a sensory apparatus, movement options and basic behavior patterns in common. The similarities between cultures are far greater than the differences," writes Jan Gehl.[111]

Sustainability, Security and Health

In the 21st century, the concept of sustainability was expanded from being a rather narrow environmental perspective to include social and economic sustainability. The need for more knowledge about what can get people to bike or walk instead of driving a polluting car has to be supplemented with more basic knowledge about the social and economic cohesion of public space. The goal of creating cities where everyone can move on foot is an elemental part of the ideology underlying public life studies.

The terrorist attack on the World Trade Center in New York City on September 11, 2001 put increasing focus on fear and security in cities. Efforts have since been made to create more open, inclusive public space with people present around the clock. Unfortunately, it also led to the opposite: gated communities that exclude public life.

Video-monitoring of public space also plays an increasing role and the ethical aspects involved were a heated topic of discussion in this period. When the objective is to broadly create a sense of security in the city, it is important to study how that can be done using the city's own structures. Here public life studies are also highly relevant.

Rallying in public space

2011 was a year that witnessed demonstrations all over the world. Protests in Arab countries encompassed entire regimes, while Western demonstrators aimed their ire at the financial sector's reckless behavior and responsibility for the global financial crisis. Public space was a significant venue despite the many new social media, which also played a prominent role.

In January 2011, more than 300,000 people took to the streets near Tahir Square in Cairo, the epicenter of protest in Egypt, to demonstrate against the rule of Hosni Mubarak. In Manama, Bahrain, a traffic hub with a monumental sculpture at its center became the meeting place for protests against the government. The monument and plaza were later razed by bulldozers and replaced by an intersection regulated by traffic lights in order to avoid its use as a rallying site.[112]

In the spring of 2011, people also protested in many Spanish cities against the increasing inequality in society, this in the wake of the global financial crisis that began in 2007. From the middle of September to mid-November 2011, Zucotti Park in the heart of New York City's financial district became the framework for the Occupy Wall Street movement demonstrating against the influence of global finance. Here too public space had not only symbolic significance, but was a place for people to meet face to face.[113]

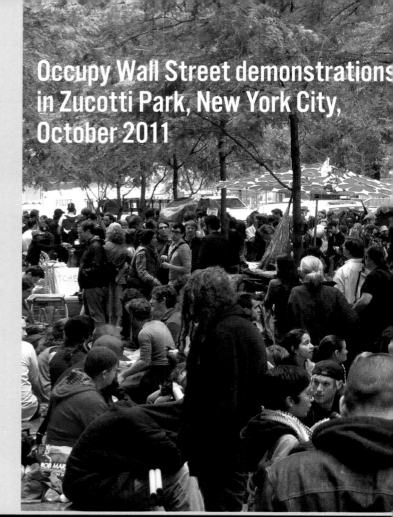

Occupy Wall Street demonstrations in Zucotti Park, New York City, October 2011

Pearl Plaza in Manama, Bahrain, spring 2011

Security has always played a key role in public life studies. For Jane Jacobs, security was central. She coupled creating a secure city together with creating a living city, because having 'eyes on the street' and interest in the life of the neighborhood can help prevent crime.[114] Architect and city planner Oscar Newman addressed crime-prevention issues in relation to designing and planning public space in his book *Defensible Space* (1972).[115]

Security has also been an ongoing topic of discussion in the field of urban planning, for example, on the basis of Mike Davis' book about Los Angeles, *City of Quartz* (1990), and more generally in a social perspective based on the concept of the 'risk society'. German sociologist Ulrich Beck coined the concept in 1986. He used the term to describe the fear tied to the consequences of globalization, the threat of environmental catastrophe and the potential impenetrability of new technology.[116]

Health is another topic that inspired more and more public debate in the course of the new millennium, also in terms of how cities are designed. This trend mirrored the increase in the share of the population dealing with obesity, diabetes, cardiac disease and other lifestyle-related diseases.

In the new century, health increasingly became an issue, with focus on lack of daily exercise, and here the role of the physical framework for daily life plays a substantial role. Politicians and urban planners deliberated about how to get people to move more on a daily basis by changing the design of cities, because walking and biking in city space is more than an environmentally friendly form of transport that also helps promote security. It promotes health as well.

Public Space as a Stage for Demonstrations and Public Assembly

The Arab Spring of 2011 bears witness to the fact that public space is still significant as the place where citizens can gather to demonstrate. Crowds of people in many Arab countries took to the streets in civil resistance to undemocratic rulers.

In Egypt, Cairo's Tahrir Square was the magnet for popular protest. In Bahrain's capital city Manama, Pearl Square, a traffic hub, was the stage for civil uprising. Later in 2011 the Bahrain government converted the square into an intersection, ordering the army to tear down the monument in the middle in order to prevent the site from further use as an assembly point for demonstrators. Examples like these emphasize the continued importance of public space as a forum for public opinion.[117]

Public space continues to have democratic, cultural and symbolic significance. Despite the new media and virtual platforms, which can also be used to rally the masses in the new millennium, public space continues to play a vital role as a meeting place for people.

Center for Public Space Research

After a period in which a good deal of public space studies were developed in collaboration with cities regarding specific projects, the need to conduct basic research in the field was gradually recognized. In 2003 the Center for Public Space Research, headed by Jan Gehl, was established at the School of Architecture, The Royal Danish Academy of Fine Arts in Copenhagen. The Realdania Foundation funded the new center for the purpose of "increasing our knowledge about the way we create living, attractive and safe urban environments."[118]

The center was tasked with generating knowledge that could provide a platform for the qualitative planning and design of public space. By selecting key research projects and training young researchers, the center was intended to help develop the public space field with the clear goal of acquiring more knowledge about the interaction between public space and public life: "We know too little about what makes for good public space. Also internationally, we need research that can provide a platform for the qualitative planning and design of public space . . . Over the years urban activities have changed character and new user groups have appeared. Whereas public life in public space used to be dominated by necessary activities, today optional and recreational activities are high on the agenda. We work, live and play in a way that makes new demands on our cities."[119] The starting point must be that the developments in city life warrant closer study.

The book *New City Life* (2006), carried out as a research project at the Center for Public Space Research, documented the way public life had gradually changed from one decade to the next. For the first time, the study was conducted in public spaces in all parts of Copenhagen, from the center to the periphery. In the 1970s and 1980s, people's reasons for being in the city were often tied to specific objectives and activities, such as shopping. In contrast, the public space studies from the middle of the first decade of the new century show that city life – understood as what is going on in the city, and looking at what is going on there and thus at society in general – had become a desirable quality in itself. Recreational activities had become more prominent, which was reflected in the furnishing of urban space: for example, the increase in number of café chairs year by year. In addition, new public space was created in the 1990s and the new century in neighborhoods outside the city center, expanding the area studied. The results of the new public life studies and expansion of the area studied underline the need for studies to capture the scope as well as the changes in public space and public life and the interaction between them.[120]

Cities do not usually have budgets to cover this type of basic research. Therefore it is crucial to find other ways to ensure that methods are developed and basic research conducted in public space studies.

Public life studies are increasingly being recognized internationally. The field is largely considered as established, despite its rather wide-ranging character. It is not a field with a specifically defined, solid position at institutions of higher education. Rather the field is an element incorporated into studies in many places – not only schools of architecture, but at technical universities with interdisciplinary programs in cultural fields, such as anthropology, sociology and geography.

New Technology – New Methods

In the 21st century, new technologies have spurred further development of the methods to study the interaction between public life and public space. In about 2000, technological development took a quantum leap with regard to data collection and dissemination via the Internet. While new technological opportunities provide a broader selection of ways in which to study public life, observations are still important, even though in some cases they can be made with cameras, mobile telephones or GPS senders.

The expansion of the Internet from the middle of the 1990s increased the accessibility of data that can inform about the character of life in the city, for example, in the form of GPS information and statistics generally. Google Street View can provide snapshots of life at eye level, and is a program that can be used by everyone regardless of technical skills.[121] And unlike other expensive technological solutions, Google Street View is even free. Technology develops constantly, making new methods cheaper and easier to use.

GPS tracking

Instead of following or shadowing people, they can be equipped with a Global Positioning System (GPS) device. The GPS device together with a positioning program can be used to gather information about movements and the duration of movements or stationary activities. GPS positioning was developed by the US military and made accessible for civilian use in the mid-1990s. Several services have been developed since then, such as registering jogging routes, but the technique is also used increasingly to study human activity in the city. It is particularly useful in mapping in widespread areas and over long periods, where physical shadowing would require too much manpower.

One of the projects to develop GPS technology to register people's behavior in public space is Henrik Harder's project at the University of Ålborg, in Denmark. Harder developed an application that registers as well as asks questions underway using special GPS devices and telephones with GPS devices.[122]

Technical Universities – GPS Registrations

Public life studies have been anchored primarily in schools of architecture since their start in the 1960s and 1970s. However, beginning at the turn of the century, researchers, primarily from technical universities, have introduced automatic observations of human behavior using, for example, tracking technology such as GPS registrations that can reveal where people go, where they stay and for how long.

Compared to manual registration, GPS senders can be used to register movements and stays over larger areas and for longer periods. Senders can provide more precise information about the position of an individual. However, there is still a margin of about 3-5 meters, which makes this technology less well-suited to register precisely where on a square people are located, or whether they are inside or outside a building.

GPS registration can outline the big picture and is typically used to register movements in public space. The people being registered wear senders. In other words, they must volunteer to participate in registration and wear the gear, which makes the process more cumbersome than simple manual observations. In addition, the equipment is relatively expensive. That may change with the expansion of GPS senders in mobile telephones – devices that have certainly become ubiquitous.[123]

The pioneers in GPS public life studies are located particularly in Holland with Stefan van der Spek in conjunction with the Technical University of Delft, at MIT, at the Hebrew University of Jerusalem with Noam Shoval, and in Denmark at Ålborg University, where Henrik Harder, among others, has used the technology to map movements in public space.

Mathematical Methods – Space Syntax

Space syntax is a set of theories and techniques for analyzing spatial configurations, originally conceived to help architects simulate the likely social effects of their designs. In contrast to studies that observe life directly by watching people's behavior, space syntax looks indirectly at life through mathematical models. The models process data in order to predict where people will probably go and which way they will probably take and how often they will take it. The objective here is to make prognoses and predict movements.

The most important tool for space syntax is computer programs that are programmed with selected principles of human behavior. The principles are based on data from observations. So while space syntax is not used as a tool in the city per se, the data that provide the basis for drawing maps and various degrees of accessibility derive from direct observations of human behavior. Knowledge about how people move in relation to urban structures is coded into the computer programs used for space syntax, for example, to calculate the probability that so and so many people will walk down a given street.

The Social Logic of Space (1984) by Bill Hillier, et al. is the textbook for space syntax.[124] The title supports the mathematical focus of Hillier and his colleagues at The Bartlett, University College of London, who were seeking logic. The book was published already in the middle of the 1980s, but it was not until the development of computer programs that could process large amounts of data after the turn of the century that space syntax targeted public life studies.

Professor of architecture and urban morphology, Hillier is the academic father figure for space syntax, while architect Tim Stonor is its main practitioner. In 1995 Stoner established the Space Syntax Laboratory at University College London, and the following year he became the managing director of Space Syntax Limited, the laboratory's private consulting arm. Just like the rest of the public space studies field, space syntax operates with a close interchange between research and practice. In recent years, the space syntax approach has seen use in a number of countries, and the methodology has moved from exclusive focus on movement to other factors such as functions and building density.[125]

Space syntax publications typically contain many colored maps showing where roads are connected in a neighborhood or city. The warmer the color, the greater the potential for movement in the area. Lines can also vary in density. For example, a street connected to many other streets is accessible from many points and will typically be red with many crossed lines. In contrast, a street that ends blind and thus is not connected with many other streets will be typically represented by a thin blue line standing alone.

Space syntax maps can be difficult for non-professionals to read. There is a greater degree of abstraction in space syntax studies than in manual public life studies. The method is more dependent on specialists due to the mathematical component of the method itself, as well as to the computer programming needed to process the data. Although space syntax represents studies of the interaction between life and form in the city, it departs from traditional manual public life studies with regard to basic values. Sacrosanct to traditionalists are the ideas that the city should be seen and depicted at eye level; being in the city is a prerequisite for understanding the interaction between life and form; ideally, the methods and means of communication should be relatively simple tools.

The consulting firm Space Syntax contributed to the development of a master plan for the Olympic City in Stratford City London (2012) by analyzing the connections in and around the Olympic area.

The map was made with the help of information from computer programs about the probability that pedestrians, bicyclists and drivers would choose one way or another, and which public spaces and parks have the greatest and least probability of being used. The color scale illustrates the results, with blue the least likely and red the most likely. Space Syntax's managing director Tim Stonor wrote about the map:

"This map captures the essence of London: people moving and interacting in space; sharing stories and ideas; trading, creating and innovating; a social and economic network, played out in streets and public spaces."[126]

The map illustrates how the starting point for Space Syntax's studies is the interaction between public space and public life. However, the way information is presented is not city life and situations at eye level, which is typically the case for public life studies. Rather space syntax represents a more technical, logical and abstract version of public life studies.

Degree of accessibility

High

Low

Automated or Manual Data Collection

These paragraphs on GPS registration, space syntax and the general influence of technological development on public life studies were written in 2012, with advanced technical solutions, on the whole, still in their infancy. Ahead are the considerable challenges of producing reliable results and designing software that can process the huge amounts of data involved, so that non-specialists too can participate. This type of specialization stands in sharp contrast to the 'Berkeley and Copenhagen School of Public Life Studies' with its emphasis on simple tools and methods that can be conducted by everyone. This does not mean that new technology will not contribute constructively to future public space studies. It is reasonable to expect that the price of equipment will fall dramatically within very few years, and that equipment use and subsequent data processing will be simplified. This development will in all probability mean that space syntax, GPS studies and similar types of methodologies will become more accessible as tools for more and more people. At present, automated and technical tools for studying public space and public life are found primarily at technical universities.

Automated data collection means that observers no longer have to be physically present in public space, which impacts on subsequent interpretation. Are we talking about abstract data or tangible data observed in situ, thereby containing more subtleties with regard to further interpretation? Life is diverse and unpredictable, and its nuances and complexity cannot really be captured by automated methods of collection.

A basic tenet of method development for traditional, manual-oriented public space researchers is to come to the city to experience and discover connections and to observe the interaction between public space and public life.

In the 21st century, qualifying the connections between city form and life in order to consider conditions for living and working is almost taken for granted. There is a broad spectrum of methods – manual and automated – for focusing on what was once often overlooked. However, the evidence shows that we are far from being able to take for granted that we have managed to get city form and life to interact. Success requires that we make sensitive, determined and focused efforts to get a grip on city life.

The Social Logic of Space (1984)

In 1984 the father figure of space syntax, Bill Hillier, together with Julienne Hanson wrote the book *The Social Logic of Space*, considered the textbook for space syntax.[127] They study the connections between social life and urban structures, and, as the title suggests, their starting point is neither personal nor activist like many of the other public life study pioneers. To map social logistics, they use observations of how people walk around in public space or data from GIS. The goal is to quantify data to such an extent that it can be used with the help of computer programs to calculate the probability that people will walk in one direction or another in existing and future buildings and city districts.

The publishing of Hillier's book marks the new technological options for the field of public life studies and a more abstract and logic-based access to public space and public life that started in the 1980s.

Urban Life in Retrospect

In the Middle Ages, building cities was largely centered on human needs. Craftsmanship, knowledge and experience were passed down from one generation to the next and utilized in the public arena and public life of medieval cities where everyone moved by foot.

The rise of modernism and the automobile shifted the focus away from life in the city. Starting in the 1960s, a number of researchers reacted to the change and their books and methods laid the foundation for public life studies. Their starting point was to go into the city to observe city life and learn from their observations.

In step with the shifting agendas of development in society, city councils and planners become more willing to accept public life studies in order to strengthen their cities in inter-city competition from the end of the 1980s. Softer themes such as sustainability, health and social responsibility begin to head up urban agendas, making public life studies all the more relevant. Hard values such as the economy also encouraged the authorities to use public space-public life studies as a tool to document the development of city life in order to attract tax-payers, tourists and investors in the increasing inter-city competition. Although working with the interaction between public life and public space became increasingly taken for granted, public life studies were by no means part of every urban toolbox here at the beginning of the 21st century.

Interdisciplinary Observations at Eye Level

Direct observations are the primary tool for studying the interaction of public space and public life. The point is to see the city at eye level from the perspective of pedestrians, not as an abstract configuration seen from an airplane or as computer-generated lines on a screen. Being able to see the city at eye level requires several skills in order to qualify the interplay of life and space in the city in dialectic between research and practice.

It is primarily Anglo-Saxon and Scandinavian researchers who are involved with this type of public space-public life

studies. They are known for a pragmatic approach that is only loosely tied to theory, understood to mean that they are not bound by the established academic discourse. Seen in retrospect, one might ask whether public life studies should have been fitted into a Marxist framework of understanding in the 1960s, or a basic theoretical discourse inspired by French philosophy at the end of the century. These and other theoretical platforms would have been an option, but public life pioneers were more pragmatic than theoretical.

The point is to come into the city to learn and develop methods in dialectic between research and practice rather than to write about public life studies as a field in an academic framework. As Jane Jacobs wrote: "Cities are an immense laboratory of trial and error, failure and success, in city building and city design. This is the laboratory in which city planning should have been learning and forming and testing theories."[128] Gehl, Whyte and many others operationalized Jacob's concerns in the years to follow.

From the Specter of Moribund Metropolis to Cities for People

The titles of the books published on the subject of public space and public life studies reflect the corresponding development from a cry for help to an established field.

Already in 1961 Jane Jacobs' book was a spirited call to arms: *The Death and Life of Great American Cities*. Jan Gehl followed a decade later by systematizing and operationalizing the challenge in his book on acquiring more knowledge about *Life Between Buildings* (1971). In the next two decades, the goal was to establish and communicate basic knowledge about and methods to study public life and its interaction with public space. Life was the essence of William H. Whyte's book *The Social Life of Small Urban Spaces* from 1980. The need to generate awareness about the lack of consideration for public life in urban planning continued, as illustrated by the polemical title of Clare Cooper Marcus' book, *Housing as if People Mattered*, published in 1985.

Once awareness had been created about life in the city and the necessity of taking city life seriously, public space, specific neighborhoods and places, found their way into book titles. Whyte had already dealt with small urban spaces and Gehl with life between buildings. Allan Jacobs took to the streets with his book *Great Streets* published in 1995, and Gehl and Gemzøe turned the focus to *New City Spaces* in their book from 2000. Life was not in the title of the latter book, nor in PPS's *How to Turn a Place Around*, also published in 2000, despite the special focus of users in PPS's approach. This bears witness to the fact that public life studies had gradually become established in the fields of architecture and urban planning and thus no longer had the same ties to sociology and psychology that they had had originally in the 1960s and 1970s. Another interpretation is that as the field became established, researchers and publications became more specialized.

Seen in a historical perspective, the book titles reflect the gradual establishment of the field. More books were published dealing with the methods used to study public space and public life: for example, *Looking at Cities* by Allan Jacobs (1985), which deals with observations, *Representations of Places* by Bosselmann (1998), which is about the problems of disseminating knowledge about public life, while a good part of *Public Spaces – Public Life* by Gehl and Gemzøe (1995) is also about the methods used to study the interaction of public space and public life.

Deciding that the time had come to document the changes that could be shown over the 40 years that Copenhagen's public life had been studied, in 2006 Gehl and Gemzøe et al. once again took up the theme, but this time focused on *New City Life*. The character of public life had moved from activities by necessity to activities by choice.

In 2008 Bosselmann provided a retrospective look through a large collection of studies of the interaction between public space and public life in *Urban Transformation*. In 2010 Jan Gehl, in his book *Cities for People*, summed up 40 years of public life studies and provided many different examples from all over the world about the work with the interaction between public space and public life from the end of the 1960s to today. The fact that several decades of work can be documented is proof that the field is indeed established. At the same time, the voices of the pioneers continue to be heard in the field of public space and public life studies.

The B001 waterfront area in Malmø, Sweden is an example of a quarter in which knowledge about the interaction between public space and public life has been incorporated in the general plan as well as in individual city spaces and buildings. The result is an attractive quarter – and with a contemporary expression.

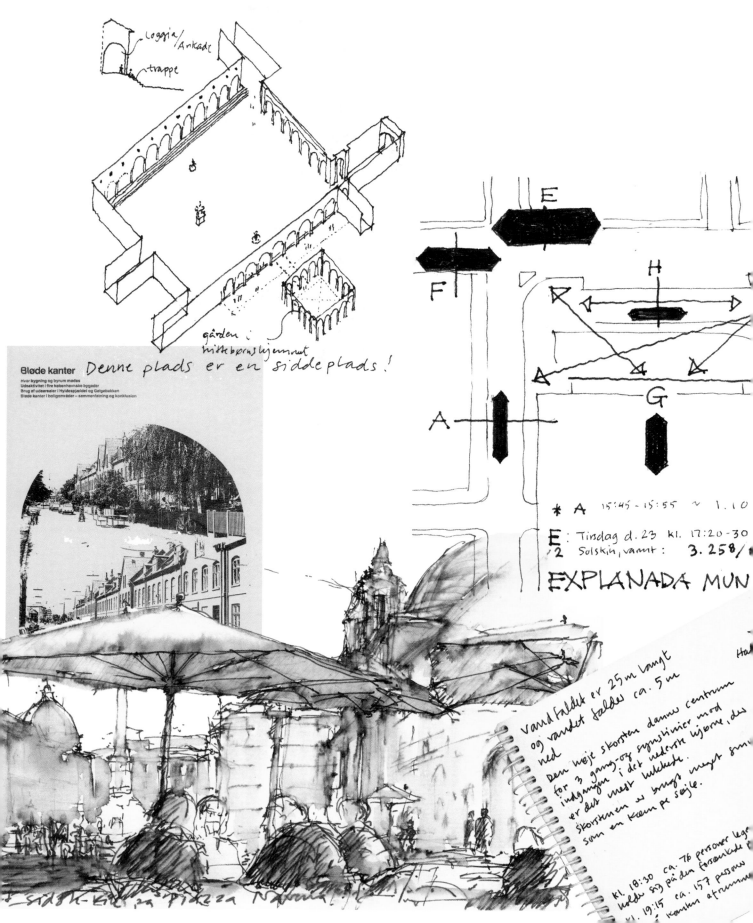

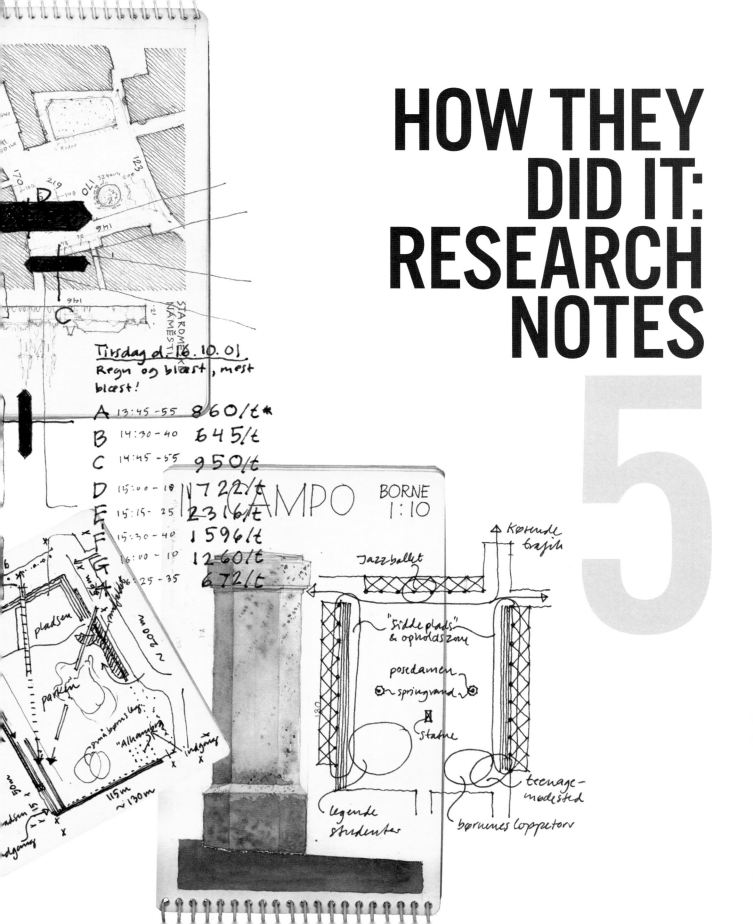

HOW THEY DID IT: RESEARCH NOTES

5

It is one thing to read about tools or adopt theories about how people might behave in public space, but something quite different to be observing out in the field.

The references in this chapter are like pages torn from notebooks: pages with notes about why and how various tools were used, which areas selected for study, etc. Together the varied stories provide a picture of the breadth of public life studies, and individually they can serve as specific inspiration for studies.

The brief research stories describe the development and use of tools for public life studies. They are told in retrospect and, as far as possible, from the field where tools are often developed and adapted to the individual situation. Emphasis is on the selection, development and use of tools rather than on the results of the individual studies. Some references are the description of a segment of a larger study.

Examples provide firsthand accounts of why and how the interaction between public life and public space is studied. While the examples are primarily from the authors and others at Gehl Architects, studies by other researchers are included to show other methods and points of view.

Every story is framed by a headline plus factual information about who conducted the study, where and how it was carried out and the source, if the study has been published. In this case the earliest reference will be given, so that the reader can find the original study.

The tools for public life studies are developed, adjusted and adapted to the purpose of individual studies and the local context in the field. The photographs opposite show observers in various cities: top left, studies in Perth, West Australia, 1978; top right, observations in Chongqing, China, 2010; middle left, close-up of the counting process in Adelaide, Australia, 2011; middle right, Jan Gehl photographing in Melbourne, Australia, 2013; bottom, public life registrations in Chennai, India, 2010.

GOOD PLACES TO STAND

Studying preferred places to stand at a public square

Who: Jan Gehl
Where: Piazza del Popolo, Ascoli Piceno, Italy
When: Friday, December 10, 1965, 5:30 pm
Method: Behavioral mapping
Published: Jan Gehl together with Ingrid Gehl, "Mennesker i byer" (*People in Cities*. In Danish),
             Arkitekten 21/1966[1]

Activities in public space can be divided fundamentally into those that are transitory and those that are stationary. Transitory activities can be recorded simply by using a counter to count the number of pedestrians who walk selected stretches. Other methods of 'counting' are needed to get an idea about stationary activities. Behavioral mapping is a simple tool well-suited for a space that is not too large.

The 1965 studies of the good places to stand at the square in the Italian town of Ascoli Piceno illustrate this method. By plotting in the position of all the people at the square who are not walking, the observer needs to make only one registration to get a good overview of the good places to stand.

On this rather cool (*9°C*) December day at Piazza del Popolo, 206 people were recorded at the square at 5:30 p.m., of which 105 were walking across the square, while 101 were standing. The study was carried out in less than 10 minutes.

Like similar studies, the one at the square in Ascoli Piceno shows that pedestrians typically crisscross the space, while people standing have carefully chosen their spots at the edge of the space.

Clearly preference is for standing by the columns of the archways, under the archways and along the facades. On the square itself, all the people found standing are involved in conversations. If someone meets an acquaintance while walking in town, they tend to stop and talk at the place where they met, even if it is in the middle of the square.

Studies like this have helped draw attention to the importance of edges, a topic that has since played a key role in our understanding of the interaction between public life and public space.

In Piazza del Popolo, behavioral mapping was used to register stationary activity, and patterns formed where there were few and many stays relative to the buildings, design of space, other people, etc. These studies clearly show what was later described as the edge effect: the fact that people were more likely to stay at the edge of spaces.[2] Behavioral mapping can provide a clear picture of how people stay in a selected public space.

Plan and photograph: Piazza del Popolo, Ascoli Piceno, Italy, 1965.
Top: Behavioral mapping is used to show where people are standing; everyone standing on the piazza at a given point in time is indicated on the plan.
Bottom: "Here in semi-darkness or by the pillars, one can be present and yet discreet, can see everything that is going on but remain partially hidden."[3]

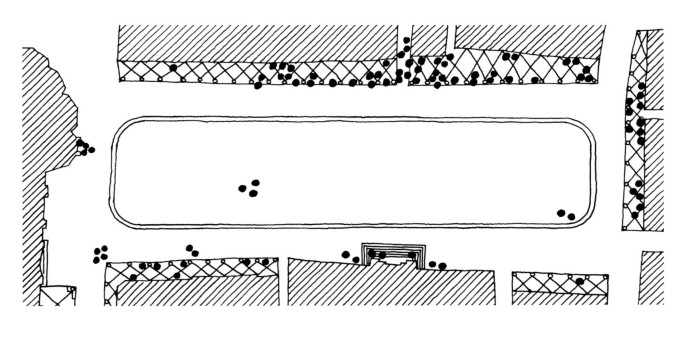

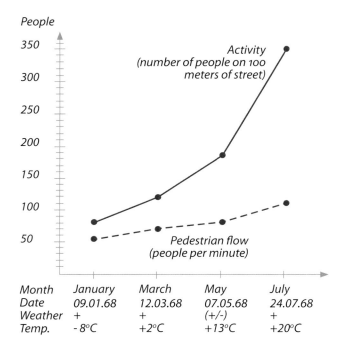

Month	January	March	May	July
Date	09.01.68	12.03.68	07.05.68	24.07.68
Weather	+	+	(+/-)	+
Temp.	- 8°C	+2°C	+13°C	+20°C

Original text from Arkitekten no. 20/1968:
Graphic representation of the relationship between pedestrian flow and activity level (crowding) on Strøget, Copenhagen's main pedestrian street, from January to July. The dashed line shows the average number of pedestrians per minute (daytime). The solid line shows the average number of people walking, standing and sitting per 100-meter stretch. Registrations like these, which include the number of people as well as staying time, can be used to evaluate pedestrian areas.

1. Activity on Strøget, January 9, 3 p.m., -8°C. Pedestrian flow is 70 people per minute, average walking speed 62 sec./100 m. It is cold and people have to keep walking to stay warm. The individual pedestrian is within sight range for 124 seconds.

2. Activity on Strøget, July 24, 3 p.m., +20°C. Pedestrian flow is 125 people per minute, average walking speed 85 sec. /100 m. The individual pedestrian is now within sight range for 170 seconds. The reduced walking speed alone means that in the summer with the same pedestrian flow, 35% more pedestrians are seen on the street.[4]

Copenhagen's main pedestrian street, Strøget, in winter and summer 1967.

WHO WALKS, HOW FAST, WHEN?

Studying walking speed, categories of people and seasons

Who: Jan Gehl
Where: The Pedestrian Street (Strøget), Copenhagen, Denmark
When: January, March, May and July, 1967
Method: Tracking
Published: Jan Gehl, "Mennesker til fods" (*People on Foot*. In Danish), *Arkitekten* 20/1968[5]

Knowing how quickly people walk in public space is important in many contexts. A five-minute walk can cover various distances depending on walking speed. In order to study the influence of the seasons on walking tempo, a study was conducted on Strøget, the main pedestrian street in Copenhagen, in both summer and winter in 1967.

At the fast end of the spectrum on the pedestrian street in 1967 were goal-oriented pedestrians, primarily single men, clocked at a speed of 100 meters in only 48 seconds (125 m/min). A fast walker can usually cover 500 meters in five minutes (6 km/hour).

At the slower end of the spectrum were older folks, people with disabilities, families with young children and people promenading at a stately tempo. The slowest time registered was for a patrolling policeman who took 137 seconds (2.5 km/hour) to cover 100 meters.

The walking tempo of pedestrians on city streets can be registered simply by the method known as 'tracking'. The observer first measures out a distance of 100 or 200 meters: a discreet chalk mark on the pavement at the start and finish of the 'test course' is useful. The observer then takes out a stopwatch, follows and times each subject for the distance measured. Naturally the observer keeps an appropriate distance from the person being followed. The observer falls into the tempo of the selected subject well before the chalked start and uses the stopwatch to register the time it takes each subject to cover the distance.

It is simple to select and register the fastest and slowest pedestrians, but it is also usually necessary to determine the average speed of all the people walking in a given area. This makes it necessary to follow a rather large number (such as 100) of randomly selected people. Random selection can be achieved by using a system such as choosing every fifth person who enters the 'test area', for example, until the observer has a timed a sufficiently large collection on which to calculate an average.

Once the observer has calculated the average walking tempo, interesting variations can be noted over the day, week and year. On Strøget, the main pedestrian street in Copenhagen, people move fastest in the morning and afternoon, while they walk more slowly in the middle of the day. As one might expect, people walk more quickly on weekdays than on the weekends.

There are also large variations throughout the year. Pedestrians on Strøget walk considerably faster in the cold winter months than in the summer. Average walking speed is 62 seconds for 100 meters on a day in January and 85 seconds in July. Naturally, people walk more quickly when it is cold in order to keep warm, but, in addition, walking in the winter tends to be more goal-oriented than in the summer, when many people go on walks for pleasure.

Walking speed plays a role in the way that public life is perceived. When pedestrians are in a hurry, they move quickly out of sight; conversely, pedestrians who are ambling along the street stay longer in the field of vision of an observer. This means that streets are experienced as more lively in summer than in winter – even when an equal number of people are on the street.

On Copenhagen's pedestrian street, pedestrians walk 35% more slowly in summer than in winter. This difference in walking speed alone means that although 35% more people are observed on the street in summer than in winter, in fact, there are not more people on the street, just people moving slower.

Top: Plan of Blågårds Square, Copenhagen. Pedestrian traffic was registered from 4 to 4:30 p.m. one Wednesday in May, 1968. The lines were not drawn with surgical precision, but rather to show the general pattern of movement.[6] If the movements are registered over a day, they can either be seen individually or compared to point out differences depending on time of day. Registrations can also be layered to provide a combined picture of the movements over the course of the day. This also works for different days, weekdays/weekends, summer/winter, and so on.

The footprints that can just be made out at the bottom of the photograph below of Blågårds Square on a winter day in 2013 show that people still cut through the middle of the square – even in the snow.

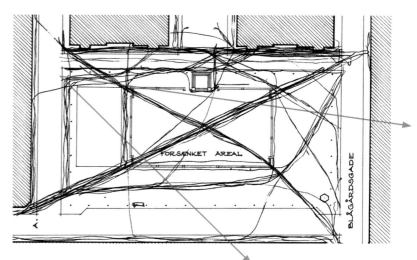

THE DIRECT PATH
Studying movement patterns across a square

Who: Jan Gehl
Where: Blågårds Square, Copenhagen, Denmark
When: Afternoon in May, 1968
Method: Tracing
Published: Jan Gehl, "Mennesker til fods" (*People on Foot*. In Danish), *Arkitekten* 20/1968[7]

This 1968 study of the lines of movement across Blågårds Square in Copenhagen served a dual purpose: to see which routes pedestrians chose to cross the square, and to shed light on what impact a four-step depression in the middle of the square had on the selection of pedestrian route.

Observations were made from a second-story window, from which there was a good view of the square. The study was made by indicating the lines of movement for all pedestrians on a drawing of the square.

After only 30 minutes of observation, the dominant movement patterns were clear from the drawing. Almost all pedestrians chose the shortest path, even though the diagonal route across the square meant walking up and down the four steps of the depression. The pedestrians who walked around the depression were almost all pushing a baby buggy or walking a bicycle.

A new pattern was observed in the evening. Almost all pedestrians crossing the square walked along the edges, which were well lit, seldom choosing the dark center of the square.

MANY GOOD REASONS

Studying activities and excuses for being in public space

Who:	Jan Gehl
Where:	City space in Italy and Denmark
When:	1965-66
Method	Photo documentation
Published:	Jan Gehl and Ingrid Gehl, "Mennesker i byer" (*People in Cities*. In Danish), *Arkitekten* 21/1966[8]

In 1965, Jan Gehl received a grant for a six-month study tour to Italy to gather basic material about the interaction between public space and public life. Situations that supported the data gathered were photographed underway.

It was clear early on in the process that people do not always have an obviously practical reason for being in public space. If you ask them directly, they might tell you that they are in town to shop or run errands. The many good reasons and sensible arguments made for being in public space often prove to be rational explanations for activity patterns that weave together errands and pleasure. In this context, rationally explained behavior can cover stays in public space for the purpose of looking at people and public life in general. The selected photographs from Italy (and one from Denmark) on the opposite page show the ambiguity of actions, including a number of excuses for staying in public space.

Later studies supported this conclusion with data, but in these early studies, it is the photographs that document a number of excuses for people to be in public space.

The observers kept their eyes and ears open while gathering data and taking photographs over a long period, which led them to conclude that people's presence in public space can often be characterized as postponed necessity. While it is true that people leave home for a rational reason, in many situations the real reason for choosing public space is simply to be there – to see and be seen, in other words.

The observations underline the importance of making sure that public space has something to offer, and that this 'something' need not be a huge display of flora and fountains.

A bench to sit on or a couple of pigeons for entertainment can be enough to create life in public space – but the most important element is other people.

The photographs illustrate several ways of embracing public space, various types of activities. Motifs are people in public space, and how public space and buildings can support – or discourage – human activity. In contrast to traditional architectural photographs, here individual architectural traits are secondary to the public life unfolding in public space.

Over the years, Jan Gehl has captured innumerable small situations that describe people's behavior in cities. These photographs from the mid-1960s were taken before the digital age, and the motifs were carefully selected indeed, because it was expensive to take and develop pictures.

The function of the city for people

Jan Gehl "Mennesker i byer" ("People in Cities". In Danish)
Arkitekten no. 21, 1966[9]

Need for social acknowledgement. Promenading is one of the ways to satisfy the need to see and be seen. (Rome, Italy)

A newspaper is a handy prop to use as an excuse for staying in an eventful place in the city. (Mantova, Italy)

The need for passivity. The city's active spaces provide highly acceptable conditions for people to be passive. (Lucca, Italy)

Supervising children at play is an excellent reason for these mothers to stay in public space. (Blågårds Square, Copenhagen, Denmark)

The need for movement, light and air. These needs are secondary in the city, because they can be satisfied in so many other places. (Arezzo, Italy)

Hungry pigeons can be the purpose of a walk as well as an acceptable excuse for staying in public space. (Milan, Italy)

THEORY AND PRACTICE
Studying walking patterns in a new residential area

Who: Jan Gehl and the Fabrin family on walks
Where: Albertslund Syd (south), Denmark
When: January, 1969
Method: Shadowing
Published: Jan Gehl, "En gennemgang af Albertslund" ("Walking through Albertslund". In Danish), *Landskab* 2/1969[10]

The housing complex Albertslund Syd, a new suburb west of Copenhagen, was built in the beginning of the 1960s based on contemporary theories regarding traffic safety, which meant consistent separation of pedestrian and vehicular traffic. Cars had a system of roads completely devoid of sidewalks, while pedestrians had their own separate system of paths, with car-free access to all housing, and long, even paths through the complex and tunnels under all roads. In theory, this was in every way the perfect, safe traffic system.

At any rate that is how it looked on the drawing board, but how did the separation of pedestrian and vehicular traffic work in practice? How did residents get around? Already from the start there were clear signs that the traffic system did not work as planned. In addition to using the car-free paths, it appeared that residents, from the youngest to the oldest, had a penchant for taking more direct routes without regard for any theories about traffic safety. While the pedestrian system was certainly free of cars, it dictated many detours and indirect connections.

A documented review of the area was arranged in order to shed light on the issue. The mother of a family and her young child, who lived in the far end of the complex, often walked through the area to shop in the city centre. It was agreed that the little family would continue to follow its usual route, but that on a day picked at random, a public-space researcher would follow and note routes, times, pleasures and problems, while taking pictures along the way. The walk was 1.3 km and took 31 minutes. It proved to be as direct and targeted as possible, and without regard to whether individual stretches were on vehicular roads, through parking lots or along pedestrian paths.

In total, almost one-third of the route was covered in areas where pedestrians were not supposed to be. The trip included crossing several vehicular roads where drivers were not expected to be watching out for pedestrians. The family walk demonstrated convincingly that the theoretical world of traffic engineers was considerably different from that of the real world inhabited by residents.

Over several years, this 'traffic-safe' area loomed large in accident statistics because many pedestrians walking on vehicular roads were struck by cars. After several more years, the entire traffic system in Albertslund Syd was rebuilt. The new design departed from the principle of separating types of traffic, using instead a new system based on the integration and coexistence of different types of traffic, which corresponds to the way the area is actually used.

Albertslund Syd, January, 1969. Walking along with residents on the route they usually take through the residential area.
Located 15 km west of Copenhagen, the Albertslund Syd residential area was designed by Fællestegnestuen in 1963-68 with separated systems for soft and hard traffic.[11]

380 meters prohibited for pedestrians

Jan Gehl, "En gennemgang af Albertslund", (Walking through Albertslund. In Danish), Landskab 2/1969[12]

Although people who don't live there are critical of the long, uniform, whitewashed paths that wind through the row-house quarters in Albertslund, Tove and Peter Fabrin don't find them a problem. True enough, Albertslund has a 100% traffic-safe pedestrian network that leads underneath all the roads for cars, but that isn't the route that the Fabrin family uses. Their usual route is across a parking lot and down streets designed for car traffic to the main road, Sletbrovej, which they traverse at a good clip.

The walk continues along Sletbrovej, where the family walks above the pedestrian tunnel designed for them by planners. There is a good view of the pedestrian paths from the low, white walls that mark the location of the pedestrian tunnel on both sides of the road. We don't really have time to enjoy the view, however; we are in a hurry.

The little family has come to the Swan Quarter and swing to the right, crossing the area quickly down the car access road. What dictates the route is simply the desire to walk the shortest and easiest way, and it is easiest to be a car in Albertslund.

So when the family reaches the parking lot for the area, they swing left and – after 380 meters prohibited for pedestrians or rather along the road for cars – they enter Albertslund's pedestrian path system for the very first time. The walk goes along a few buildings, down some stairs, and passes the empty lot where the church will one day be built, reaching Canal Street, the backbone and main nerve of Albertslund.

Selected photos from the series accompanying the article, which included all the segments of the walk.

ACTION RESEARCH

From empty stretch of gravel to active playground in one day

Who: Residents from the area and students from Copenhagen universities
Where: Høje Gladsaxe, newly built public housing complex in a suburb of Copenhagen, Denmark
When: Saturday, April 29, 1969
Method: Action research
Published: Gehl et al., "SPAS 4. Konstruktionen i Høje Gladsaxe" (*SPAS 4. The Construction in Høje Gladsaxe*. In Danish), Akademisk Forlag 1969[13]

"Our Fathers on High" was the title of a highly critical review of the newly built 13-story public housing complex in Høje Gladsaxe. The starting point of the review, written by Jan Gehl and published in the journal *Landskab* (*Landscape*. In Danish) no. 7, 1967, was that the outdoor areas were boring in the extreme: 'Less is more' modernism converted into public housing. Several preliminary activity studies were conducted at the site, which showed that the outdoor areas were seldom used, and that primarily only women and children were in residence during the day. Clearly neither the architecture nor the landscape planning was aimed at these groups, but rather at the fathers of the households in the top stories, who could see all the way to Sweden while they ate dinner.[14]

The article created quite a stir and became one of many critical pieces about the wave of modernistic housing being built at the time. This was also the period in which the first studies appeared showing the difficulty children had in using outdoor areas in multi-story housing complexes. All in all, it became clear that there were special problems concerning multi-story housing complexes, and that in Høje Gladsaxe in particular, the outdoor areas were unusually rigid and uninspired.

A large group of parents who lived in the complex lobbied the housing societies and the local authorities to improve playground opportunities for their children, but to no avail. Then the group contacted SPAS (a study group consisting of sociologists, psychologists and architects) at The Royal Danish Academy of Fine Arts, School of Architecture. On April 29, 1969, after intensive and close cooperation, residents and students were ready to embark on the unauthorized building of a large adventure playground on an empty stretch of gravel in front of the multi-story complex.

Working from early morning until late at night, 50 residents and 50 students built the large playground in only one day. The action was so comprehensive and the goal so popular that the authorities made no attempt to halt the illegal endeavor. The playground became a huge success – both while it was being built – and for many years later.

Extract from the original caption from SPAS 4, 1969 for the drawing (above right) from the magazine Bo Bedre: 1. The sandbox for the youngest children was located near the housing blocks 9. A playground in the rain is a sad sight, but this playground has a covered area.[15]

The playground action at Høje Gladsaxe was carried out as a protest against modernism's neglect of human needs. The goal was to give residents – especially children – in Høje Gladsaxe better opportunities for expression, as well as to stir up debate about modernism's ideals and buildings. The before-and-after pictures show how the playground breaks with the straight geometric lines of modernism by 'bridging' the borderlines.

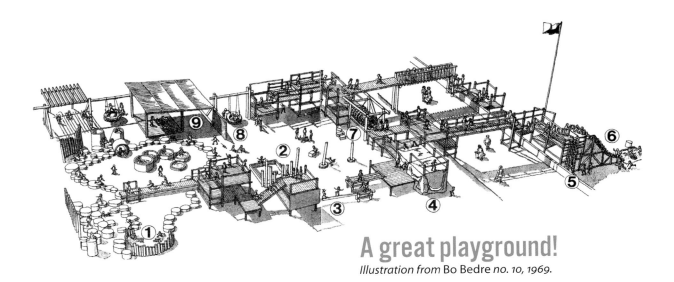

A great playground!

Illustration from Bo Bedre *no. 10, 1969.*

Before

After

The diary method came into its own on a residential street in the Fitzroy neighborhood in Melbourne in 1976. The observers kept a diary to register details of the activities on the street – from early in the morning until late at night.

The bubble contains excerpts from a similar diary kept in connection with later studies in Melbourne.[16]

EXCERPTS FROM SUNDAY DIARY

9.53 MR Nº 8 COMES OUT OF HOUSE YELLS TO BRUNO, HIS DOG, WHO IS FIGHTING WITH DOG AT Nº 15. COMES DOWN ROAD WITH CHAIN IN HAND, PUTS LEAD ON DOG AND DRAGS HIM HOME.

12.48 LADY (WHO LIVES IN Nº 18) COMES OUT OF Nº 9, GOES OVER TO Nº 10 & ASKS MAN TO DINNER.

1.26 MR. Nº 9 (ABOUT 40) COMES OUT TO WASH OUT CUP FROM TAP ON FRONT VERANDAH.

3.37 TWO MEN (BOTH ABOUT 30) ARE CHATTING ON THE VERANDAH OF Nº 8. ONE LEAVES AND GOES INTO Nº 11 TO HELP MAKE WINE. HE CHATS TO GIRL AT THE DOOR AS HE GOES IN.

4.37 FOUR CHILDREN FROM Nº 9 GO DOWN STREET ON SCOOTERS, CARRYING A BUCKET OF FISH.

DIARY METHOD
Capturing details and nuances

Who: Jan Gehl with a study group from the School of Architecture, University of Melbourne
Where: Fitzroy, Melbourne, Australia
When: Saturdays in March, 1976
Method: Keeping a diary
Published: Not published

In March of 1976, students from the School of Architecture in Melbourne were tasked with spending 24 hours in a self-selected site in the city in order to document their experiences. They were divided into groups of two or three and given free choice of tools with which to document their observations by drawing, photographing, counting, writing, making sound recordings or using other techniques. The student groups were spread throughout the city: zoo, market, train station, prison, local newspaper offices, etc.

Two students decided to spend 24 hours in a typical residential street of one- and two-story townhouses, all with front yards. They selected a 100-meter section of the street, and took up their positions in the middle of the night in order to wait for dawn and for residents to begin appearing in their yards and street.

Based on several pilot studies, the decision was made to record all of the activities on the street in the form of a diary. Recording would cover everything that happened on the street from façade to façade, that is, in the front yards, the area around the front fences, the street and sidewalk.

A complete record of everything that happened was noted in the diary. Every time someone came out of one of the houses or passed along the street, the gender, age and street address (if relevant) were noted. Also written down was the type of activity the person was involved in, where it took place, and whether it was a social activity (conversation, greeting, children playing, etc.). A very important element in the process of notation was registering how much time people spent on each activity.

The fact that there were observers on the street noting down everything happening from dawn to dusk naturally aroused the curiosity of the street's residents. In anticipation,

the two students had concocted a cover story: that they were architecture students carrying out a study of traffic safety in residential streets. That seemed plausible and residents indicated that such a study was a meaningful activity for architecture students. The acceptance of the residents meant that after a bout of initial curiosity, they quickly ignored the observers, who were able to record hundreds of activity notes from just one day spent observing a 100-meter section of the street.

Their notes provided an overview of what took place along the street: how many people were outside, who they were (gender and age), what happened, what part of the physical environment was used for activities by whom and for what kinds of activities. The more activities on the street, the more meetings between people and social activities. All very interesting indeed.

However, what was most interesting is that by being on site as observers for a long cohesive period, the students were able to note not only activity patterns in rough outline, but also a large number of brief activities that could be measured in seconds: greetings, waves, short stops on otherwise fast walks, heads turning, etc. By far the majority of the day's activities were these brief, spontaneous episodes. In combination with longer activities, these bits and pieces could be formed into a complex and dramatic 'street ballet' in this ordinary residential street.

Being on site for a long uninterrupted period was the key to gaining a detailed understanding of the interaction between public space and public life. Most other methods used to study public life are based on studying limited periods as 'samples' and thus overlook many of the small but important details.

THE IMPORTANCE OF FRONT YARDS

Studying the connection between the design of residential streets and the extent and character of activities

Who: Jan Gehl with a study group from the School of Architecture, University of Melbourne
Where: 17 streets in older sections of the city and new suburbs, respectively, in Melbourne, Australia
When: Sundays in April-May, 1976
Method: Behavioral mapping and keeping a diary
Published: Jan Gehl et al. *The Interface Between Public and Private Territories in Residential Areas*, 1977[17]

Thirty-three architecture students from the University of Melbourne conducted a comprehensive and ambitious study in April-May of 1976. The study comprised a total of 17 streets in older parts of the city of Melbourne as well as in newer suburbs. The streets represented a wide spectrum of types of residents plus ethnic, economic and social factors. The purpose of the study was to illuminate the connection between the physical conditions in the streets - the design of street space, front yards and building facades - and the activities that took place in the various types of street space. In short: what is the influence of the physical conditions on the extent and character of life in the individual streets?

Characteristic of older city streets in Melbourne was a semi-private zone in front of residences in the form of a front yard, typically bordered by a low fence facing the street space. While many streets had this typically traditional Australian transition zone, some did not have this feature in front of the houses, and in the suburbs a small lawn encircling the whole house was typical. Did the semi-private front yards have an influence on life in the streets, and what significance did street design and housing density have on the pattern of activities?

The studies were conducted on days with good weather for staying outdoors, and Sunday was selected as the specific study day because many residents were expected to be home then. Each study area comprised a 100-meter stretch of street, and the studies included measuring the physical relationships of the street as well as registering activities according to the 'diary method' developed in preliminary pilot studies. With this starting point, all activities on the streets were registered for an entire Sunday from sunrise to sunset, including noting the time expended on each activity. At the same time, a map was plotted once an hour throughout the day in order to have a graphic depiction of how the various activities took place in the individual spaces.

Together, the registrations gave a comprehensive and detailed picture of life - or in some cases lack of life - in the various streets. It was possible to determine with great accuracy that the semi-private front yards played a decisive role on the extensive activity level of the streets with 'soft edges'.[18]

The studies illuminated many interesting sub-topics. For example, there were often as many activities taking place per household in the suburbs as in the more densely populated city streets with front yards, but the activity patterns were very different. While many people were outside in the suburbs, they were all engaged in mowing lawns or maintaining large gardens. In the denser city streets, residents sat in their front yards and spent time on minor tasks, eating and recreation, and engaged in far more social activities. These studies also showed that by far the majority of all events taking place on residential streets were brief. They also showed that the many brief events were a prerequisite for bigger and longer events.

After the studies were published showing that front yards played a large role in the social life of city streets, building regulations were tightened to ensure that front yards could not be isolated behind walls or fences. In addition, public housing regulations were changed in favor of building more housing in the style of row houses with front yards rather than large concentrated multi-story complexes. All in all, many small observations had large – and positive – consequences.

General information and registration of interaction and activities on Y Street, Prahran, Melbourne.

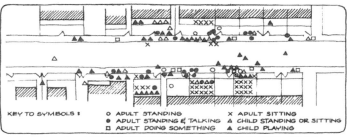

KEY TO SYMBOLS :
- O ADULT STANDING
- ● ADULT STANDING & TALKING
- □ ADULT DOING SOMETHING
- X ADULT SITTING
- △ CHILD STANDING OR SITTING
- ▲ CHILD PLAYING

MAP A SHOWING POSITIONS OF ALL PEOPLE IN AREA AT 38 PREDETERMINED TIMES ON SUNDAY & WEDNESDAY

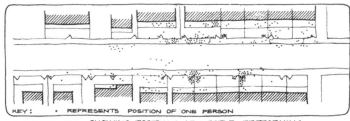

KEY : • REPRESENTS POSITION OF ONE PERSON

MAP B SHOWING POSITIONS OF PEOPLE PERFORMING INTERACTIONS & ACTIVITIES - SUNDAY 8·00-6·30

General information and registration of interaction and activities on C Avenue, Vermont, Melbourne.

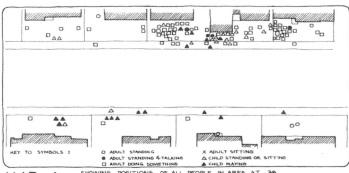

KEY TO SYMBOLS :
- O ADULT STANDING
- ● ADULT STANDING & TALKING
- □ ADULT DOING SOMETHING
- X ADULT SITTING
- △ CHILD STANDING OR SITTING
- ▲ CHILD PLAYING

MAP A SHOWING POSITIONS OF ALL PEOPLE IN AREA AT 38 PREDETERMINED TIMES ON SUNDAY

Map A shows activities on residential streets plotted in according to type of activity. Map B shows social activities exclusively, such as greetings. A comparison of the street with more dwellings and more clearly defined front yards (above) with the street with fewer dwellings and open lawns (below) shows clearly that there are more social activities on the street with front yards.[19]

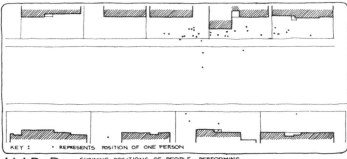

KEY : • REPRESENTS POSITION OF ONE PERSON

MAP B SHOWING POSITIONS OF PEOPLE PERFORMING INTERACTIONS & ACTIVITIES - SUNDAY 8·00-6·30

TIME IS CRUCIAL

Studying the duration of various activities in residential streets

Who: Jan Gehl with a study group from the School of Architecture, University of Waterloo, Ontario, Canada
Where: 12 streets with semi-detached and detached houses, respectively, Kitchener and Waterloo, Ontario, Canada
When: Summer weekdays, 1977
Method: Keeping a diary
Published: Jan Gehl, *Life Between Buildings*, New York: Van Nostrand Reinhold, New York, 1987[20] (reprinted by Island Press, 2011)

What is it that actually brings life to residential streets? In 1977 the activities on 12 streets with semi-detached and detached houses, were studied in Kitschener and Waterloo, Ontario, Canada, respectively. In order to compare results and gain an overview, an area measuring approximately 100 yards (90 meters) was studied in each of the 12 streets. The study was conducted on summer days with optimal weather for outdoor stays, that is, not too hot and not too cold: days with good weather for the time of year.

The number and types of activities were registered for each street. Types of activities were divided into the most common, with emphasis on a category for social activities such as greetings and other types of interaction.

It was interesting to find that the most common activity was going to and from a dwelling. However, while arriving and leaving by foot and car accounted for half of all activities recorded, it represented only 10% of life in the streets, because when calculated in amount of time spent, coming and going took very little time. There were a moderate number of stays on the street, but when this activity was calculated in time spent, staying accounted for some 90% of life in the streets.

The study made clear that staying activities last considerably longer than transient activities. Perhaps that seems obvious, but it is nonetheless important to stress that time and thus staying activities can be a decisive factor in how animated a street scene appears. The longer people stay, the more people are seen in public space. Time can indeed be a decisive factor for life in residential streets and public space.

Diagrams of the frequency and duration of activities in public space on 12 residential streets in Waterloo and Kitchener, Ontario, Canada, 1977.[21]

A: Interaction
B: Stays
C: Gardening, etc.
D: Play
E: Pedestrian traffic within the area
F: Pedestrian traffic, to and from
G: By car, to and from

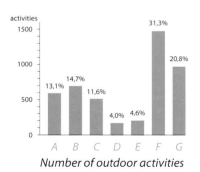

Number of outdoor activities

Duration of each category of activities, average

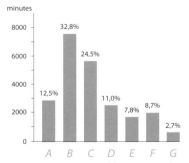

Minutes spent in public space related to the various types of activity (total)

101

MEASURING FEAR AND APPREHENSION

Studying the influence of traffic on the behavior of adult and child pedestrians

Who: Jan Gehl with study groups from the School of Architecture, Royal Melbourne Institute of
                Technology and the University of Melbourne, 1978
Where: Traffic streets and pedestrian areas in Adelaide, Melbourne and Sydney
When: October 1978
Method: Counting, behavioral mapping, systematic observation of parents and children
Published: Jan Gehl, *Life between Buildings*, Van Nostrand Reinhold, New York, 1987[22]
                (reprinted by Island Press, 2011)

In 1978, study groups from the two schools of architecture in Melbourne conducted a series of field studies to gain knowledge about pedestrian behavior in streets with different traffic statuses. They sought answers to what vehicular traffic means to the way people move and stay in various types of streets. Three street types were studied: traffic streets with sidewalks, pedestrian streets with limited traffic (such as streetcar-pedestrian streets) and totally traffic-free pedestrian streets.

The methods used to study selected streets in Adelaide, Melbourne and Sydney included counting pedestrians, behavioral mapping and systematic observations of selected themes.

The result was that traffic-free streets provided the opportunity for more – and more varied – activities for all age groups. The traffic streets were crowded, noisy, noxious, and pedestrians needed to take many safety precautions. The behavior patterns of pedestrians on pedestrian streets with streetcars or limited traffic were much closer to the results from traffic streets than from areas that were

totally free of cars. Even limited traffic apparently placed surprisingly great limitations on opportunities for human activities.

One of the themes studied was how safe pedestrians felt in the various types of streets. Some of the students observed that young children apparently had different opportunities to roam freely in the different types of streets. Their observations were systematized by noting whether children under the age of six were held by the hand or were allowed to walk on their own. The study showed clear distinctions between traffic streets and streets that were free of cars. Almost all children (approximately 85%) were held by the hand on sidewalks along traffic streets, while most children were allowed to move about freely on pedestrian streets – to the obvious delight of both children and adults.

This little study is an example of inventiveness with regard to new but simple ways of illuminating complex and important aspects of the interaction between public space and public life that heavily influence urban life quality.

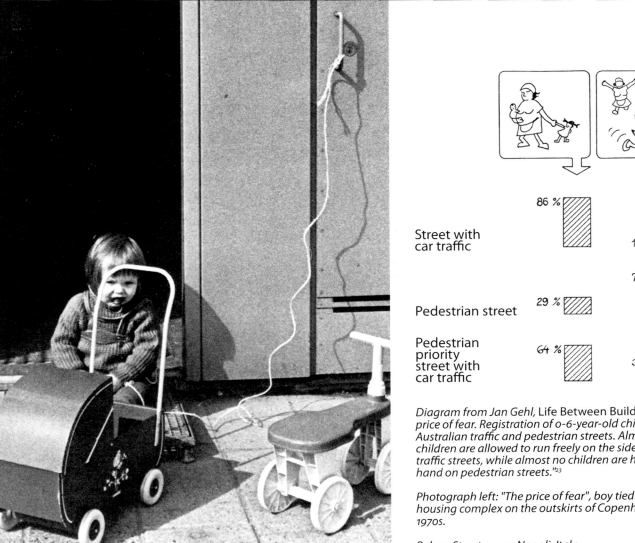

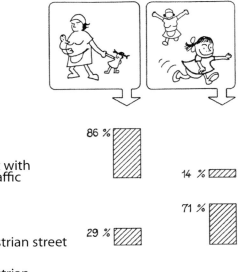

	Street with car traffic	Pedestrian street	Pedestrian priority street with car traffic
	86 %	29 %	64 %
	14 %	71 %	36 %

Diagram from Jan Gehl, Life Between Buildings: *"The price of fear. Registration of 0-6-year-old children in Australian traffic and pedestrian streets. Almost no children are allowed to run freely on the sidewalks on traffic streets, while almost no children are held by the hand on pedestrian streets."[23]*

Photograph left: "The price of fear", boy tied outside housing complex on the outskirts of Copenhagen in the 1970s.

Below: Street scene, Napoli, Italy.

ACTIVE OR PASSIVE FAÇADES
Studying life in front of open and closed façades

Who: Jan Gehl, Solvejg Reigstad and Lotte Kaefer at the Center for Public Space Research,
              The Royal Danish Academy of Fine Arts, School of Architecture
Where: Seven city streets in Copenhagen
When: Morning, noon, afternoon on summer days, evening on autumn days, 2003
Method: Counting and observations
Published: Jan Gehl, Solvejg Reigstad and Lotte Kaefer, "Close Encounters with Buildings."
              Special issue of *Arkitekten* 9/2004[24]

The human eye is developed primarily for horizontal vision: we seldom look up, although we occasionally look down to see where we are going. However, most of what we take in visually is at eye-level, and in relation to buildings, it is primarily the ground-floor level that catches our eye. Numerous studies have pointed to edges, the transition between building and public space, as significant for how many and which activities take place.[25]

In this study, shop façades and activities on the sidewalks, lining the shops were studied based on the assumption that there would be more activities in front of ground-floor façades with an open and varied character compared to those that were closed and monotone. Seven 100-meter segments along Copenhagen shopping streets were selected for study in order to test the theory.

The selected study areas contained a stretch of open, active façades with many details, door openings, contact between inside and outside, and further down the same street, the direct opposite: closed, inactive façade sections with few details, blind windows or none at all. The character of the façades was defined with the aid of façade assessment tools, which had been developed for public life-public space studies. Within the 100-meter segments, the most representative 10-meter sections of A and E façades, respectively, were selected. In order to make comparisons as direct as possible, the goal was to select sections without side streets, with about the same climatic conditions, traffic intensity and other factors that could influence the activity level.

Life along the façades was calculated by registering: number of passing pedestrians, their speed, how many turned their heads towards the façade, how many stopped

or went in or out of a door, and how long the activities on the sidewalk lasted.

Time of day was noted for each section: morning, noon, or afternoon on summer days with good weather for the time of year. In addition, evening activities were registered for autumn days between 5 and 8 p.m. with good weather for the time of year.

The study showed clearly that façade design can have great influence on the pattern of activities on shopping streets. There was a considerably greater level of activity in front of open facades than in segments with closed façades. People walked slower, turned their heads more often to look in shop windows, and stopped more frequently. And although people sometimes stopped to look at the shops, interesting enough, many of their stops were made somewhere besides an active façade: for example, people stopped to tie their shoes, talk on their cell phones, adjust their shopping bags, and so on. As Jane Jacobs wrote: "the sight of people attracts still other people". In total, up to seven times as many activities could be seen before the open façades than in front of closed façades.

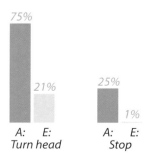

Of the passersby along the selected course of A façades, 75% showed interest by turning their heads, while only 21% did the same along the closed E façades. One-quarter stopped in front of the open façades, while only 1% stopped in front of the closed façades.[26]

Façade Categories

Jan Gehl, Cities for People, 2010[27]
(originally developed for public life study in Stockholm in 1990)[28]

A – active
Small units, many doors
(15-20 doors per 100 m/328 feet)
Large variation in function
No blind and few passive units
Lots of character in façade relief
Primarily vertical façade articulation
Good details and materials

B – friendly
Relatively small units
(10-14 doors per 100 m/328 feet)
Some variation in function
Few blind and passive units
Façade relief
Many details

C – mixture
Large and small units
(6-10 doors per 100 m/328 feet)
Some blind and passive units
Modest façade relief
Few details

D – boring
Large units, few doors
(2-5 doors per 100 m/328 feet)
Almost no variation, uninteresting units
Few or no details

E – inactive
Large units, few or no doors
(0-2 doors per 100 m/328 feet)
No visible variation in function
Blind or passive units
Uniform façades, no details, nothing to look at

GOING FROM 43 TO 12 CRITERIA

Developing a check-list to assess public space qualities

Who: Jan Gehl et al (1974-)
Where: Department of Urban Design, The Royal Danish Academy of
             Fine Arts, School of Architecture, Copenhagen, Denmark
When: Ongoing
Method: Checklist for assessing public space qualities
Published: Not published[29]

What makes a public space a pleasant place to be and thus used? For several decades, numerous criteria for evaluating this question have been gathered, sorted and categorized into a tool known as "the 12 quality criteria".[30]

These 12 quality criteria (and there used to be many more) can be used in a delimited public space, where the observer evaluates and notes the extent to which the individual public space lives up to the criteria for inviting people to come and stay. A three-point scale is usually used for graphic illustration; for example, in three shades of gray, in order to compare public spaces.

The list of quality criteria was developed on the basis of fundamental knowledge about human senses and needs, as well as many years of public space studies in all parts of the world.[31] The underlying knowledge about human senses, needs, and what it takes to make people feel comfortable and stay in public space has been adapted over the years in a close dialogue with practice, so that it is functional.

The keyword chart on the opposite page was drawn up in the 1970s by Jan Gehl at The Royal Danish Academy of Fine Arts, School of Architecture for classroom use. Many more criteria were described in the beginning, because criteria important for urban and site planning were included, in addition to those relevant for public space.

Over the years, the idea has evolved into a checklist so simple that it is self-evident to most people and can serve as a tool that is easy to grasp, for example, in comparing various public spaces. At the same time, the checklist has to have a sufficient amount of detail and dimensions to enable assessments of the extent to which the individual public spaces meet the human need for protection and expression.

Today the tool is used as the starting point for dialogue. For example, a project team might use the checklist to examine how people experience the extent to which an existing or planned public space lives up to specifications about places to walk and stay, scale and climate conditions.

The drawing from 1974 shown opposite illustrates some of the categories found in later versions. Points were later redefined or eliminated, and those remaining were structured according to three main themes: protection, comfort and enjoyment.[32]

Even though the list was drawn up at a school of architecture, there is only a single point – the last one on the list – dealing with aesthetic qualities. This means that public space assessment does not take its starting point in aesthetic parameters. First we must consider people's need for protection from cars, noise, rain and wind, as well as their need to walk, stand, sit, look, speak, listen and express themselves. People also need to be able to utilize the positive aspects of the local climate and surroundings on a human scale. Experience has shown that much more than aesthetic qualities determine whether a public space is valued and used. However, it is important for overall quality that all the functional and practical aspects are dealt with within an architectural framework that respects visual qualities. Many of the world's best public spaces beautifully fulfill the 12 quality criteria on the list. Piazza il Campo in Siena, Italy is a prime example.

Opposite: A checklist devised by Jan Gehl for urban design students at The Royal Danish Academy of Fine Arts, School of Architecture, Copenhagen, 1974.

URBAN DESIGN — A LIST OF KEY WORDS

A. TASK ANALYSIS ~ DECISION ~ BASIC PROGRAMME

TASK ANALYSIS
DECISION
PRIMARY PROGRAMME

ANALYSING THE TASK
who is giving the task?
what are the objectives?
who will benefit?
etc.

– DECISION –
can task be accepted?
– if yes on what
conditions?

BASIC PROGRAMME / GROWTH & CHANGES
overall goals
– what is to be planned and what is not?
– what is to be planned now and what is not?
– future developements
alternations – growth / changes
– who decides?

B. PROGRAMME

SOCIAL STRUCTURE

1. A POLICY FOR THE SOCIAL STRUCTURE
considerations on the subdivision into:
– primary groups
– secondary groups
– neighbourhoods
– townships
– town etc.

2. A POLICY FOR THE DECISION MAKING
– who is to decide what?
– how can the decision making strengthen social structure?

3. A POLICY FOR INTEGRATION / SEGREGATION
– living / manufacturing / service
– different age groups
– social classes
– private - public spaces

4. A POLICY FOR THE PUBLIC SPACES
– how can social structure be strengthened by public spaces?
– what kind of public spaces? active / inactive diverse / specific inviting / inspiring / repulsive
– location of different activities

SERVICES AND COMMUNICATIONS

1. SERVICES
which services and facilities are needed?
where are they to be located in social structure?
where are they to be located on site?

2. INTERNAL COMMUNICATIONS
– see below –

3. RELATIONS BETWEEN INTERNAL & EXTERNAL COMMUNICATIONS
– distances to points of exchange
– quality of way
– quality of exch. point
– waiting time, frequency
emergency traffic

4. EXTERNAL COMMUNICATIONS
kind of traffic
public / private
distances
speed - frequency
directions
etc.

C. DESIGN

STRUCTURE OF PEDESTRIAN SYSTEMS
– organizing the movements

1. NUMBER OF DIRECTIONS (LENGTH OF WALK)
to concentrate:
– one direction (compact ped. system)
to disperse:
– several directions (widespread ped. system)

2. NUMBER OF ALTERNATIVE ROUTES
to concentrate
– one street
to disperse
– several parallell streets
– skywalks etc.

3. NUMBER OF ALTERNATIVE TRANSP. SYSTEMS
to concentrate
– one system: walking
to disperse
– several systems

4. STRUCTURABILITY
– a logical "easy to find your way around in" overall structure
– using topography
– etc.

– organizing the buildings / functions in relation to the pedestrian systems

1. DISTANCES BETWEEN BUILDINGS / FUNCTIONS
to concentrate
– compact ped system
– attractions close together
– narrow facades
to disperse
– attractions far apart

2. NUMBER OF STOREYS / LEVELS
to concentrate
– one level
to disperse
– several levels

3. ORIENTATION OF BUILDINGS / FUNCTIONS
(entrances, doors, windows etc.)
to concentrate
– orientation towards public spaces
to disperse
– orientation away from public spaces

4. RELATIONS BETWEEN MOBILE & STATIONARY PEDESTRIAN ACTIVITIES
to concentrate
– same spaces for moving and staying
to disperse
– separate spaces

DESIGNING THE SPACES
DESIGNING THE EDGES

1. DIMENSIONS (LENGTH, WIDTH, AREAS)
– designing in relation to human senses / no. of persons
– small dimensions
– "small spaces / big ones"

2. STRUCTURE / FORM
– spatial sequences
– closed vistas

1. INTERFACE BETWEEN PUBLIC & PRIVATE SPACES
to concentrate
– soft borders / overlapping
– semi-public front yard
– phys. & psych. accessibility
to disperse
– hard edges / walls

2. DEGREE OF TRANSPARENCY BETWEEN PUBLIC & PRIVATE
to concentrate
– windows
to disperse
– short distances

DESIGNING / DETAILING THE PUBLIC SPACES
(the pedestrian landscape)

1. PROTECTION AGAINST TRAFFIC & ACCIDENTS
– traffic accidents
– fear of traffic
– other accidents

2. PROTECTION AGAINST CRIME & VIOLENCE
– lived in / used
– streetlife
– streetwatchers
– social structure & identity
– overlapping / cohesion in space & time
– lighting (when dark)

3. PROTECTION AGAINST UNPLEASANT CLIMATE
– wind
– rain, snow
– cold / heat
– draft

4. PROTECTION AGAINST UNPLEASANT SENSE-EXPERIENCES
– noise
– smog
– stench - smell
– dirt - dust
– blinding

5. POSSIBILITIES FOR WALKING
– space for walking (dimen.)
– lines of walk (organized)
– distance of walk (m/feet)
– distance of walk (experienced)
– surface (materials)
– surface conditions (snow)
– change of level etc.

6. POSSIBILITIES FOR STANDING
– standing zones
– standing spots
– support for standing

7. POSSIBILITIES FOR SITTING
zones for sitting
maximizing advantages
– primary sitting poss.
secondary sitting poss.
benches for resting

8. POSSIBILITIES TO SEE
seeing - distances
unhindered lines of vision
views
lighting (when dark)

9. POSSIBILITIES FOR HEARING / TALKING
– noise level
– talking distances
– bench arrangements
a.o.

10. POSSIBILITIES FOR PLAY / UNWINDING
– play
– dance
– music
– theatre
– soapbox speeches a.o.
different age groups
different people

11. POSSIBILITIES FOR A MULTITUDE OF OTHER ACTIVITIES
– space / area
– permission / accept
– "challenges"
– "generators"
summer / winter / day / night

12. POSSIBILITIES FOR PEACE / ISOLATION / INACTIVITY

13. PHYSIOLOGICAL NEEDS
– eat / drink
– rest
– run / jump / play
– public toilets!

14. SMALL SCALE SERVICES (FRIENDLY GESTURES)
– signs
– telephonebooths
– postboxes
– notice boards
– maps of town
– pushcarts / babycarts
– waste paper baskets

15. DESIGNING FOR ENJOYING POSITIVE CLIMATE ELEMENTS
– sun
– warmth / coolness
– breeze / ventilation

16. DESIGNING FOR POSITIVE SENSE-EXPERIENCES
– aesthetic qualities
– views
– nature · plants trees, flowers, animals

THE 12 CRITERIA

D. MAINTENANCE / CHANGE

1. DAILY MAINTENANCE
"built in" reasonable possibilities for:
– cleaning
– snowremoval
– icemelting
– etc.

2. REPAIR / UPKEEPING
"built in" sturdiness
– repairing
– painting
– re - planting
– etc.

3. BUILT IN CHANGE-ABILITY - FLEXIBILITY
– daily
– day to day
– summer / winter
– time to time

4. A POLICY FOR PUBLIC DECISIONMAKING - ON CHANGES

JAN GEHL OCT. 19??

SENSES AND SCALE IN PRACTICE

Experiencing distances in an ordinary context

Who: Jan Gehl, et al.
Where: Copenhagen, Denmark
When: 1987-2010
Method: Testing theories, measuring, taking photos, collecting examples
Published: Jan Gehl, *Cities for People*, Washington DC, Island Press 2010[33]

In order to focus more closely on public life and its interaction with public space, it has been essential to learn more about human senses. We need this knowledge in order to carefully adapt the city to the human scale. American anthropologist Edward T. Hall and environmental psychologist Robert Sommer, among others, have written on the topic.[34] However, it is one thing to read about human senses in relation to the scale of the city and public space, and quite another to test them in practice.

Distance is a significant aspect of the work with human senses in relation to public space. Often the scale of city space is much too large relative to the movement possibilities and senses of humans. Despite technological and social development, we are still pedestrian animals at a height of about 175 centimeters and with a predominantly horizontal field of vision with clear limitations as to what we can see, at what distance and within what angles.

Our sight allows us to detect human movements at a distance of 100 meters, but we can first interact socially and determine detail at much shorter distances. This impacts on how we arrange our surroundings – whether outside in public space, at the opera, in the classroom, or home around the dining table.

Naturally, the best kind of testing is to go to the opera or other public space and sense in relation to one's own body whether the spaces seem to large, too small, or perhaps just right. Personally experiencing spatial relationships and scales will always have the most useful impact.

Once we begin to measure, gather and systematize our own observations and examples, concepts like human scale, human senses and need take on a more concrete meaning.

They are no longer incorporated as an afterthought at the end of a project, but can naturally form the starting point for designing cities, buildings and public space for people.

The increasing use of computer simulations to design cities, public space and buildings increases the importance of personally experiencing the interaction between public space and public life.

The page opposite shows an example of our knowledge about distance and human senses and scale tested in practice. The underlying idea is for the observer to go out and experience how the existing situation functions by conducting small tests that turn abstract knowledge into ordinary situations in order to better understand the practical consequences, as well as to better communicate this information to laymen and professionals. Testing scale is also highly recommended as a teaching method.

From Jan Gehl's book, Cities for People, *2010, illustrating one example of the theories of human senses tested in practice. The diagram and photographs show a test of the contact between people on the ground floor and various upper floors in a high building. Contact is already lost above the fifth floor.*[35]

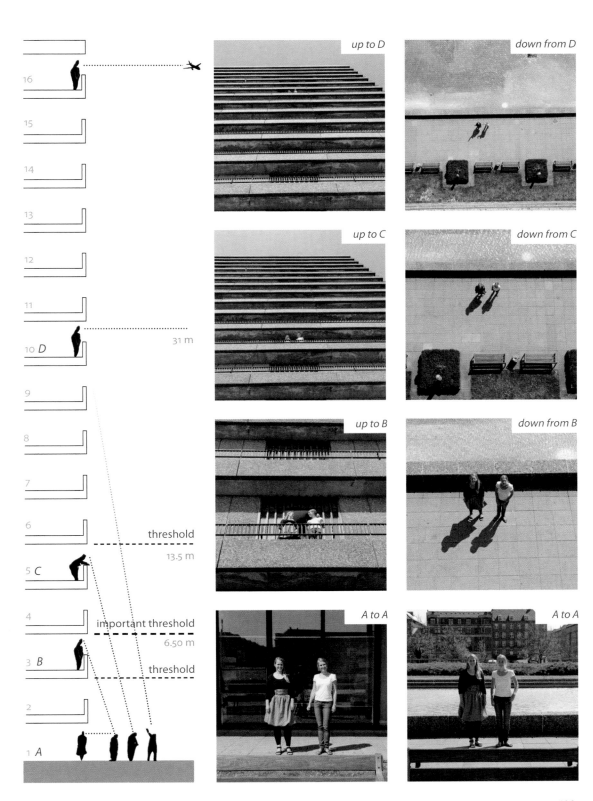

16

15

14

13

12

11

10 D

31 m

9

8

7

6

threshold

13.5 m

5 C

4

important threshold

6.50 m

3 B

threshold

2

1 A

up to D

down from D

up to C

down from C

up to B

down from B

A to A

A to A

LIVELY CITY SPACE

William H. Whyte's statistics from New York tested in a small Norwegian city

Who: Camilla Richter-Friis van Deurs, Gehl Architects and workshop participants
Where: Arendal, Norway
When: Monday afternoon, 23 January 2012, cold, snowing
Method: Testing theories about how public life and public space are experienced
Published: Not published

How many people does it take to make a public space lively, and is it at all possible to generate public life in small communities? Planners from small Norwegian towns were presented with William H. Whyte's theory that it takes about 16.6 pedestrians within the human visual field to make a public space urban and stimulating.[36] At a workshop that included public life studies, Whyte's thesis was tested by sending workshop participants across a central public space: first two of them, then four, then ten, then 14 and finally 20. The remaining participants were asked to evaluate whether the square seemed urban and stimulating. They didn't think so with two to ten pedestrians on the square, but they agreed that the sight of 14 to 20 people on the square gave the impression of an urban, stimulating public space.[37]

The figures from a small Norwegian town support Whyte's test carried out in Manhattan in the 1970s. In the small Norwegian town 14 people were sufficient to make the square seem vibrant. The experiment and Whyte's figures emphasize the importance of gathering functions and thus also people in order to make places lively – in small towns as well as large cities. But it is one thing to hear about it in theory and another to test it in practice.

Subsequently most of the 20 participants were asked to stay along the edge, where people most often stay, and the remaining participants were asked to evaluate what effect that had on the experience of vibrancy. Not surprisingly – and yet quickly and unswervingly – they found the square far less lively. This exercise illustrates the importance of scale, if public space is not to end up devoid of people, because a great deal of public life takes place along edges.

In the middle

On the edge

Workshop participants occupy Sam Eydes Square in Arendal, Norway (710 m²), while the rest of the participants evaluate whether or not the square seems lively. The photo shows 20 participants, which in the context was characterized as urban and stimulating

THE EFFECT OF MORE SEATING

When the number of seats is doubled, do more people sit?

Who: Gehl Architects
Where: Aker Brygge in Oslo, Norway
When: August 1998 and August 2000
Method: Registering the amount of seating and the extent of people sitting before and after the
              area was renovated
Published: Jan Gehl, *Cities for People,* Washington DC, Island Press 2010[38]

"People tend to sit the most where there are places to sit," concluded William H. Whyte in his book *The Social Life of Small Urban Spaces*, based on numerous studies in Manhattan. About his conclusion, he stated: "This may not strike you as an intellectual bombshell, and, now that I look back on our study, I wonder why it was not more apparent to us from the beginning."[39] It certainly sounds obvious, but does it really work that way? Whyte's theory was tested in Oslo at the end of the 1990s.

In 1999, the public spaces of the Aker Brygge quarter at Oslo harbor were renovated on the basis of a study of public life in the area. In the summer of 1998, the public space, furniture and details plus the way the many visitors to the area used the space were carefully studied in a public space-public life study. It was determined that there were apparently too few opportunities for seating in the area, and the quality of those options was poor.[40] As part of the renovation project, old benches were replaced with Parisian-style double park benches placed about where the old benches had been. In total, the changes meant that after renovation of the area there were slightly more than double (+129%) the seating options for visitors.

Exactly two years to the day after the first study, and also on a summer day with good weather, the use of the benches in the area was recorded once again. Four head counts were taken between 12 noon and 4 p.m., and it was possible to determine that the average number of people seated at Aker Brygge had increased by 12%.[41] Put simply, the conclusion was that doubling the amount of bench seating meant a doubling of the number of people seated.

Doubling the amount of seating at Aker Brygge in Oslo, Norway doubled the number of people sitting.

Upper, marked in white: 100-meter street; Østergade, Copenhagen, Denmark.
Lower, marked in red, a direct extension of Østergade: 100-meter square; Amagertorv.

100 M STREET

100 M SQUARE

100-METER STREET
100-METER SQUARE
Studying walking speed

Who: Kristian Skaarup and Birgitte Svarre
Where: 100-meter segment on Strøget (pedestrian street) and Amagertorv Square,
             Copenhagen, Denmark
When: Weekdays in December 2011
Method: Tracking
Published: Not published

Generally speaking, cities are made of spaces for movement and spaces for staying: streets and squares. The question to be answered in this little study was basic: How quickly do we move in streets and squares, respectively? The assumption was that pedestrians would walk slower across squares than on streets due to the character and psychological signal of squares as places to experience and to stay. This assumption was tested by studying the speed of pedestrians on a street that changed character by leading into a square. Would walking speed slow for pedestrians moving across the square rather than along the street?

Selecting the right observation site was tested by registering movements on various squares connected to Copenhagen streets. The best suited site proved to be Amagertorv Square on Strøget, the walking street. The surrounding buildings and functions had the same character, which made it less likely that other factors would influence walking speed. Potential study sites were rejected if there were any hindrances that could lower speed, or if there were great differences in how interesting facades were to passersby.

The study was conducted by measuring 100 meters on the square as well as on the street. Out in the field the observer started a stopwatch when someone walked over the starting line and stopped it when the person crossed over the finish line 100 meters later. Another stop watch was started at the moment someone entered the square and the stopwatch was then stopped when the person had traversed 100 meters.

In order to get a representative sample, the observer followed every third person who passed the selected starting line. Speed measurements were made of a total of 200 people. Quite a few observations were made on the street

with the observer following the study object, but after a while the observer found a good outlook post – a shop with rooms on the second floor, from which there was an unhindered view of the entire course under study.

The speed studies confirmed the thesis that pedestrians reduce their speed when moving from a street space to a square. However, the reduction in speed was modest: from 4.93 km/hour on the street to 4.73 km/hour on the square, that is, about 5%. However, most of the pedestrians reduced their speed. They slowed down despite the relatively cold weather in which the studies were conducted – about $5°C$ on gray winter days, not exactly typical promenading weather.

Because the difference in speeds was so relatively slight, calculations took into consideration whether there were many fast or slow pedestrians going one way or the other. The speeds that looked suspicious relative to the average results were then removed from the calculation as a test. However, it was apparent that these registrations did not have a significant influence on the results.

When observers go into town to study people's walking speed, it can be difficult to calculate exactly how quickly they are moving. That was also the case in these studies, where it was not possible to determine with the naked eye a difference in pedestrian speed along street or square. But by measuring how long it takes to walk 100 meters on the street and 100 meters on the square, it could be documented that there is a difference.

It took a lot of patience to register enough measurements, because very few people actually went directly from point A to point B – another well-known conclusion that the observer could once again bring home from this study.

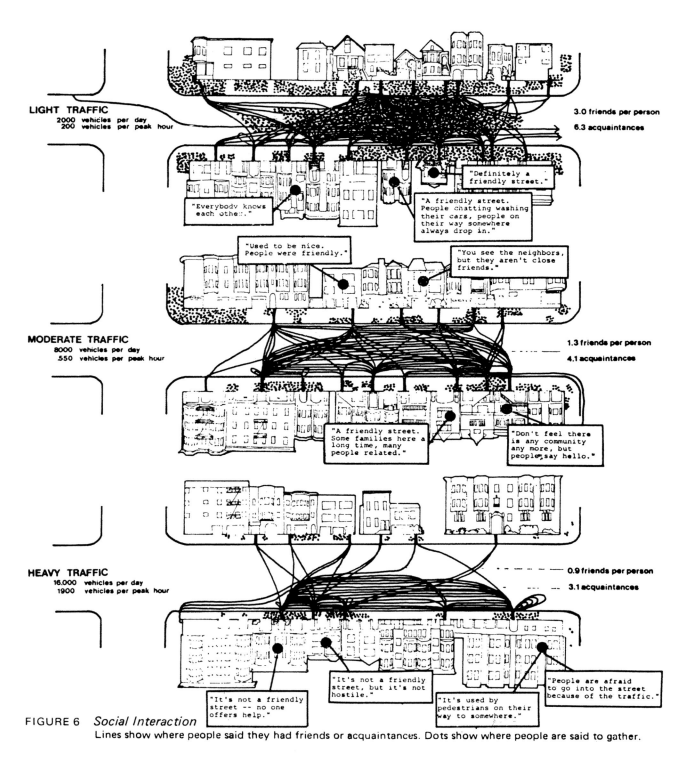

LIGHT TRAFFIC
2000 vehicles per day
200 vehicles per peak hour

3.0 friends per person

6.3 acquaintances

"Definitely a friendly street."

"Everybody knows each other."

"A friendly street. People chatting washing their cars, people on their way somewhere always drop in."

"Used to be nice. People were friendly."

"You see the neighbors, but they aren't close friends."

MODERATE TRAFFIC
8000 vehicles per day
550 vehicles per peak hour

1.3 friends per person

4.1 acquaintances

"A friendly street. Some families here a long time, many people related."

"Don't feel there is any community any more, but people say hello."

HEAVY TRAFFIC
16,000 vehicles per day
1900 vehicles per peak hour

— — — 0.9 friends per person

— ·— 3.1 acquaintances

"It's not a friendly street -- no one offers help."

"It's not a friendly street, but it's not hostile."

"It's used by pedestrians on their way to somewhere."

"People are afraid to go into the street because of the traffic."

FIGURE 6 *Social Interaction*
Lines show where people said they had friends or acquaintances. Dots show where people are said to gather.

114

TRAFFIC CORRIDORS OR LIVELY CITY STREETS

Social relationships and traffic

Who: Donald Appleyard and Mark Lintell
Where: Parallel streets: Franklin Street, Gough Street and Octavia Street, San Francisco, California
When: 1969
Method: Mapping and interviews
Published: Donald Appleyard and Mark Lintell, "The environmental quality of city streets:
            The residents' viewpoint," *Journal of the American Institute of Planners*, March 1972[42]

The increasing amount of traffic in the 1960s was the catalyst for Donald Appleyard and Mark Lintell to study the effect of car traffic on life in residential streets. Until then, the social consequences of traffic had been largely overlooked: "Studies of urban streets (...) have concentrated almost exclusively on increasing their traffic capacity, through devices such as street-widening, signalization, and one-way streets, with no parallel accounting of the environmental and social costs of these alternatives."[43]

Appleyard and Lintell selected three residential streets in San Francisco that were identical in character, but had different amounts of traffic. The three streets were all 23 meters wide and lined by two- and three-story houses and a mix of rental apartments and condominiums. The great difference was the traffic load. In a 24-hour period, 2,000 cars drove down the street with the least amount of traffic, while the next busiest street had 8,700 cars and the most heavily trafficked street 15,750 per day. In order to study the effect of traffic on the activity patterns in the three streets, Appleyard and Lintell plotted their observations on a street map. They also noted which age groups used the various public spaces.

They supplemented their observations by interviewing residents about where they gathered on the street, and about acquaintances in the neighborhood. Friendships and acquaintances were marked with lines between the various residences, while dots marked meeting points on the street.

The diagram opposite shows three streets with heavy, moderate and light traffic, respectively. Lines show where people have friends or acquaintances back and forth across streets, and dots show where people gather. With strong graphic clarity, the maps illustrate the conclusion of the study: the more traffic, the less life and social interaction.[44]

Registration showed clearly that there were considerably fewer street activities and far fewer social relations on the street with heavy traffic compared to the one with the least amount of traffic. The conclusion was easy to see graphically, because acquaintances between people on the street were drawn as connecting lines rather than more abstractly with figures and diagrams.

In terms of staying activities, it was also clear that there were by far the most staying places (dots) on the street with the least traffic, and stays absorbed more areas. Children played in the street where there was least traffic, and numerous people stayed on stoops and entrances to houses. There were fewer activities in the street with a moderate amount of traffic, and these took place on the sidewalks. And in the street with the heaviest traffic, which also had narrow sidewalks, activities were restricted to the entrances to buildings.

In order to illuminate the consequences of various amounts of traffic, the focus of the study was not on obvious topics such as traffic safety and accident statistics. Instead the observers studied the influence of traffic on the social life of residents.

Subsequently, Appleyard conducted similar studies on streets with various income levels and mixture of residents. These later studies supported the conclusions of the pilot study about the influence of traffic on social life. Appleyard's study is considered a classic in the field of public life studies. One of the reasons that the study has become so widely known is because the conclusions were communicated graphically in such an unusually clear and visually powerful way. Anyone who looks can see that there is something terribly wrong in the heavily trafficked street.

Bosselmann compares spatial relationships by making figure ground maps of the 14 study areas: 1. Berkeley Campus, University of California; 2. Downtown San Francisco, California; 3. Chinatown, San Francisco, California; 4. Times Square, New York City; 5. Strøget, Copenhagen, Denmark; 6. Pennsylvania Avenue, Washington DC; 7. Old quarter, Toronto, Canada; 8. Old part of Kyoto, Japan; 9. Piazza Novona, Rome, Italy; 10. Trafalgar Square, London, England; 11. Marais, Paris, France; 12. La Rambla, Barcelona, Spain; 13. Gated community, Laguna Niguel, Orange County, California; 14. Stanford Shopping Center, Palo Alto, California. The lines mark the 350-meter routes.

LONG OR SHORT MINUTES

Studies about experiencing public space while on the go

Who: Peter Bosselmann
Where: Various locations
When: 1982-1989
Method: Four-minute walks
Publiceret: Peter Bosselmann, *Representation of Places,* Berkeley: University of California Press, 1998[45]

After drawing sequences in an attempt to reproduce a four-minute walk rich with impressions in Venice, Bosselmann wanted to study other 350-meter routes, which in principle would take just as long to walk as the route in Venice, but would perhaps be experienced differently in terms of time.

Bosselmann selected 14 different routes in various parts of the world with widely different urban structures. In order to compare the spatial characteristics, he worked with figure/ground maps of the study areas. The graphically clear maps showed the different spatial characters of the various routes: from dense traditional urban structures in

Barcelona, Spain, for example, to an open campus area in Berkeley, California; a gated community with winding residential streets in Orange County, California; and the large expanses of a shopping center and open space in Palo Alto, California. The maps are accompanied by short texts that describe Bosselmann's experience of the route with the walk in Venice as a reference point. Bosselmann asks whether the routes are experienced as shorter or longer than the 350 meters in Venice. A four-minute walk can be used as a tool for comparing the experience of various routes.

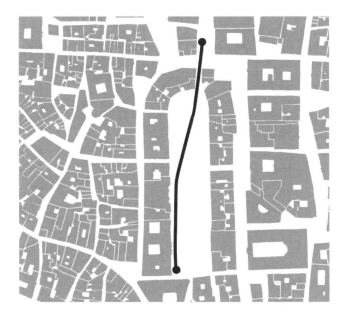

Peter Bosselmann comments on the experience of walking all the routes compared with a four-minute walk in Venice. This is what he says about the walk across the Piazza Navona in Rome (left): "To my great surprise, the walk in Venice equals a stroll through the Piazza Navona in Rome. Although I claim to know it well, I had underestimated its size, assuming that it took only half the time of the Venice walk; but, in fact, crossing the plaza takes four minutes."[46]

STREET BALLETS ON FILM
Time-lapse studies of small scenes in public space

Who:	William H. Whyte
Where:	Street life project, New York, USA
When:	1971-1980
Method:	Time-lapse photography
Published:	William H. Whyte, *The Social Life of Small Urban Spaces*, New York: Project for Public Spaces, 1980[47]

Life in public space consists of numerous small, unremarkable situations, but how can we register and illustrate these small everyday happenings?

Anyone who has ever tried to photograph telling situations in public space knows how much patience is required to capture the narrative moment one has just witnessed, if that is even possible. Many moments are exactly that: moments. Or perhaps situations cannot be reduced to a single photograph, because while the situations may play out in a split second, over time they are sequences that cannot be frozen into a single snapshot.

William H. Whyte had an eye for the way that small everyday situations provide much information about how people use public space. He used time-lapse photography to reproduce what Jane Jacobs called small street ballets, which are performed on the city's streets, squares and sidewalks, particularly street corners.

On this page and the next is shown one of the scenes Whyte captured with time-lapse photography on a street corner in Manhattan in the 1970s: A businessman is showing another how to swing a golf club. The first businessman adjusts the position of the second man's arm, the invisible golf club swings through the air, and the golfer finishes the swing with final adjustments being made to his back leg. Whyte was in the city to capture and describe situations that take place and to understand why it was precisely this corner and not in the middle of the sidewalk that the two men stopped to talk.

Whyte's point is that this type of situation does not happen just anywhere, and he describes what characterizes the best street corner: "One of New York's best corners is 49th Street

and the Avenue of the Americas, alongside the McGraw-Hill building. This corner has all of the basics: sitting space, a food vendor, and a heavy pedestrian flow, the middle of which is a favorite place for conversations."[48]

The top sequence of pictures shows another example taken by time-lapse photography, of a woman moving her chair just a bit – not to move into the sun or away from it or anything else, but to own the space or to show she is in charge. She has the opportunity to mark where she will sit. Illustrating someone's desire to mark their surroundings with a little photo sequences is stronger than any verbal description – even though Whyte's lively description in words supplements the pictures with an interpretation that guides the reader.

There has been a technological development in time-lapse photography since Whyte conducted these studies in the 1970s. All the same, Whyte's in-depth description of the use of time-lapse photography at the end of his book *The Social Life of Small Urban Spaces* continues to be useful and instructive. For example, Whyte writes about placing the camera so that it is not visible from the street, what time-lapse cannot capture and about interpreting the material: "Let me emphasize again that you have to know what to look for or you will not see it. Direct observation is the prerequisite."[49] For Whyte, direct observations are a prerequisite for being able to make a qualified analysis of the photographic material.

Captions from The Social Life of Small Urban Spaces.
Top series: "The impulse to move chairs, whether only six or eight inches, is very strong. Even where there is no functional reason for it, the exercise of choice is satisfying. Perhaps this is why the woman above moved her chair a foot – neither into the sun nor out of it."[50]
Bottom series: "A corner of Wall Street is a great place for business conversations."[51]

400 m   800 m

400 m   800 m

CAR DRIVERS ARE ALSO PEDESTRIANS

GPS studies of pedestrians' routes in three European city centers

Who: Stefan van der Spek with a team from Delft University of Technology
Where: City centers in Norwich, United Kingdom; Rouen, France; and Koblenz, Germany
When: Norwich, June 2007, Rouen and Koblenz, October 2007
Method: GPS registrations and questionnaires
Published: Stefan van der Spek, "Tracking pedestrians in historic city centers using GPS" in
             Street-level desires. Discovering the city on foot, ed. Hoeven, Smit and Spek, 2008[52]

In 2007, architect Stefan van der Spek from the University of Technology in Delft, Holland, studied the movements of pedestrians in three European city centers. He equipped pedestrians with a GPS sender in order to map which streets and areas they visited and did not visit. The goal was to be better able to target shopping and recreational opportunities.

The GPS senders were provided to visitors who parked their cars in parking garages at the edge of the city centers. In each of the three cities, Norwich, Rouen and Koblenz, two parking garages on each side of the city center were selected – it was a requirement that they were located with direct access to the city center. The reason that parking garages were selected was to ensure that participants would return with the GPS senders.

Participants were selected by asking what they planned to do in the city center, as shopping and recreation were the selection criteria. If they met the criteria, they were equipped with a GPS sender as well as an information sheet about the purpose and set-up of the study. When they returned to the parking garage a questionnaire with background information was filled in.

As shown on the opposite page, the information from the GPS sender was illustrated by dots on a map of the area studied. The dots mark the positions of participants every five seconds, and with an accuracy of from three to five meters – the precision that GPS senders had in 2007. Each line represents a person or group, and the goal was to make the general lines of movement readable.

In all three cities, car drivers from the parking garages used large parts of the city. There were parts of the city that were not visited, perhaps due to barriers of some kind, but the large picture was clear: the pedestrians from the parking garages walked in the entire city center.[53] The study supports an obvious but important point: car drivers are also pedestrians.

At this time GPS studies are being developed rapidly and in many different contexts, and we assume that this method will become very popular in future.

Above: When participants returned from walking in the city, an interviewer filled in a questionnaire with background information.

Opposite left: Map of Norwich, England. Top: Capelfield parking garage at the edge of Norwich city center, where GPS devices were handed out. Bottom: St. Andrews parking garage, the other access point for the city center, where participants were also equipped with GPS devices. The dots show where participants stayed and moved around in Norwich's city center.

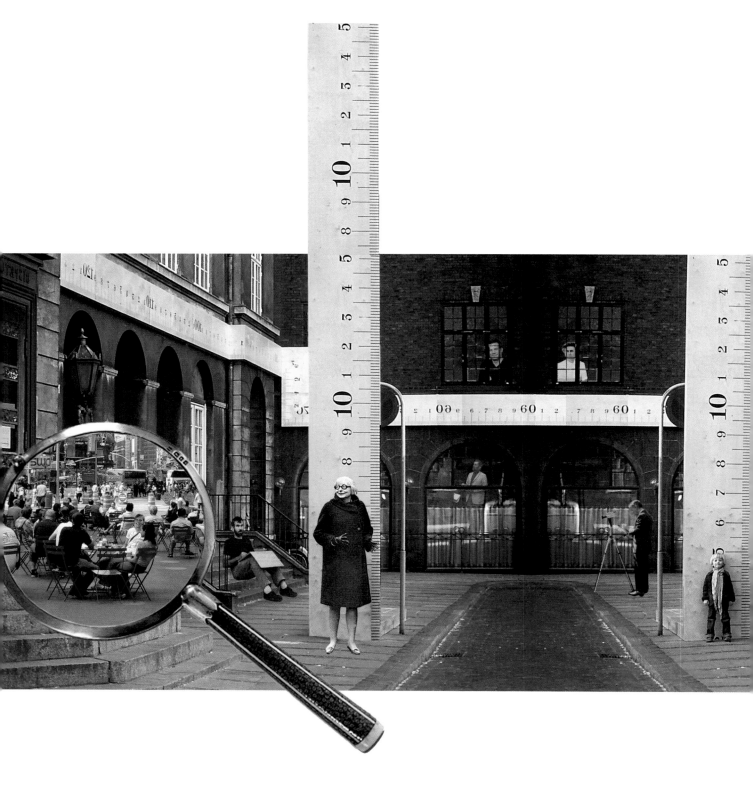

PUBLIC LIFE STUDIES IN PRACTICE

6

This chapter presents 'public space-public life' studies from different types of cities – large and small, modern and traditional. Some studies cover several years, others a shorter interval. All of the examples were conducted by Jan Gehl and Gehl Architects, respectively.

As the name indicates, public space-public life studies provide knowledge about physical frameworks as well as how people use them. The purpose of conducting these studies is to improve the physical conditions for people in cities by acquiring specific knowledge about individual public spaces and how and when they are used.

The studies can provide decision-making input in political debates on plans and strategies, or be used more concretely to assess the effect of initiatives already carried out by comparing before and after registrations. Acquiring more tangible and systematized knowledge about the interaction between public space and public life has proven useful in qualifying and targeting discussion – particularly across the lines of disciplines and administrative departments. While public life studies generally can provide a platform for professional and political debate, the information can also contribute to broader public debate.

Many people have conducted public life studies in practice, including Allan Jacobs and Peter Bosselmann in San Francisco, just to name two examples.[1] What is special about the public space-public life studies conducted by Jan Gehl and Gehl Architects is that they have been conducted in many cities in different countries and cultures over several decades, enabling comparisons across geographic lines and over time. That results in interesting research perspectives, and allows cities to follow their own development and compare their city with others.

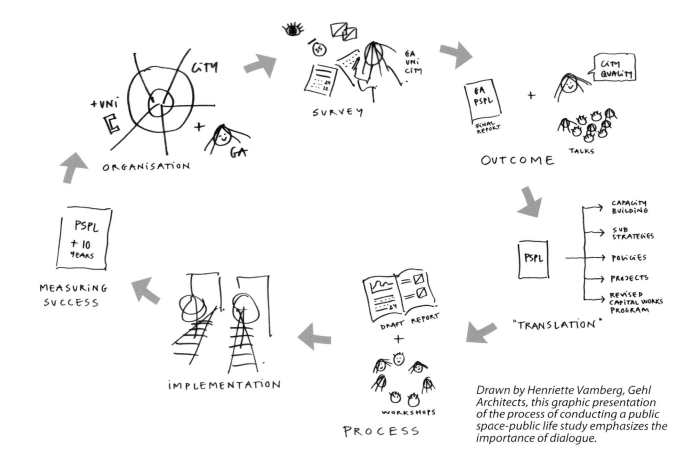

Drawn by Henriette Vamberg, Gehl Architects, this graphic presentation of the process of conducting a public space-public life study emphasizes the importance of dialogue.

Public Space-Public Life Studies

The content of Jan Gehl's and later Gehl Architects' public space-public life studies varies from study to study and from place to place. However, some elements are constant, such as counting pedestrians and registering stationary activities. The results are presented together with recommendations for improvements in report form to the client, which is typically a city.

In 1968 the first large study of city life was conducted in Copenhagen as a research project. The 1986 Copenhagen study also had a research aim. The first actual practice-oriented study – called a public space-public life study – was conducted in 1996 with the earlier city life studies as a strong platform.[2]

Later public space-public life studies were conducted in a close dialogue with local partners: a city, an urban region, NGOs, local business people, a local university or others with an interest in city development.

If a local university provides observers, the studies are usually part of a course. Training observers is more than simply giving instructions about a task. The goal is to inspire students about their future work – in terms of method but also more generally concerning prioritizing people in the planning process and specific design.

Even if what is being measured is tangible – here-and-now registrations of where, when and how many people are in the city and what they are doing – the long-term goal of public space-public life studies is always to make people a more visible part of planning. It is essentially a way of thinking and working with cities that considers people before infrastructure, buildings, pavements, and so on.

Area Studies or Acupuncture

In the planning stage, the size of the city or focus area very much determines how the study can be conducted. If the focus area is delimited to a public space or street, the site for registration is often obvious. It frequently proves valuable to study the connections to and from a public space.

If a larger area such as a city district is in focus, it is still possible to understand the entire context and to point

Acupuncture study: London

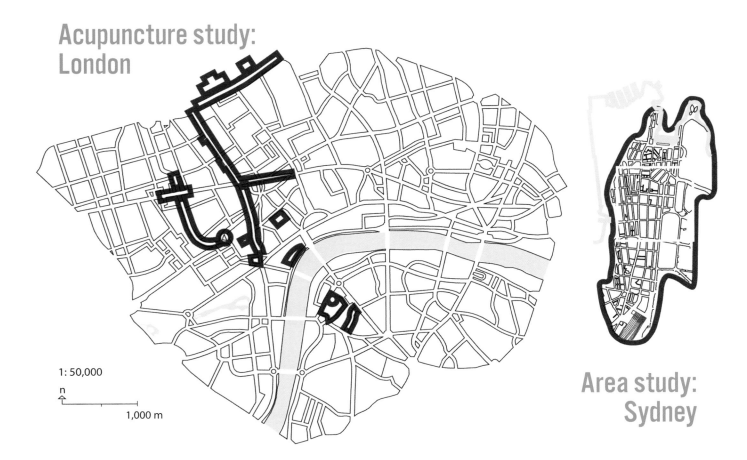

1: 50,000

n

1,000 m

Area study: Sydney

out the most interesting places for registration. Most of the public space-public life studies have been made in this way dealing with a larger cohesive area such as the city center.

In this context, many city centers have proven to be surprisingly uniform in size: typically 1x1 km (or a bit more) with an area of 1-1.5 km², even though the population varies from 500,000 to several million. One obvious explanation for the rather uniform size of city centers is that 1x1 km corresponds to an acceptable walking distance, that is, all parts of the city center can be reached on foot. We can call this a standard size determined by biology.

That so many city centers are about 1-1.5 km² in area simplifies comparison. Size also makes the study area relatively simple and doable, and the whole city center can be studied in what is called an 'area study'. Area studies have been conducted in Copenhagen, Stockholm, Rotterdam, Riga, Sydney and Melbourne, among others, as well as in all the smaller cities in which public space-public life studies have been conducted.

Since the target area in Sydney covers only 2.2 km², it was possible to conduct an area study of the entire city center. However, in London's congestion charging zone, which is 24.7 km², the acupuncture method was selected instead: 5.5 km of streets, 53,800 m² of parks and 61,200 m² of squares and plazas.[3]

Area studies are too extensive for city centers or districts considerably larger than 1 km², so the 'acupuncture' method is employed in these cases. Meaning that representative streets, squares, parks and local areas are selected. By studying typical elements of a larger city, it is possible to piece together a picture of the problem fields and opportunities that generally characterize the city under scrutiny. Acupuncture studies have been the method used to conduct studies in London, New York and Moscow.[4]

40 years: Copenhagen

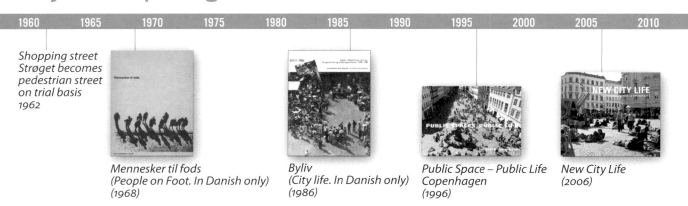

| 1960 | 1965 | 1970 | 1975 | 1980 | 1985 | 1990 | 1995 | 2000 | 2005 | 2010 |

Shopping street Strøget becomes pedestrian street on trial basis 1962

Mennesker til fods (People on Foot. In Danish only) (1968)

Byliv (City life. In Danish only) (1986)

Public Space – Public Life Copenhagen (1996)

New City Life (2006)

10 years: Melbourne

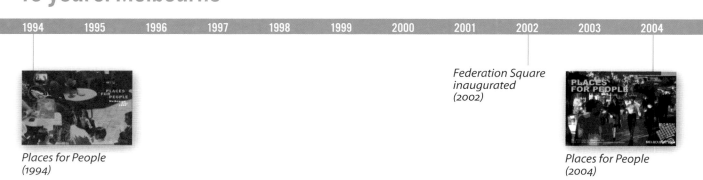

| 1994 | 1995 | 1996 | 1997 | 1998 | 1999 | 2000 | 2001 | 2002 | 2003 | 2004 |

Federation Square inaugurated (2002)

Places for People (1994)

Places for People (2004)

2 years: New York

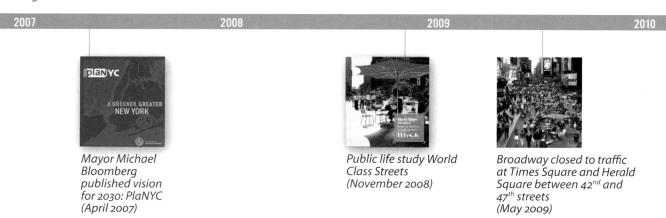

| 2007 | 2008 | 2009 | 2010 |

Mayor Michael Bloomberg published vision for 2030: PlaNYC (April 2007)

Public life study World Class Streets (November 2008)

Broadway closed to traffic at Times Square and Herald Square between 42nd and 47th streets (May 2009)

The Effect of Public Space-Public Life Studies

In her PhD thesis *Rediscovering urban design through walkability: An assessment of the contribution of Jan Gehl* (2011) written at Curtin University Sustainability Policy Institute in Western Australia, Anne Matan interviewed several of the urban planners who used public space-public life studies conducted by Jan Gehl and Gehl Architects.[5]

One of the most frequent responses to her question of what public space-public life studies can be used for is that they provide statistics rather than assumptions about what is actually happening. The studies also make it possible for public space and its uses to be seen in a larger context. Providing a holistic view of the city, the studies illustrate how the various public spaces can be seen in relation to each other at different times of day, week and year, rather than as individual urban projects. One urban designer involved in the study said: "Before that we had some general ideas, but [through the public space-public life survey] we were able to see the patterns more clearly."[6] Thus the studies can provide knowledge about a more general pattern and place patterns in a larger context.

In addition to serving as an analytical tool to assess existing status, public space-public life studies make it possible to set specific targets that are easy to follow up and use to adjust initiatives so that they function optimally. Based on her interviews with participants in the city's public space-public life studies, Anne Matan's conclusion is that the studies enable cities to implement simple, effective and logical changes. But it was also found important for cities to have the opportunity to compare themselves with other cities.

Clear communication of the study results is crucial for giving politicians and the public an understanding of the current condition of their city and the most desirable future direction for it.

This chapter contains several examples of cities where public space-public life studies were conducted and then used to improve urban quality.

Car-free areas in Copenhagen have been increased in a gradual process starting in 1962. The graph on the right illustrates the extent of stationary activities in the city center in 1968, 1986 and 1995. The figures given are an average of four registrations in the timeframe 11 a.m. to 4 p.m. on summer weekdays. Stationary activities quadrupled over the period in step with almost the same enlargement of the car-free area.[7]

The Long Haul – Copenhagen

In 1996, Copenhagen became the first city in which an actual public space-public life study was conducted. Before that time city life studies had been conducted over several decades as research projects at The Royal Danish Academy of Fine Arts, School of Architecture.

No radical changes have been made to Copenhagen's street pattern, which stems from the Middle Ages. However, minor yet distinctive changes have been made over a longer period, such as converting 2-3% of the city's parking places into people spaces and bicycle paths. These changes have helped create Copenhagen's international reputation as a city that has consistently made targeted efforts to improve conditions for pedestrians and bicyclists.

These changes were made over many years, and the major city life studies conducted about once a decade have documented the effect of the initiatives. For example, a direct connection between the number of car-free square meters and the extent of staying activities in the city has been documented. The more room, the more life!

By repeating the studies using exactly the same methods under the same conditions every two, five or ten years, changes in the way the city is used can be documented. The city's public space-public life studies become a knowledge bank that can be continuously updated. Repeated public space-public life studies have been conducted in many other cities, including Oslo, Stockholm, Perth, Adelaide and Melbourne.

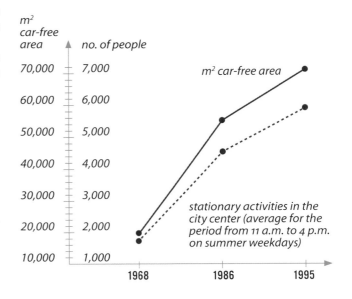

m² car-free area

stationary activities in the city center (average for the period from 11 a.m. to 4 p.m. on summer weekdays)

Dramatic growth in number of housing units and cafes in Melbourne over 20 years

1982: 204 housing units, two outdoor cafes

1992: 736 housing units, 95 outdoor cafes

2002: 6,958 housing units, 356 outdoor cafes

The 2004 study documents that within a decade the groundwork was laid so that many more people stayed in public space, and even more took up residence in the city center. The number of inhabitants increased from around 1,000 in 1992 to almost 9,400 in 2002.

The number of café chairs expanded from 1,940 in 1992 to 5,380 in 2002. The increase reflects changes in city culture generally, as well as putting numbers on the extent to which people to spend time in downtown Melbourne.[8]

● Official residence (one dot = five units)

● Apartments (one dot = five units)

● Student housing (one dot = five units)

● Café with outdoor service

▲ Under construction

Major Results in a Decade – Melbourne

In 1994, when Jan Gehl first conducted a public space-public life study in Melbourne, the starting point was a city center totally dominated by commercial activities and offices and very few residents.

This initial study served as a baseline to which later initiatives could be compared. It was a tool for documenting the effect of the changes implemented by the city between studies. A number of initiatives were adopted from 1994 to 2004. For example, narrow passageways through blocks of buildings were converted into attractive places for staying or sauntering. A central square and a new city hall plaza were established. Art projects beautified public space. These and many other initiatives made downtown Melbourne a more attractive place to live and to visit – by day and by night.

From 1994 to 2004, 71% more square meters of public space with staying options were established. In other words, the city made a massive effort to invite the city's residents and visitors not only to walk more in the city, but to stay awhile. The 2004 report documents that the efforts paid off. Pedestrian traffic in the city center in the evening took off by 98%, and in general the number of people who stayed a while almost tripled.[9]

It was not the city's public space-public life studies that brought about the changes in Melbourne, but a great number of actors: politicians, urban planners, business people and residents. However, having a public space-public life study as a tool in the process increased understanding of the importance of providing quality public space "designed and managed for people," as one of the city's urban designers put it.[10]

Melbourne now takes for granted that you have to have more knowledge about how public space is used and not used in order to make it function well. Ongoing studies are made of city life; staying and other social activities are registered as a matter of course. Prioritizing people and making them visible in planning has become an integrated part of daily planning work.

The reports were prepared in collaboration between the city of Melbourne and Jan Gehl in 1994 and Gehl Architects in 2004. Collaboration was a way for the city to take ownership of the study from the beginning in order to conclude with a report that was integral to a large planning project instead of being an isolated external document. The city council approved the goals and recommendations, which are integrated into concrete projects as well as strategic work. According to city architect Rob Adams, who headed up the studies in both 1994 and 2004, collaboration goes a long way in explaining the success of the Melbourne study.[11]

Below are photos of typical Melbourne lanes, many of which have been converted into vibrant city space. Left: traditional Melbourne lane. Right: revitalized Melbourne lane.

Dramatic Changes in Very Few Years – New York

There was a strong political will in New York City to implement changes to make the city more sustainable. In 2007 Mayor Michael Bloomberg launched an ambitious plan, *PlaNYC 2030. A Greener, Greater New York.*[12] The plan described how New York could be a more sustainable and better city for its many residents and the anticipated one million new arrivals expected to move to the city in the years from 2007 to 2030. The goal was to provide more quality of life for all New Yorkers, and a good deal of the work was to improve city streets, reduce private car traffic, and rethink public space. Gehl Architects contributed by conducting a comprehensive public space-public life study for the city.

Typically, a city's public space-public life study ends in a report that is published, but the New York study was not published in its entirety. Instead a substantial part of the results were incorporated in the vision *World Class Streets* prepared by the New York City Department of Transportation in 2008.[13]

Broadway, near Times Square, was one of the places selected to contribute to realizing the vision of a better New York for everyone. Work was also carried out on other projects in Manhattan and adjacent areas, but Times Square became the most dramatic picture of changes in New York.

For many years on New Year's Eve, news broadcasts from Times Square showed the world crowds of people gathered on the street. However, for the rest of the year Times Square was primarily a place for car traffic.

The exact ratio was illustrated by calculating how large an area of Times Square was dedicated to cars and how much left for people. This simple calculation had a thought-provoking result: 89% of Times Square was for cars, leaving only 11% of the area for pedestrians. This tiny area consisted largely of sidewalks and narrow pedestrian islands, where people could seek refuge as yellow cabs swept by. Large numbers of pedestrians were counted in the scant space available to them. These numbers were a focal point in the debate on what kind of a city New York would be in the 21st century.

Taking on Times Square as a possible public space was not uncontroversial. New York is known as one of the world's most modern cities with speed and yellow cabs as symbols. (The fact that car traffic moved more quickly and smoothly after the changes is another story.)[14] It took a massive communication campaign from the city before Times Square and other squares along Broadway could be converted into car-free public spaces.

New York City acted quickly by converting traffic streets to pedestrian-friendly streets and by laying down 322 kilometers of bicycle paths in just the first two years from June 2007 to November 2009. At Times Square changes were literally made overnight: the area was cordoned off, the asphalt painted, barriers and other temporary measures set up – including new opportunities to sit in quickly purchased, simple folding chairs next to temporary flower boxes.

Headcounts were made before and after in order to evaluate the effect of the temporary measures. The numbers could be used in support of the projects, as they clearly documented the fact that many, many people took advantage of the new initiatives. Documentation served as an evaluation tool in the process of adjusting the temporary measures with regard to optimal placement and so on.

The studies were an ongoing part of the rapid changes being made in New York City and used to measure the individual pilot projects as well as changes in the city generally. The Commissioner for the Department of Transportation in New York City, Janette Sadik-Khan, described it as a completely new way of looking at the streets of the city: "Until a few years ago, our streets [in New York] looked the same as they did fifty years ago. That's not

Pedestrians in the street

Pedestrians walking in the space for traffic on 7th Avenue between 45th and 46th Street, that is, at Times Square, before and after the area was closed to through traffic. Headcounts were made between 8:30 a.m. and 1:00 p.m.

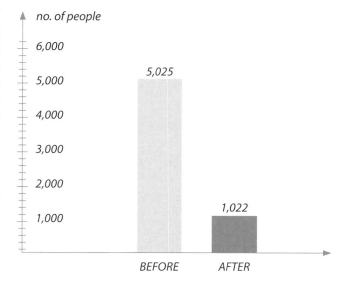

good business... We're updating our streets to reflect the way people live now. And we're designing a city for people, not a city for vehicles."[15]

Documenting public life in public space supported the political will to change the urban culture of New York City – or perhaps it would be more accurate to say that it supported cultural change by updating the physical framework.

Public space-public life studies start with existing conditions. As Annie Matan concludes in her PhD thesis: "Discussions about cities often focus on what they should be, what they have been and their problems, not on what they currently are and how they currently operate. [Public Space-Public Life] surveys offer an opportunity to view a city for what it is – to examine its everyday life and to focus on the present, not on the future."[16]

While the changes in New York City have been made at breathtaking speed, cities with other norms for planning and political leadership are pursuing a more stately tempo. Nonetheless, the changes in NYC have had widespread implications as inspiration to cities in the rest of the USA, and the world for that matter. In this context, before-and-after statistics and photographic documentation are essential for communicating the results.

Broadway was closed at Times Square and Herald Square as an experiment, but the change is now permanent, thanks to before and after studies and the immediate popularity of the new public spaces. A total of 35,771 m² of public space have been returned to people, while transport time for vehicular traffic has improved by 17%. There are also far fewer pedestrians walking in the street, and the number of pedestrians injured in traffic has fallen by 35%.

Headcounts before and after the changes show that Times Square has become a place for stationary activities in the city. While the increase in number of pedestrians is slight, 11%, there has been an 84% increase in the number of people standing and sitting at Times Square.[17]

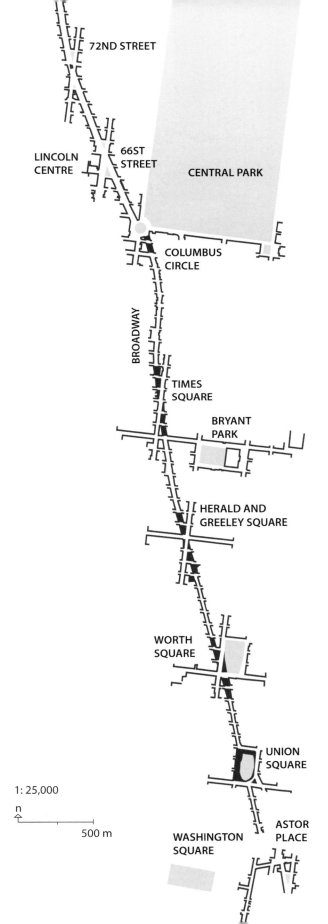

72ND STREET

LINCOLN CENTRE

66ST STREET

CENTRAL PARK

COLUMBUS CIRCLE

BROADWAY

TIMES SQUARE

BRYANT PARK

HERALD AND GREELEY SQUARE

WORTH SQUARE

UNION SQUARE

ASTOR PLACE

WASHINGTON SQUARE

1: 25,000

n

500 m

Times Square spring 2009

Times Square summer 2009

From Report to Streets and Squares – Sydney

A public space-public life study was conducted in Sydney, Australia in 2007. One conclusion was the urgent need for a cohesive pedestrian network to make Sydney a better city to walk in. It was also considered crucial to define a main street as the backbone of the city, and to select three squares along that backbone to help build a stronger identity for the city.[18] George Street was selected as the potential backbone. The report was published in 2007, and work to upgrade George Street began.

In 2013, it was decided to close George Street to cars and busses and instead introduce a new light rail system in the pedestrian street.

A public space-public life study was conducted in Sydney in 2007. Since then, the recommendations have been developed into design principles for selected streets pinpointed in the report. This includes George Street, the major north-south connection. As illustrated below, a detailed design strategy for George Street and adjoining plazas was made in 2013.

George Street Concept Design

City of Sydney with Gehl Architects

This document sets out the design principles that will guide the detailed design of George Street. It outlines strategies and concepts for improving the public realm in concert with the State Government's light rail project.

The ideas and images in this document have been tested to ensure that the City's $180 million investment is spent wisely and can achieve the public benefit that we strive for.

6 years: Sydney – George Street

2007   2008   2009   2010   2011   2012   2013

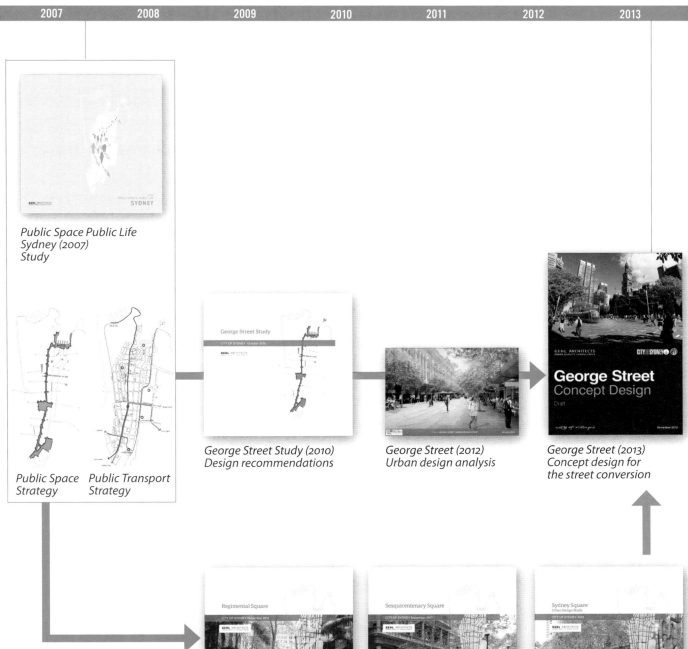

*Public Space Public Life
Sydney (2007)
Study*

*Public Space
Strategy*   *Public Transport
Strategy*

*George Street Study (2010)
Design recommendations*

*George Street (2012)
Urban design analysis*

*George Street (2013)
Concept design for
the street conversion*

*Regimental Square (2011)
Design recommendations*

*Sesquicentenary Square (2011)
Design recommendations*

*Sydney Square (2013)
Design recommendations*

An Important Contribution to Debate – London

Sometimes it is difficult to read the direct effects of a public space-public life study. One reason is that it takes time to implement initiatives, and another that the study is only one of several change elements. It is not possible to equate recommendations and subsequent projects, and the most important effect of a study is not necessarily visible. The most important contribution of a study can be that it changes the way the city's future is debated among professionals, politicians and the public at large.

A public space-public life study was conducted in London in 2004.[19] Subsequently, Patricia Brown, head of Central London Partnership, commented that people were talking about "streets for people" in London for the first time. The study provided a thought process and access route to the city that would mean a tangible platform for the city to build on.[20]

The report from 2004 pinpointed several specific areas as starting points. There were several sidewalks so crowded that the number of pedestrians far exceeded comfortable walking conditions. In other words, there can be too much city life in places not designed for it! The public space-public life study in London used photo documentation as well as headcounts for the large streams of pedestrians. The number and location of pedestrians was seen in relation to the design of the public space they traversed, that is, sidewalk width, position of entrances to underground stations, installations and other barriers.[21]

Results were not visible in London as quickly as in New York. While improving conditions on specific street corners was certainly a concern, London planners were also dealing with new political agendas and routes of access to provide streets for people.

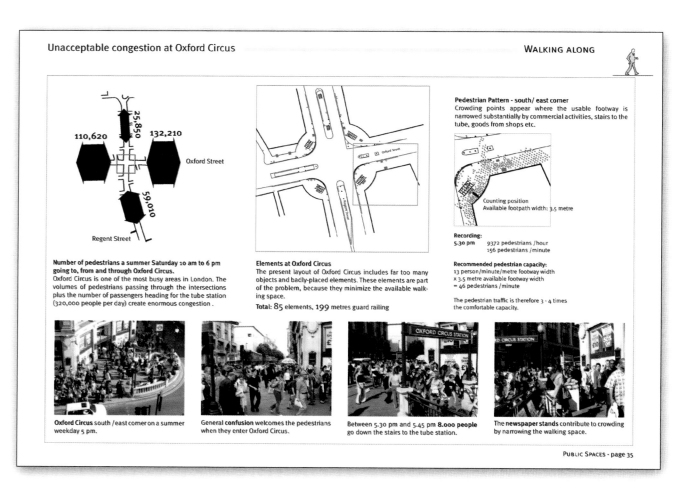

Unacceptable congestion at Oxford Circus

WALKING ALONG

Number of pedestrians a summer Saturday 10 am to 6 pm going to, from and through Oxford Circus.
Oxford Circus is one of the most busy areas in London. The volumes of pedestrians passing through the intersections plus the number of passengers heading for the tube station (320,000 people per day) create enormous congestion.

Elements at Oxford Circus
The present layout of Oxford Circus includes far too many objects and badly-placed elements. These elements are part of the problem, because they minimize the available walking space.
Total: 85 elements, 199 metres guard railing

Pedestrian Pattern - south/ east corner
Crowding points appear where the usable footway is narrowed substantially by commercial activities, stairs to the tube, goods from shops etc.

Counting position
Available footpath width: 3.5 metre

Recording:
5.30 pm   9372 pedestrians /hour
           156 pedestrians /minute

Recommended pedestrian capacity:
13 person/minute/metre footway width
x 3.5 metre available footway width
= 46 pedestrians /minute

The pedestrian traffic is therefore 3 - 4 times the comfortable capacity.

Oxford Circus south /east corner on a summer weekday 5 pm.

General **confusion** welcomes the pedestrians when they enter Oxford Circus.

Between 5.30 pm and 5.45 pm **8.000 people** go down the stairs to the tube station.

The **newspaper stands** contribute to crowding by narrowing the walking space.

However, the thought process and numerous projects have sprouted from the recommendations of the 2004 study in the intervening years. In the summer of 2013, the plan is to test various options for closing main shopping streets like Regent Street to through traffic – perhaps inspired by New York City's bold and symbolically significant closing of parts of Broadway to car traffic. Other projects large and small to improve conditions for pedestrians have been implemented.

The revamping of Oxford Circus in 2010 is a successful example of one of the new improvement projects.

Opposite: a page from the report, Towards a Fine City for People. Public Spaces and Public Life – London 2004, *which illustrates the congestion on the sidewalks in central London around Oxford Circus.*[22]

In 2010 Oxford Circus was converted so that pedestrians can cross diagonally, instead of being redirected behind fences and other barriers to prevent them from taking the direct route. As evidenced by the report from 2004 and later studies conducted by Atkins, who designed the new plan, prior to the conversion many people took shortcuts anyway by jumping the barrier.[23] *People have a tendency to take the shortest route – even when there are barriers and safety arguments to the contrary.*[24]

Below: a photo of Oxford Circus after the conversion in 2010.

When Opportunity Knocks – Cape Town

It is characteristic of the cities in which public space-public life studies have been conducted to have the political will to improve conditions for walking, public life and bicyclists. The studies are a useful tool for giving people a more prominent position in urban planning. However, despite good will, there are examples of public space-public life studies being put on the shelf for economic, political or other reasons. The shelf might belong to urban planners or a new mayor who does not want to carry on his predecessor's projects.

Sometimes after several years, one of these shelved studies is rescued from oblivion. Perhaps the political climate has changed, or there is another incentive to work on individual elements or the recommendations of the study as a whole.

Gehl Architects conducted a public space-public life study in Cape Town, South Africa in 2005.[25] Nothing much happened until Cape Town was named one of the host cities for the 2010 FIFA World Cup soccer championship games, which provided the impetus for the city to go to work on selected parts of the conclusions and recommendations of the study.

The Fan Walk, Cape Town, South Africa, during World Cup Soccer 2010. Built for the 2010 championship games, the pedestrian street connects the new stadium to the city center. The street was envisioned as a means of moving crowds of people during the World Cup games by foot rather than having to provide other means of transport. In addition, the street serves as a much needed new connection and meeting place for Cape Town's own residents. World Cup Soccer 2010 was the catalyst for realizing large projects like The Fan Walk, inspired by recommendations from the public space-public life study conducted in 2005.

Comparability

Taking stock can be useful on the local level. However, seen in a wider perspective – in relation to practice as well as in research terms – it is important to be able to compare studies across the lines of geography or over time. Comparisons can be made for the same city over the years, or across city and national lines. Main streets can be compared, for example, in order to gain an idea of how well visited the main street of one city is compared to those of other cities similar in size or character. There are many ways of making comparisons.

For research purposes, it can be wise to look at how public space-public life studies are conducted over a longer timeframe that can provide the opportunity to draw general conclusions about the historic development of city life. However, in practice city planners often want a shorter time perspective in order to be able to show results.

A systematic approach is necessary for comparisons over time and across geographic lines. What this means basically is that every single time studies are made, it is important to document actual weather conditions, time of day, week and year, registration method and other factors that are significant in making comparisons with other studies and cities.

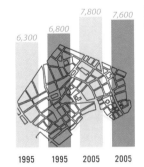

6,300 6,800 7,800 7,600

1995 1995 2005 2005

Number of lighted windows one winter night

The total number of lighted windows in central Copenhagen one winter night at 11 p.m. in 1995 and 2005, respectively.

Number of inner city inhabitants

The total number of inhabitants in central Copenhagen.

In the 1996 study of Copenhagen, lighted windows at night were registered as an indicator of life in the inner city. It was a problem at the time that so many city centers were unpopulated and therefore empty once the working day was over. Observers biked through the streets of inner Copenhagen registering the number of lighted windows and compared their findings to the statistical data on number of inhabitants. The result was a very concrete way of recording one of the benefits of residences in the inner city, namely the sense of safety. A decade later the increasing number of inhabitants in the heart of Copenhagen was reflected in the increased number of lighted windows at night.[26]

Copenhagen, Denmark

Copenhagen, Denmark

Oslo, Norway
Odense, Denmark

Odense, Denmark

Stockholm, Sweden

Perth, Australia
Melbourne, Australia

Copenhagen, Denmark

Odense, Denmark
Edinburgh, Scotland

1968   1986   1987   1988   1989   1990   1991   1992   1993   1994   1995   1996   1997   19

Public Space – Public Life Studies

*Maps of sites for public space-public life studies
conducted by Jan Gehl and Gehl Architects. The many
studies allow comparisons across time and place.*

London, Great Britain
2004

Copenhagen, Denmark
1968, 1986, 1996, 2006

Oslo, Norway
1988, 2013

Odense, Denmark
1988, 1998, 2008

Stockholm, Sweden
1990, 2005

Edinburgh, Scotland
1998

Perth, Australia
1994. 2009

Melbourne, Australia
1994, 2004

Wellington, New Zealand
2003

Cape Town, South Africa
2005

Sydney, Australia
2007

Vejle, Denmark
2002

1: 50,000

n

1,000 m

Riga, Latvia

Adelaide, Australia
Vejle, Denmark

Wellington, New Zealand

Zürich, Switzerland
London, England
Melbourne, Australia

Cape Town, South Africa
Stockholm, Sweden

Copenhagen, Denmark

Sydney, Australia
New York City, New York, USA
Rotterdam, Holland

Svendborg, Denmark
Odense, Denmark

Seattle, Washington, USA

Perth, Australia
Christchurch, New Zealand

Istanbul, Turkey
Auckland, New Zealand
Chongqing, China

Hobart, Australia
Launceston, Australia
Melbourne Docklands, Australia

Adelaide, Australia
Oslo, Norway
Moscow, Russia

2000 2001 2002 2003 2004 2005 2006 2007 2008 2009 2010 2011 2012

Moscow, Russia
2013

Riga, Latvia
2001

Manhattan,
New York, USA
2007

Rotterdam, Holland
2007

Svendborg, Denmark
2008

Seattle, USA
2009

Auckland, New Zealand
2010

Adelaide, Australia
2002, 2012

Christchurch, New Zealand
2009

Hobart, Australia
2011

Launceston, Australia
2011

Zürich, Schwitzerland
2004

Istanbul, Tyrkey
2010

Chongqing, China
2010

Summer weekday

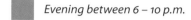 Evening between 6 – 10 p.m.

Daytime between 10 a.m. – 6 p.m.

* New York between 8 a.m. – 8 p.m.

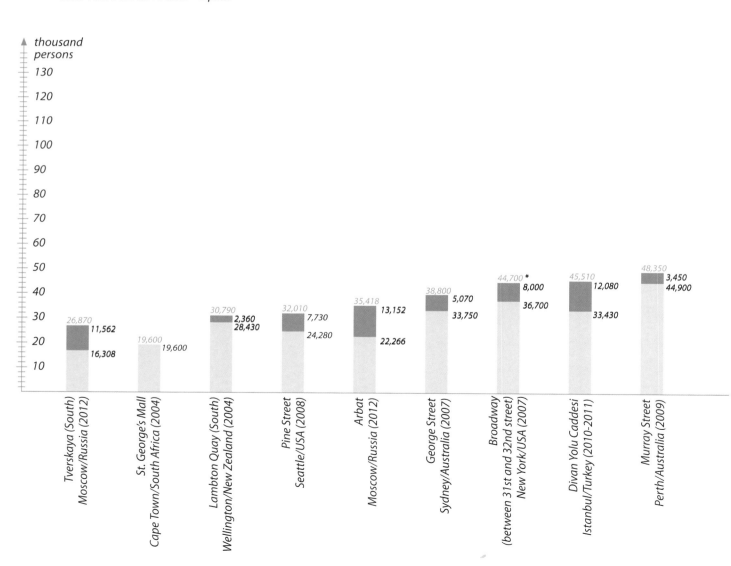

Public Space-Public Life Studies –
Across Geographic Lines

How many are many and how few are few? To get a feeling for what the numbers mean for a specific city, comparison with other cities can show the relative amount of activity in a square or the number of pedestrians on a street.

On the basis of their registrations in numerous cities, Jan Gehl and Gehl Architects have gathered material that makes it possible to compare cities across the lines of geography. It might seem obvious to compare cities of the same size or same population, but as shown on this page, when studying the numbers for main shopping streets, for example, it is not necessarily the major streets in the largest cities that attract the most pedestrians. For example, Oslo's shopping street outranks a street like Regent Street in London, between which streets the counts referred to were made, in number of pedestrians on a Saturday. Moscow, with its millions of inhabitants, ranks quite low on the list.

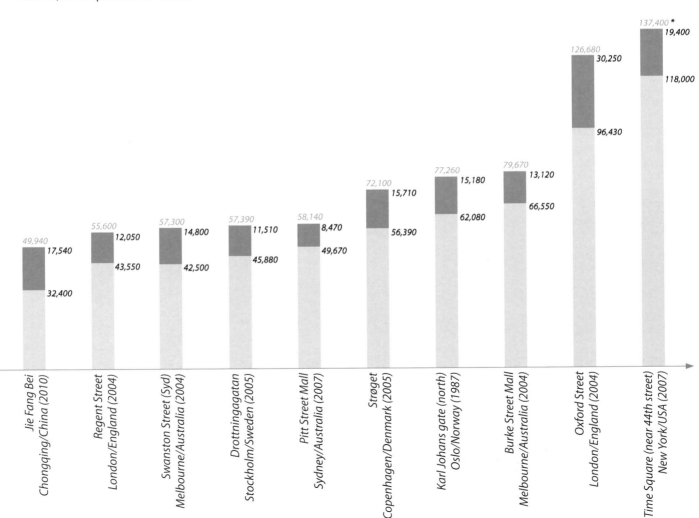

Public Space-Public Life Studies – Over Time

Looking at public space-public life studies over time is interesting for individual cities in a local perspective. As more and more of these studies are conducted, it is possible to draw more general conclusions about the development of city life over the years in keeping with other changes in society.

Public life studies have been conducted in Copenhagen since 1968 using the same methods, which makes it possible to see decades of life in the city from a historical perspective. Copenhagen has had a significant increase in the number of optional recreational activities, for example. The historical development from necessary to optional activities – the product of changes in society generally – impacts how public space is used. By registering what kinds of activity take place, these changes can be documented and the city spaces adapted accordingly.

When it is no longer absolutely essential for people to spend time in public space, it takes more to get them to come there rather than staying indoors or at home. The four decades of studies from Copenhagen document that inviting people to stay by establishing quality public space

gets results. The more square meters provided for staying, the more people that stay in public space – if the space is designed in keeping with human needs, that is.

The most recent study from 2006 shows how a more active public life takes place. In order to chart new types of activities, the tools and categories must be adjusted along the way, so that they capture the new activity patterns and other changes in how and for what purpose public space is used.[27]

This photo of Copenhagen Harbor (2010) shows the changes made as industrial buildings were vacated and converted to housing and recreational areas. For many years, the harbor was too polluted to allow swimming. Next to the harbor swimming pool, which opened in 2002, is the public harbor bath, which exists thanks to the efforts of local citizens, who fought plans to build multi-story buildings on this side of the harbor, which gets the prized western and evening sun. Here, only one kilometer from the city center and Copenhagen Town Hall, is a venue for versatile, recreational public life – day after day throughout the summer months.

Development of public life from 1880 to 2005

OPTIONAL
ACTIVITIES
*Urban
recreation*

ACTIVE

PASSIVE

NECESSARY
ACTIVITIES

1880   1900   1910   1920   1930   1940   1950   1960   1970   1980   1990   2000

NECESSARY ACTIVITIES
DISREGARD QUALITY OF
PUBLIC SPACE

OPTIONAL ACTIVITIES REQUIRE GOOD QUALITY
PUBLIC SPACE

CAR INVASION

RESEARCH AND
PLANNING
REGARDING
RENAISSANCE
OF PUBLIC SPACE
*- pedestrian
streets
- public life and
urban activities
- re-emergence
of bicycles
- calming traffic*

A diagram in the book New City Life *sums up the history
of urban life from 1880 to 2005. At the beginning of the
20th century, many activities took place in public space by
necessity. This was before vans and trucks made their way
into cities, so goods were transported through the city by
foot or horse, and most of remaining traffic was pedestrian.
Many people also used the streets as their workplace. But over
the course of the 20th century, goods moved inside or over to
other forms of transport, and city space gradually became an
arena for recreational and leisure activities. In this context the
quality of public space becomes all-important.*[28]

147

Villo Sigurdsson
Mayor for City Planning
1978-1986

Otto Käszner
City Architect
1989-1998

Bente Frost
Mayor for Building and Construction
1994-1997

Søren Pind
Mayor for Building and
Construction
1998-2005

Tina Saaby
City Architect
2010-

Gunna Starck
Mayor for City Planning
1986-1989

Jens Rørbech
City Engineer
1987-1999

Klaus Bondam
Mayor for the Technical and
Environment Administration
2006-2009

Ritt Bjerregaard
Mayor of
Copenhagen
2004-2009

Ayfer Baykal
Mayor for the Techni
and Environment
Administration
2011-

PUBLIC LIFE STUDIES AND URBAN POLICY

Copenhagen, Denmark. The first city in the world in which comprehensive studies of public life were conducted systematically for decades. The city where these studies made a decisive difference in how public life policies were designed and qualified for more than 40 years. The city where the local government and business community gradually began to see public life studies as a valuable tool for user-friendly urban development, and to such an extent that these studies long ago moved from School of Architecture research to the auspices of the city. In the city of Copenhagen, it has become only natural for public life to be documented and followed just like other elements that make up the city's combined policies. This is how it happened.

A Pedestrian Street since 1962

Copenhagen's main street, Strøget, was converted from a traffic street to a pedestrian street in November 1962. It didn't happen without the rattling of sabers and vociferous debate: "We are Danes, not Italians, and car-free public space is never going to work in Scandinavian weather and Scandinavian culture."[1] But the street was closed to car traffic all the same. Nothing was renovated at this point; it was still an ordinary street with asphalt lanes, curbs and sidewalks, just minus car traffic as an experiment.

In many ways, closing Strøget to car traffic in 1962 was a pioneering effort. It was not the first street closed to cars in Europe, but one of the first major streets that marked willingness to reduce the pressure from cars in the city center. Inspiration came largely from various German cities that had established pedestrian streets in connection with re-building after World War II. In these cities as well as in Copenhagen, the motive was primarily to strengthen trade and give customers in the inner city more room and better conditions for shopping. While that was indeed good for customers, it also proved beneficial for the inner city, as downtown was increasingly forced to compete with the new, American-inspired shopping centers that began sprouting up on the outskirts of cities in the 1960s.

The conversion of Strøget comprised the entire street - 11-meters wide and 1.1 kilometers long – interspersed by several small squares. Despite the many dire prophecies about the impossibility of car-free streets being able to function in a Danish environment, the new pedestrian street quickly became popular. Pedestrian traffic grew by 35% already the first year. In 1965 the pedestrian status of the street was made permanent, and by 1968 the City of Copenhagen was ready to resurface the street and squares. Strøget became an established success story.[2]

Top: Amagertorv, Copenhagen, view from the south, 1953.
Bottom: Amagertorv, Copenhagen, same view, 2013.

Public Life Studies in Copenhagen

Mennesker til fods
(People on foot. In Danish only)
Offprint by Arkitekten *no. 20,*
1968

Byliv
(City Life. In Danish only)
Offprint by Arkitekten, *1986*

Public Spaces Public Life
Book, The Danish Architectural
Press and the School of
Architecture, The Royal Danish
Academy of Fine Arts, 1996

New City Life
Book, The Danish Architectural
Press, 2006

Showing the major public life studies conducted in
Copenhagen approximately ten years apart over 40 years.
Starting out as articles, the studies grew into solid book
publications.

Public Life Studies at the School of Architecture, initial studies 1966-71

In 1966 Jan Gehl was offered a research position at The Royal Danish Academy of Fine Arts, School of Architecture in Copenhagen with "People's use of outdoor space in cities and residential neighborhoods" as the research theme. Gehl had conducted several studies in Italy on the same theme, and he and his wife, psychologist Ingrid Gehl, wrote about their findings in several articles published in the Danish architectural journal *Arkitekten* in 1966. The articles described how Italians use public squares and space on a daily basis, and the studies created quite a stir, because the topic had not really been studied previously. New territory was being charted.[3]

Next came the invitation to continue the research at the School of Architecture for a four-year period. Timing seemed almost to dictate the use of Copenhagen's newly opened pedestrian street, Strøget, as a large outdoor laboratory where people's use of public space could be studied.

The Copenhagen studies were most definitely basic research. Very little was known on the subject, and all types of research questions had to be answered. So the Strøget studies became an extensive project in 1967 and subsequent years, with basic data such as the number of pedestrians and the extent of various types of activities making up only a small part of the total material collected.

The studies were conducted by studying life along the various stretches of the pedestrian street every Tuesday throughout the year, supplemented by gathering data in selected weeks and weekends, and during festivities and holidays. How did the street function when Her Majesty Queen Margrethe II rode through in her horse-drawn carriage on her birthday? How did the narrow street handle the Christmas crush? Daily rhythms, weekly rhythms and yearly rhythms were charted, differences between winter and summer behavior were studied, as well as questions such as, how fast do people walk down the street? How are the benches used? What is the most popular seating? How warm does the temperature have to get before people use seating at all? What is the impact of rain, wind and cold, and what about sun and shadow? What is the influence of darkness and lighting? And to what extent are the various user groups influenced by the changing conditions? Who goes home first, and who holds out the longest?

All in all, an immense amount of material was collected, which formed the basis for the book *Life Between Buildings*, published in 1971, incorporating primarily the studies from Italy and Copenhagen.[4] Prior to the book, the studies from Copenhagen had also been published in articles in Danish professional magazines, and these articles attracted considerable attention from the city's planners, politicians and business community. Here was detailed data describing how the city center was used throughout the year, and what conditions enticed pedestrians to come and spend time in the city.

An ongoing dialogue between the School of Architecture's public life researchers and the city's planners, politicians and business people had begun.

Public Life Studies in Copenhagen, 1986

In the meantime, another series of changes had been made in the city center. New pedestrian streets and car-free plazas were added to the public space that had already been transformed. In the first phase in 1962, car-free public space totaling 15,800 m² had been established. By 1974 car-free public space had grown to 49,000 m², and with the inclusion of the canal street Nyhavn by the harbor, the pedestrian area was more than 66,000 m² after 1980.

Another comprehensive public life study was conducted in Copenhagen in 1986 – once again as a research project under the auspices of The Royal Danish Academy of Fine Arts, School of Architecture.[5] The compendious results of the studies in 1967-68 made it possible to conduct a follow-up study in 1986 to shed light on the changes in public life that had occurred in the intervening 18 years. The 1967-68 study had established a baseline providing an overall view of how the city functioned at that point in time. By carefully following the methods and prerequisites set down in 1967, it was possible 18 years later to gain an overview of how public life had changed, as well as to see the effect of the considerably larger car-free areas that had been established.

In an international context, the 1986 study marked the first time that a baseline study was conducted in a city, a study that could proclaim, "This is the situation in this city at this moment." Now it was possible to document development in public life seen over a longer period of time.

Just as with the first public life study, the one conducted in 1986 was published as an article in the architectural journal *Arkitekten*, and, once again, the results attracted widespread interest from the city's planners, politicians and business community. Not only did the study provide good documentation of the current public life situation, but it also made it possible to get an overview of what had changed since 1968. In brief, it could be concluded that there were considerably more people and activities in the city in 1986, just as it could be clearly shown that the new

From a street in Denmark... to universal recommendations

Since its publication in 1971, *Life Between Buildings* has been reprinted many times in English and Danish and translated into many other languages – from Farsi to Bengali and Korean. Despite the fact that the examples in the book are largely taken from Denmark and other Western countries, the book's wide appeal may be because the observations and principles described in the book are universal to people. Regardless of continent and culture, all people are pedestrians to some degree.

The book covers have changed over the years in keeping with cultural changes and the fact that the book has acquired a more international status. The picture on the left shows the original cover of the first Danish edition published in 1971. The street party motif was taken on Sjællandsgade in Århus, Denmark's second largest city, around the year 1970 and captures the focus on togetherness at that time. It almost looks like a depiction of hippie life between buildings. The cover of a later edition from 1980 shows more sedate public life in a classic small-town Scandinavian framework, while the cover from 1996 and following editions is almost timeless and placeless thanks to the graphics. Also in terms of its covers, the book has become a classic that crosses the lines of time and geography.

1971

1980

2003

public space had meant a corresponding reinforcement of life in the city. Better space in the city could be seen to equal correspondingly more activities going on.

The 1986 study was the starting point for what became known as public space-public life studies. The studies comprised (and continue to comprise) the registration of numerous spatial relationships (public space) supplemented by the study of life in the city (public life), which together document how the city functions on the whole and in individual spaces.

The 1986 study was the catalyst for closer cooperation between researchers at the School of Architecture and planners at City Hall. Seminars and meetings were held, where the development of public life was presented and the city's plans debated. The Copenhagen public space-public life studies also attracted attention in the capitals of Denmark's Scandinavian neighbors. Soon afterwards, corresponding studies were being conducted in Oslo, Norway and Stockholm, Sweden, with the assistance of the School of Architecture in Copenhagen.

Top: Gammeltorv/Nytorv, Copenhagen, 1954
Bottom: Gammeltorv/Nytorv, Copenhagen, 2006

Studies in Copenhagen 1996 and 2006

Ten years later in 1996, Copenhagen was selected as the European City of Culture for the year, and an abundance of activities were planned to signal the event. The School of Architecture decided that one of the school's contributions to the festivities would be to conduct another comprehensive public space-public life study.[6] These studies had gradually become a Copenhagen specialty. Public life had been documented in 1968 and 1986 and now, 28 years after the first study, the development in public space and public life would be documented once again.

The 1996 study was ambitious and extensive. In addition to the many headcounts and observations, this study included interviews seeking answers to questions that the earlier observation studies had been unable to answer: Who visits the city center? Where do visitors come from? What forms of transport do visitors use for their trips to the city? From where, why, how long and how often, as well as questions concerning the positive and negative experiences of visitors to the city. These questions could be probed by asking the city's users and would add a valuable extra layer of information to the observation studies.

Although researchers from the School of Architecture were also the driving force of the studies in 1996, the project was no longer a narrow academic endeavor, but a project supported by several foundations, the City of Copenhagen, tourist and cultural institutions and the business community. Public space-public life studies had definitely grown from the status of basic research to becoming a generally recognized means of gathering knowledge to manage the development of the city center.

The 1996 studies were published in book form, *Public Spaces, Public Life* with Jan Gehl and Lars Gemzøe as co-authors. In addition to the results of the studies from various years, the book also presented a combined overview of the development of Copenhagen's city center from 1962 to 1996, and a description of the transformation from crowded car-urbania to a city that took the concerns of pedestrians and public life seriously. The book was published in Danish and English, the first time that the public space-public life studies were presented in an English-language version.

Over the years, the public space-public life studies from Copenhagen and the city-life orientation of Copenhagen's development generally have become internationally recognized, and information about the Copenhagen success story has traveled widely. A Chinese version of *Public Spaces, Public Life* was published in 2005.

In 2006, a comprehensive public life study was conducted by the School of Architecture for the fourth time. The framework was the school's newly established Center for Public Space Research, and this time the goal was to illuminate the development of public space and public life not only in the city core, but in all parts of the city: from the center to the periphery, from the Medieval heart of the city to its newest additions. The city of Copenhagen financed data collection, while researchers from the School of Architecture conducted the analyses and handled publication. The result was a hefty volume entitled *New City Life*, authored by Jan Gehl, Lars Gemzøe, Sia Kirknæs and Britt Søndergaard.[7]

The title of the book sums up the main conclusion of the study: that more leisure time, increased resources and changes in society have gradually produced a 'new city life' where a great deal of what is happening in the city center is rooted in recreational and cultural activities. Whereas two or three generations ago, necessary, goal-oriented activities dominated the urban scene, today the city boasts a much broader spectrum of human activities. At the start of the 21st century, 'recreational city life' was at the hub of the way public space was used.

Focus on Public Space and Public Life as City Policy

From the 1960s to the 1990s, Copenhagen developed on two fronts. The Royal Danish Academy of Fine Arts, School of Architecture, developed a special field of research with focus on public space and public life, while the city continued to convert streets, squares and plazas into car-free or nearly car-free areas in order to invite people to use public space. In principle the two fronts were separate – research in one corner and urban transformation in the other. However, Copenhagen – and all of Denmark for that matter – is a relatively small society with short lines of communication between the various environments. People from Copenhagen's City Hall and planners and politicians throughout Denmark follow what is happening at the School of Architecture, and in turn researchers at the school keep their fingers on the pulse of what is happening in the cities.

Over the years ongoing exchanges were made, and gradually it became apparent that the way of thinking about the city and urban development in Denmark was increasingly influenced by the many publications, studies and media debates engendered by the public life research conducted in Copenhagen. The importance of topics such as public space and public life for the attractiveness of cities and inter-city competition became increasingly clearer.

This change in focus took form as work with city life moved from the research world to actual urban policy. The Copenhagen public space-public life studies became an established part of city planning in the same way that studies of traffic development had served as the cornerstone of traffic planning for decades.

It could be seen that documenting public life development and knowledge of the connection between city quality and city life served as useful tools in the debates about the city's transformation, assessing plans already carried out and setting goals for future development.

Through the years, Copenhagen gradually established a position as a very attractive and inviting city from an international perspective. The city's concern for pedestrians, city

In later years, the City of Copenhagen has steadily published planning documents that incorporate public life into city planning. In A Metropolis for People *from 2009, the city council describes its new strategy for making Copenhagen the best city in the world for people.[8]*

Top: Nyhavn, Copenhagen, 1979
Bottom: Nyhavn, Copenhagen, 2007

life and bicyclists plays a key role in that image. On many occasions, the city's politicians and planners have pointed to the interesting connection between the public life research developed in Copenhagen and the city's concern for public space and public life. "Without the many studies from the School of Architecture, we politicians would not have had the courage to carry out the many projects to increase the city's attractiveness," said Bente Frost, mayor for city planning, in 1996.[9] It is significant that Copenhagen – in an ongoing process – became more and more oriented towards public space and public life as crucial factors for the city's overall quality and good international image.

The experiences gained from systematically documenting public life and using the results to shape public policy were not restricted to Copenhagen. Soon cities in other parts of the world were following suit. The term 'Copenhagenization' is often used to describe the results developed from systematic data-driven urban improvements. To 'Copenhagenize' has become the description of a process as well as a term to describe a particular way of thinking and planning with regard to people and life in the city.

Already in 1988 and 1990, respectively, Oslo, Norway and Stockholm, Sweden began to conduct their own public life studies. In 1993-94 Perth and Melbourne in Australia introduced public space-public life studies modeled on Copenhagen. After that the methods began to spread at a galloping pace, and in the years from 2000 to 2012 Adelaide, London, Sydney, Riga, Rotterdam, Auckland, Wellington, Christchurch, New York, Seattle and Moscow added their names to the circle of cities that use public space-public life studies as the starting point for urban quality development.

Cities conduct basic studies primarily in order to gain an overview of how people use the city in daily life. After that, plans for development and changes can be made.

Just as in Copenhagen, more and more cities gradually use new follow-up public space-public life studies to chart how city life has developed since their original baseline studies were conducted. Oslo, Stockholm, Perth, Adelaide and Melbourne have all used follow-up public space-public life studies as a city policy tool 10-15 years after the first baseline studies. The follow-up studies in Melbourne in 2004 are a prime example of how it has been possible to show dramatic development in city life as the direct result of targeted policy. The positive Melbourne results from 2004 have again provided grounds for setting new ambitious goals, which will be studied in the years to come.

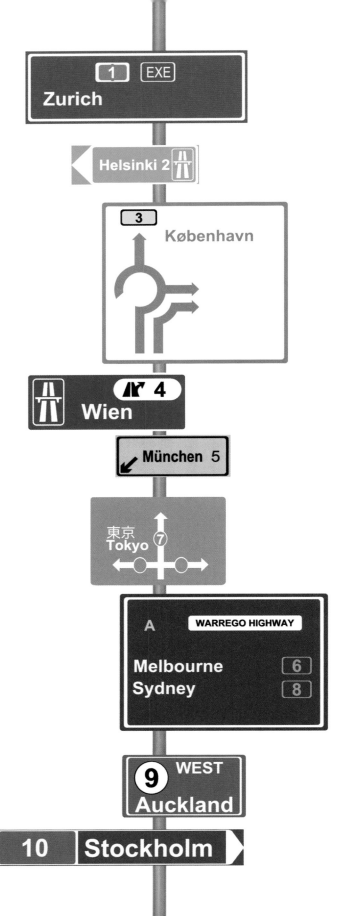

1 EXE
Zurich

Helsinki 2

3 København

Wien 4

München 5

東京
Tokyo 7

A WARREGO HIGHWAY

Melbourne 6
Sydney 8

9 WEST
Auckland

10 **Stockholm**

Reflection

There has been considerable development regarding public space, public life and methods for studying them in the 50 years since Jane Jacobs wrote about the prospect of dead, empty cities in 1961. At the time, there was essentially no formalized knowledge about how form influenced life in cities. Throughout history, public life had been borne by tradition and experience. In fact, cities were to a great extent built with public life as the starting point. But from about the year 1960, in what had become car-dominated and rapidly expanding cities, the planning profession had neither experience nor tradition to call upon. First the problems of the lifeless cities had to be described, and then knowledge of the subject had to be gathered. The first efforts were tentative and intuitive, eventually enhanced by a degree of overview and continuity. Here, 50 years later we can see that not only has an extensive knowledge base been established, but practical methods and tools have been developed so that policy and planning can systematically be used to invite people's use of public space.

Through a long process, public space-public life studies have made the people who use cities visible to politicians and planners. Now it is possible to actively plan to reinforce life in the cities, or, at a minimum, to ensure that public space is useable and pleasurable for urban inhabitants. Life in cities, once overlooked, is now an established field recognized as having great impact on the attractiveness of cities. It has become a legitimate field that can be systematically taught and studied, as well as a sector considered equally with other urban planning sectors.

Humanistic city planning has become an academic field with theories, knowledge, methods and many visible results. Examples from Copenhagen and Melbourne show how research, public space-public life studies, visions, political will and action can put cities on the world-class map – not because of their skylines or monuments, but because of good public space and a versatile public life. Focus on people in the city has ensured that they are really good cities to visit, live and work in. On the lists of the 'World's Most Livable Cities' in the 21st century, it is no coincidence that year after year Melbourne and Copenhagen continue to rank among the best.

Good cities are all about people.

What we can learn from diverse lists of the most livable cities in the world can be discussed. However, an increasing number of such lists have been published in recent years. The magazine Monocle *began making its list of "most livable cities" in 2007.*
In 2012 the cities on Monocle's *top 10 list were:*
1. Zürich 2. Helsinki 3. Copenhagen 4. Vienna 5. Munich 6. Melbourne 7. Tokyo 8. Sydney 9. Auckland 10. Stockholm.[10]
What is remarkable about Monocle's *top 10 list for 2012 is that public space-public life studies have been conducted in six of the ten cities listed. These cities made a dedicated effort to become more people-friendly by studying public space and life, among other means: Zürich, Copenhagen, Melbourne, Sydney, Auckland and Stockholm.*

NOTES, BIBLIOGRAPHY, PHOTOS AND ILLUSTRATION CREDITS

NOTES

Chapter 1

1. Among others: Jane Jacobs, *The Death and Life of Great American Cities* (New York: Random House, 1993 (1961)); Jan Gehl, *Life Between Buildings* (Copenhagen: The Danish Architectural Press, 1971, distributed by Island Press); William H. Whyte, *The Social Life of Small Urban Spaces* (New York: Project for Public Spaces, 1980).
2. Jane Jacobs, op. cit., unpaginated
3. Georges Perec (1936-1982) was a French novelist, filmmaker, documentarist and essayist. His first novel, *Les choses* (*Things: A Story of the Sixties*), was written in 1965. His most famous work is *La vie – mode d'emploi* (*Life – A User's Manual*), from 1978. Minor works with urban cultural interest are *Espèces d'espaces* (*Species of Spaces and other Pieces*), 1974, and *Tentative d'épuisement d'un lieu parisien* (*An Attempt at Exhausting a Place in Paris*), 1975.
4. Georges Perec, *Species of Spaces and Other Pieces* (London: Penguin, 1997).
5. Ibid., 50.
6. Jane Jacobs, op. cit., xxiv.
7. According to the Macmillan online dictionary, to observe means "to watch or study someone or something with care and attention in order to discover something". http://www.macmillandictionary.com/dictionary/british/observe (07-24-2013).
8. The Danish Union of Journalists, *Fotografering og Privatlivets Fred.* (*Photographing and Privacy.* In Danish) (Copenhagen: Dansk Journalistforbund, March, 1999).
9. For 'sidewalk ballets', see among others, Jane Jacobs, op. cit., 50.
10. Jan Gehl, "Mennesker til fods." ("People on Foot." In Danish), in *Arkitekten* no. 20 (1968): 444.
11. Ibid., 444.

Chapter 2

1. Jan Gehl and Lars Gemzøe, *New City Spaces* (Copenhagen: The Danish Architectural Press, 2000): 72-77.
2. Ibid., Chapter 1, note 14.
3. Clare Cooper Marcus is a public life study pioneer. She stressed the need to focus on women, children and the elderly. See Clare Cooper Marcus and Carolyn Francis, *People Places: Design Guidelines for Urban Open Spaces* (New York: Van Nostrand Reinhold, 1990).
4. Presentation for Gehl Architects by Bryant Park Corporation (BPC) President Dan Biederman, October 2011 in Bryant Park. Although public, the park is privately run and financed by the Corporation.
5. Material sent from Bryant Park plus the presentation by President Dan Biederman, October 2011 in Bryant Park.
6. Jan Gehl, "Mennesker til fods." ("People on Foot." In Danish), in *Arkitekten* no. 20 (1968): 432.
7. Jan Gehl and Lars Gemzøe, et al., *New City Life* (Copenhagen: The Danish Architectural Press, 2000).
8. Ibid., 9.
9. Jan Gehl, op. cit., *Cities for People*: 32.
10. William H. Whyte, *The Social Life of Small Urban Spaces* (New York: Project for Public Spaces, 1980): 94-97.
11. Jan Gehl, op. cit., "People on Foot": 435.
12. Ibid., 435.
13. Studies of the correlation between types of activities and their duration: Jan Gehl, op. cit., *Cities for People*: 92-95.

Chapter 3

1. A steady stream of people is a prerequisite for being able to conduct 10-minute headcounts. Counting has to be for longer intervals if there are fewer people. 10-minute headcounts are based on numerous studies conducted by Jan Gehl since the end of the 1960s.
2. Gehl Architects, *Chongqing Public Space Public Life Study and Pedestrian Network Recommendations* (Chongqing: City of Chongqing, 2010).
3. Jan Gehl, "Mennesker i byer." ("People in Cities." In Danish), in *Arkitekten* no. 20, 1968): 425-443.
4. Tracking registrations were made in December 2011 on Strøget, Copenhagen's main pedestrian street, by landscape architect Kristian Skaarup together with Birgitte Bundesen Svarre, Gehl Architects.
5. Jan Gehl, *The Interface between Public and Private Territories in Residential Areas* (Melbourne: Department of Architecture and Building, 1977): 63.
6. Ibid., Observations in connection with the Melbourne study were published here.
7. Jan Gehl, *Public Spaces and Public Life in Perth* (Perth: State of Western Australia 1994). Although pedestrian waiting time was reduced in the period up to the next public life study conducted in 2009, the second study documented that pedestrians in downtown Perth still had to push a button for a green light and do a considerable amount of waiting: Gehl Architects, *Public Spaces and Public Life Perth 2009* (City of Perth, 2009): 39. Sydney report: Gehl Architects, *Public Spaces Public Life Sydney 2007* (Sydney: City of Sydney, 2007).
8. Gehl Architects, *Public Spaces Public Life Sydney 2007* (Sydney: City of Sydney, 2007): 56.

Chapter 4

1. Gordon Cullen, *The Concise Townscape* (London: The Architectural Press, 1961).
2. Denmark adopted its first urban planning legislation in 1925. See Arne Gaardmand, *Dansk byplanlægning 1938-1992* (*Danish Urban Planning*. In Danish), (Copenhagen: The Danish Architectural Press, 1993): 11.
3. Camillo Sitte, *The Art of Building Cities* (Westport, Connecticut: Hyperion Press reprint 1979 of 1945 version). Originally published in German: Camillo Sitte, *Städtebau nach seinen künstlerischen Grundsätzen* Vienna: Verlag von Carl Graeser, 1889).
4. Le Corbusier, *Vers une architecture* (Paris: Editions Flammarion 2008 (1923)). First edition in English: Le Corbusier, *Towards a New Architecture* (London: The Architectural Press, 1927).
5. Ibid., The Athens Charter was drawn up at the Congrès International d'Architecture Moderne (CIAM) in Athens in 1933. Le Corbusier was a co-founder of the CIAM congresses.
6. Key figures on cars per household: Statistics Denmark, *Nyt fra Danmarks Statistik* (*Latest Release*. In Danish.), no. 168 (March 2012).
7. Key figures in diagram about household size: Statistics Denmark, *Danmark i Tal 2012* (*Statistics Yearbook 2012*. In Danish): 7.
8. National Institute of Public Health, *Folkesundhedsrapporten* (*Public Health Report*. In Danish), ed. Mette Kjøller, Knud Juel and Finn Kamper-Jørgensen (Copenhagen: National Institute of Public Health, University of Southern Denmark, 2007): 159-166. Ibid., "Dødeligheden i Danmark gennem 100 år." ("A Century of Mortality in Denmark." In Danish), 2004: 58 (age standardized). *Sundheds- og sygelighedsundersøgelserne* (*Health and Disease Studies*. In Danish), 2010: 73-98.
9. The Radburn principle gets its name from a 1928 plan for a new community, Radburn, in New Jersey. See Michael Southworth and Eran Ben-Joseph, *Streets and the Shaping of Towns and Cities* (Washington DC: Island Press, 1997): 70-76.
10. The Garden City Movement began in England, and the principles are stated in the form of a manifesto by the movement's founder: Ebenezer Howard, *Garden Cities of To-Morrow* (1898 or 1902) (Cambridge, MA: MIT Press, 1965, with an introductory essay by Lewis Mumford).
11. For example, in 1967 Jan Gehl criticized the newly built Høje Gladsaxe complex, then on the outskirts of Copenhagen, for its 'poverty of experience' and thus lack of inspiration for human creativity: Jan Gehl, "Vore fædre i det høje!" ("Our Fathers on High!" In Danish), in *Havekunst*, no. 48 (1967): 136-143.

12. Information on working hours (in Danish): http://www.den-storedanske.dk/Samfund,_jura_og_politik/%C3%98konomi/L%C3%B8nteorier_og_-systemer/arbejdstid (08.04.2013). Information on length of vacation (in Danish): www.den-storedanske.dk/Samfund,_jura_og_politik/%C3%98konomi/L%C3%B8nteorier_og_-systemer/arbejdstid (04-08-2013).

13. City of Copenhagen, *Copenhagen City of Cyclists. Bicycle Account 2010* (Copenhagen: City of Copenhagen, 2011).

14. Jane Jacobs, *The Death and Life of Great American Cities* (New York: Random House, 1993 (1961)): 3.

15. Ibid., back cover.

16. Gordon Cullen's book is the written foundation for the Townscape Movement, which started in England. The book is about creating connectivity and richness of experience for pedestrians between buildings, city space and streets. Gordon Cullen, *The Concise Townscape* (Oxford: The Architectural Press, 2000 (1961)).

17. Aldo Rossi, *L'Architettura della città* (Padova: Marsilio 1966); reprinted (Macerata: Edizione Quodlibet 2011); published in English in 1984 with an introduction by Peter Eisenman: Aldo Rossi, *The Architecture of the City* (Cambridge, MA: MIT Press, 1984).

18. Jane Jacobs, op. cit.

19. Ibid., 21-34.

20. Alice Sparberg Alexiou, *Jane Jacobs – Urban Visionary* (New Jersey: Rutgers University Press, 2006): 9-26, 57-67. Jan Gehl, "For you, Jane." in Stephen A. Goldsmith and Lynne Elizabeth (ed.): *What We See – Advancing the Observations of Jane Jacobs* (Oakland, California: New Village Press, 2010): 235.

21. Jane Jacobs: "Downtown is for People." (reprinted in *Fortune* Magazine, September 18, 2011). Originally published in 1958, written on the basis of a speech Jane Jacobs held at Harvard University in 1956. William H. Whyte invited Jane Jacobs to turn her speech into an article for the magazine.

22. The quote is from Paul Goldberger, architecture critic for the New York Times, in his foreword to *The Essential William H. Whyte*, ed. Albert LaFarge (New York: Fordham University Press, 2000): vii.

23. The Street Life Project received financial support from New York City's Planning Commission as well as a number of foundations.

24. William H. Whyte, *The Social Life of Small Urban Spaces* (New York: Project for Public Spaces, 1980).

25. William H. Whyte, *The Social Life of Small Urban Spaces*, film produced by The Municipal Art Society (New York, 1990).

26. William H. Whyte, op. cit.

27. Kevin Lynch, *The Image of the City* (Cambridge Mass.: MIT Press, 1960).

28. Christopher Alexander, *A Pattern Language* (Oxford: Oxford University Press, 1977).

29. Christopher Alexander, *The Timeless Way of Building* (Oxford: Oxford University Press, 1979).

30. Christopher Alexander, "The Timeless Way." In *The Urban Design Reader* (New York: Routledge 2007): 93-97.

31. Christopher Alexander, op. cit., *The Timeless Way of Building*: 754.

32. Christopher Alexander, op. cit., *A Pattern Language*: 600.

33. Clare Cooper Marcus and Wendy Sarkissian, *Housing as if People Mattered. Site Design Guidelines for Medium-Density Family Housing* (Berkeley: University of California Press, 1986): 43.

34. Ibid., vii-viii.

35. Clare Cooper Markus and Carolyn Francis, *People Places: Design Guidelines for Urban Open Spaces* (New York: Van Nostrand Reinhold, 1990): 6.

36. Clare Cooper Markus and Marni Barnes, *Healing Gardens, Therapeutic Benefits and Design Recommendations* (New York: Wiley, 1999).

37. The studies were published in a book about the driver's experience of the city seen in movement: Donald Appleyard, Kevin Lynch and John R. Myer, *A View from the Road* (MIT Press, 1965).

38. Summary of *Livable Streets* (1980) in Donald Appleyard, "Livable Streets: Protected Neighborhoods?" (*Annals*, AAPSS, 451, September, 1980): 106. Ironically, Appleyard was hit and killed by a car.

39. The study was conducted at the end of the 1960s, but first published in the book: Donald Appleyard, *Livable Streets* (Berkeley: University of California Press, 1981): 16-24.

40. Jane Jacobs, op. cit., *The Death and Life of Great American Cities*.

41. Donald Appleyard, op. cit., *Livable Streets*.

42. Peter Bosselmann studied architecture in Germany and Los Angeles, and has been a professor of Urban Design at UC Berkeley since 1984.

43. Peter Bosselmann, *Representation of Places. Reality and Realism in City Design* (California: University of California Press 1998): xiii

44. Peter Bosselmann et al., *Sun, Wind, and Comfort. A Study of Open Spaces and Sidewalks in Four Downtown Areas* (Berkeley, CA: Institute of Urban and Regional Development, College of Environmental Design, University of California, Berkeley, 1984).

45. Peter Bosselmann, "Philosophy." Portrait on UC Berkeley's website: www.ced.berkeley.edu/ced/people/query.php?id=24 (06-15-2011).

46. Peter Bosselmann et al., op. cit.

47. Jan Gehl, *Cities for People* (Washington DC, Island Press, 2010): 183-184.

48. Peter Bosselmann, op. cit., *Representation of Places: Reality and Realism in City Design*.

49. Peter Bosselmann, *Urban Transformations* (Washington DC: Island Press, 2008).

50. Allan Jacobs, *Great Streets* (Cambridge Massachusetts: MIT Press, 1993): 15.

51. The "We like cities" quote comes from the manifesto that Allan Jacobs co-authored: Allan Jacobs and Donald Appleyard, "Toward an Urban Design Manifesto." In *The Urban Design Reader* (New York: Routledge, 2007, ed. Michael Larice and Elizabeth Macdonald): 108.

52. Allan Jacobs, "Conclusion: Great Streets and City Planning." In *The Urban Design Reader* (New York: Routledge, 2007, ed. Michael Larice and Elizabeth Macdonald): 387-390.

53. Allan Jacobs and Donald Appleyard, op. cit., 98-108.

54. Ibid., headlines and main points: 102-104.

55. Ibid., 104-108.

56. Ibid., 108.

57. Allan Jacobs, *Looking at Cities* (Cambridge, MA: Harvard University Press, 1985).

58. Allan B. Jacobs, op. cit., *Great Streets*.

59. Ibid., 170.

60. Reference is to Jan Gehl's book by the same name, which has become a classic in city life studies. Jan Gehl, *Life Between Buildings* (Copenhagen: The Danish Architectural Press, 1971, distributed by Island Press).

61. Inger and Johannes Exner, Amtsstuegården at Hillerød, 1962 (project not realized). See Thomas Bo Jensen, *Exner* (Risskov: Ikaros Academic Press, 2012).

62. See criticism of the newly built modernistic suburban buildings outside Copenhagen in: Jan Gehl, op. cit., "Our Fathers on High!": 136-143.

63. Jan and Ingrid Gehl, "Torve og pladser." ("Urban squares." In Danish), in *Arkitekten* no. 16, 1966: 317-329; Jan and Ingrid Gehl, "Mennesker i byer." ("People in Cities." In Danish), in *Arkitekten* no. 21, 1966: 425-443; Jan and Ingrid Gehl, "Fire italienske torve." ("Four Italian Piazzas." In Danish), in *Arkitekten* no. 23, 1966: 474-485.

64. Study of Piazza del Popolo, op. cit., "People in Cities.": 436.

65. Jan and Ingrid Gehl, op. cit., "Four Italian Piazzas.": 477.

66. Ibid., 474.

67. Jan and Ingrid Gehl, op. cit., "People in Cities.": 425.

68. Ibid., 425-27.

69. Jan and Ingrid Gehl, op. cit., "Four Italian Piazzas.": 484.

70. Jan Gehl, *Life Between Buildings* (New York: Van Nostrand Reinhold, 1987).

71. Jan Gehl, *Life Between Buildings* was published in Danish (1971), Dutch (1978), Norwegian (1980), English (1st edition, Van Nostrand Reinhold, 1987), Japanese (1990), Italian (1991), Chinese (1991), Taiwanese (1996), Danish (3rd edition, The Danish Architectural Press, 1996), English (3rd edition, The Danish Architectural Press, 1996), Czech (2000), Korean (2002), Spanish (2006), Bengali (2008), Vietnamese (2008), Polish (2010), Serbian (2010), Rumanian (2010), English (2010, new edition, Island Press) German (2012), Japanese (reissued 2012), Italian (reissued, 2012), Russian (2012), Thai (2013) and Greek (2013).

72. Ingrid Gehl, *Bo-miljø* (*Housing Environment*. In Danish), (Copenhagen: SBI report 71, 1971).

73. See Jan Gehl, "Soft Edges in Residential Streets." in *Scandinavian Housing and Planning Research*, no. 2, 1986: 89-102.

74. Jan Gehl, op. cit., *Life Between Buildings*, foreword.

75. Jan Gehl, Ibid., 82.

76. Claes Göran Guinchard, *Bilden av förorten* (*Playground Studies*. In Swedish) (Stockholm: Kungl. Tekniska Högskolan 1965); Derk de Jonge, "Seating preferences in restaurants and cafés." (Delft 1968); Derk de Jonge, "Applied hodology," *Landscape* 17 no. 2, 1967-68: 10-11. Since 1972 Rolf Monheim has studied pedestrian streets in the midst of many German cities, counting pedestrians, registering stationary activities, etc. For a summary, see: Rolf Monheim, "Methodological aspects of surveying the volume, structure, activities and perceptions of city centre visitors." In *GeoJournal* 46, 1998: 273-287.

77. For a treatment of public life studies and urban design, see: Anne Matan, *Rediscovering Urban Design through Walkability: an Assessment of the Contribution of Jan Gehl*, PhD thesis (Perth: Curtin University: Curtin University Sustainability Policy (CUSP) Institute, 2011).

78. As evidenced by the comprehensive collections of papers published in conjunction with the annual EDRA conferences. See for example: *Edra 42 Chicago, Conference Proceedings*, ed. Daniel Mittleman and Deborah A. Middleton, The Environmental Design Research Association, 2011.

79. *Variations on a Theme Park – The New American City and the End of Public Space*, ed. Michael Sorkin (New York: Hill and Vang, 1992).

80. About the late or postmodern conditions for society and the

rise of the network society, see, for example: Manuel Castells, *The Rise of the Network Society, The Information Age: Economy, Society and Culture Vol. I.* (Cambridge, MA; Oxford, UK: Blackwell, 1996); Frederic Jameson, *Postmodernism: The Cultural Logic of Late Capitalism*, (Durham, NC: Duke University Press, 1991); Edward Soja, *Thirdspace: Journeys to Los Angeles and Other Real-and-Imagined Places* (Oxford: Basil Blackwell, 1996).

81. Jan Gehl and Lars Gemzøe, et al., *New City Life* (Copenhagen: The Danish Architectural Press, 2000): 18

82. Ibid., 29.

83. Gehl Architects continues the tradition of collaboration with institutions of higher education, and studies are often conducted together with a local university and contain an educational element for observers.

84. For example, this is the case for Jan Gehl of Gehl Architects, Allan Jacobs as an independent consultant and the Project for Public Spaces (PPS) in New York.

85. 1968 study: Jan Gehl, "Mennesker til fods." ("People on Foot." In Danish), in *Arkitekten* no. 20 (1968): 429-446; 1986 study: Jan Gehl, Karin Bergdahl and Aase Steensen, "Byliv 1986. Brugsmønstre og Udviklingstendenser 1968-1986." ("Public Life 1986. Consumer Patterns and Development Trends 1968-1986." In Danish), in *Arkitekten* no. 12 1987: 285-300; 1996 study: Jan Gehl and Lars Gemzøe, *Public Spaces Public Life* (Copenhagen: The Danish Architectural Press and The Royal Danish Architecture School, 1996); 2006 study: Jan Gehl and Lars Gemzøe et al., *New City Life* (Copenhagen: The Danish Architectural Press, 2006)

86. Jan Gehl, Karin Bergdahl and Aase Steensen, "Byliv 1986." ("Public Life 1986." In Danish) in *Arkitekten*, 1986: 294-95; Jan Gehl and Lars Gemzøe, *Public Spaces Public Life* (Copenhagen: The Danish Architectural Press, 1996); Jan Gehl and Lars Gemzøe, et al., op. cit.

87. Jan Gehl, *Stadsrum og Stadsliv i Stockholms city* (*Public Space and Public Life in the City of Stockholm*. In Swedish) (Stockholm: Stockholm Fastighetskontor og Stockholms Stadsbyggnadskontor, 1990); Gehl Architects, *Stockholmsforsöket og Stadslivet i Stockholms Innerstad* (*Stockholm Study and Public Life in the Inner City*. In Swedish) (Stockholm: Stockholm Stad, 2006); City of Melbourne and Jan Gehl, *Places for People*, (Melbourne: City of Melbourne, 1994); City of Melbourne and Gehl Architects, *Places for People* (Melbourne: City of Melbourne, 2004); Jan Gehl, Government of Western Australia og City of Perth, *Public Spaces & Public Life in Perth* (Perth: Department of Planning and Urban Development, 1994); Gehl Architects, *Public Spaces and Public Life* (Perth: City of Perth, 2009); Gehl Architects, *Byens Rum og Byens Liv Odense 1998* (*Public Space and Public Life Odense 1998*. In Danish) (Odense: Odense Kommune, 1998); Gehl Architects, *Odense Byliv og Byrum* (*Odense Public Life and Public Space*. In Danish) (Odense: Odense Kommune, 2008).

88. Project for Public Spaces, Inc., *How to Turn a Place Around. A Handbook for Creating Successful Public Spaces* (New York: Project for Public Spaces, 2000): 35.

89. Ibid.

90. Jay Walljaspar, *The Great Neighborhood Book. A Do-it-yourself-Guide to Placemaking Book* (New York City: Project for Public Spaces, 2007).

91. Project for Public Spaces, Inc., op. cit., *How to Turn a Place Around*.

92. Leon Krier, *New European Quarters*, plan for New European Quarters (Luxembourg, 1978). Aldo Rossi, op. cit.

93. Donald Appleyard, op. cit., *Livable Streets*; Clare Cooper Marcus, op. cit., *Housing as if People Mattered*; Allan Jacobs, *Looking at Cities* (Cambridge, MA: Harvard University Press, 1985); Peter Bosselmann, op. cit., *Representation of Places. Reality and Realism in City Design*; Peter Bosselmann et al. op. cit., *Sun, Wind, and Comfort: A Study of Open Spaces and Sidewalks in Four Downtown Areas*.

94. Aldo Rossi, op. cit.

95. Richard Rogers and Philip Gumuchdjian, *Cities for a Small Planet* (London: Faber and Faber, 1997).

96. Congress for the New Urbanism, *Charter of the New Urbanism*, 2001, see www.cnu.org (04.19.2012). Although the charter is formulated in general terms, the work of the New Urbanists is concentrated on precisely formulated design guidelines.

97. Jan Gehl, op. cit., *Life Between Buildings*; Clare Cooper Marcus, op. cit., *Housing as if People Mattered*.

98. Jan Gehl, Ibid., 77-120.

99. Clare Cooper Marcus, op. cit.

100. Jan Gehl and Lars Gemzøe, et al. op. cit., 34-39.

101. For example, see chapter 6 in Jan Gehl, op. cit., *Cities for People*: 222-238.

102. While the term livable can be used to mean places that are barely tolerable to live in, the term is also used more positively about cities and places. Here the term is used as an expression of attractiveness and life quality.

103. The results of the studies can be found in Donald Appleyard, op. cit., *Livable Streets*.

104. The magazines *Monocle*, *The Economist* and *Mercer*, among others.

105. The U.S. Department of Transportation about livability, strategies and initiatives: www.dot.gov/livability (04-19-2012).

106. Ray LaHood, U.S. Secretary of Transportation, quoted from: www.dot.gov/livability (04-19-2012).

107. City of Copenhagen, *Metropolis for People* (Copenhagen: City of Copenhagen, 2009).

108. Ed. Stephen A. Goldsmith & Lynne Elizabeth, op. cit.

109. Jan Gehl, op. cit., *Cities for People*.

110. Ulrich Beck, *Risk Society: Towards a New Modernity* (London: Sage, 1992), originally published in German in 1986; United Nations, *Our Common Future* (Oxford: Oxford University Press, 1987); Hugh Barton, Catherine Tsourou, *Healthy Urban Planning* (London: Taylor & Francis, 2000); *Monocle* magazine launched its livability list in 2007, which was called 'The Most Livable City Index' from 2009. The statistics for the percentage of the population that lives in cities in Denmark is from Statistics Denmark *Befolkningen i 150 år* (*The Population for 150 Years*. In Danish) (Copenhagen: Statistics Denmark, 2000): 39% in 1900; more than two-thirds by 1950 and 85% in 1999.

111. Jan Gehl, op. cit., *Cities for People*: 239.

112. Ethan Bronner, "Bahrain Tears Down Monument as Protesters Seethe" in *The New York Times*, March 18, 2011, see: www.nytimes.com/2011/03/19/world/middleeast/19bahrain.html?_r=2& (04-08-2013).

113. *Beyond Zucotti Park. Freedom of Assembly and the Occupation of Public Space*, ed. Shiffman et al. (Oakland, CA: New Village Press, 2012).

114. Jane Jacobs wrote about the street's importance to safety, in particular that there are people on the street to act as a natural monitoring system, which she called having 'eyes on the street' Jane Jacobs, op. cit., *The Death and Life of Great American Cities*: 35.

115. Oscar Newman, *Defensible Space* (New York: Macmillan, 1972).

116. Mike Davis, *City of Quartz: Excavating the Future in Los Angeles* (Verso Books, 1990); Ulrich Beck, op. cit.

117. Ethan Bronner, op. cit.

118. The Realdania Foundation funded several centers in addition to the Center for Public Space Research, including the Center for Strategic Urban Research (2004-2009), Center for Housing and Welfare (2004-2009), and Center for Management Studies of the Building Process (2004-2010). During this period, Realdania invested approximately DKK 150 million in interdisciplinary environments primarily intended to study elements in the fields of architecture and urban planning that are not necessarily architectural works, such as strategies, welfare and life between buildings: public space. See www.realdania.dk (04-19-2012).

119. Quote from Jan Gehl on the purpose of the Center for Public Space Research in a press release from Realdania in conjunction with the inauguration of the Center: http://www.realdania.dk/Presse/Nyheder/2003/Nyt+center+for +byrumsforskning+30,-d-,10,-d-,03.aspx (12-20-2011).

120. Jan Gehl and Lars Gemzøe et al., op. cit.

121. Google Street View was introduced in 2007 (and came to Denmark in 2010). http://da.wikipedia.org/wiki/Google_Street_View (04-19-2012).

122. Henrik Harder, *Diverse Urban Spaces*, GPS-based research project at Aalborg University: www.detmangfoldigebyrum.dk (04-08-2013).

123. Noam Shoval, "The GPS Revolution in Spatial Research." In *Urbanism on Track*. Application of Tracking Technologies in Urbanism, ed. Jeroen van Schaick and Stefan van der Spek (Delft: Delft University Press, 2008): 17-23.

124. Bill Hillier and Julienne Hanson, *The Social Logic of Space* (Cambridge, UK: Cambridge University Press, 1984).

125. Bill Hillier, *Space as the Machine. A Configural Theory of Architecture* (Cambridge: Press Syndicate of the University of Cambridge, 1996) (London: Space Syntax 2007): vi.

126. www.spacesyntax.com (09-13-2012).

127. Bill Hillier and Julienne Hanson, op. cit.

128. Jane Jacobs, op. cit., *The Death and Life of Great American Cities*: 6.

Chapter 5

1. Jan Gehl and Ingrid Gehl, "Mennesker i byer." ("People in Cities." In Danish) in *Arkitekten* no. 21 (1966): 425-443.

2. For the edge effect, see Jan Gehl, *Life Between Buildings*, (Copenhagen: The Danish Architectural Press, 1971, distributed by Island Press): 141, with reference to Dutch sociologist Derk de Jonge, who studied the order in which recreational areas are used. Edges of woods, beaches, copses and clearings are chosen in preference to open fields and coastal areas: Derk de Jonge, "Applied Hodology." In *Landscape* 17, no. 2, 1967-68: 10-11. There is also a reference to Edward T. Hall for his explanation of the edge effect as mankind's penchant for being able to oversee space with back covered and suitable distance to others: Edward T. Hall, *The Hidden Dimension* (Garden City, New York: Doubleday, 1990 (1966)).

3. Plan, pictures and captions from Jan Gehl and Ingrid Gehl, op. cit., "People in Cities.": 436-437.

4. Photographs, diagram and captions on this page from Jan Gehl, "Mennesker til fods." ("People on Foot." In Danish), in *Arkitekten* no. 20 (1968): 430, 435.

5. Ibid., 429-446.

6. Ibid., 442.

7. Ibid., 442.

8. Jan Gehl and Ingrid Gehl, op. cit., "People in Cities.": 427-428.

9. Ibid.

10. Jan Gehl, "En gennemgang af Albertslund." ("Walking through Albertslund." In Danish), in *Landskab* no. 2 (1969): 33-39.

11. Ibid., 33-39. (Pictures and original text on opposite page)

12. Ibid., 34.

13. Torben Dahl, Jan Gehl et al., *SPAS 4. Konstruktionen i Høje Gladsaxe* (*Building in Høje Gladsaxe*. In Danish) (Copenhagen: Akademisk Forlag, 1969). SPAS: Sociology-Psychology-Architecture-Study group.

14. Jan Gehl, "Vore fædre i det høje!" ("Our Fathers on High!" In Danish), in *Havekunst*, no. 48 (1967): 136-143.

15. Torben Dahl, Jan Gehl et al., op. cit., *Konstruktionen i Høje Gladsaxe*: 4-16.

16. Jan Gehl, Freda Brack and Simon Thornton, *The Interface Between Public and Private Territories in Residential Areas* (Melbourne: Department of Architecture and Building, 1977): 77.

17. Ibid.

18. The importance of edges is a recurring theme in Jan Gehl's studies. For a summary see the section on "soft edges in residential areas" in Jan Gehl, *Cities for People* (Washington D.C.: Island Press, 2010): 84-98.

19. Map and captions from Jan Gehl, Freda Brack and Simon Thornton, op. cit., *The Interface Between Public and Private Territories in Residential Areas*: 63, 67.

20. The study of the Canadian residential streets was published initially in the first English edition of Jan Gehl's seminal work: Jan Gehl, *Life Between Buildings* (Copenhagen. The Danish Architectural Press, 1971, distributed by Island Press).

21. Jan Gehl, Ibid., 174.

22. First published in: Jan Gehl, Ibid., 164.

23. Jan Gehl, Ibid., 164.

24. Jan Gehl, Solvejg Reigstad and Lotte Kaefer, "Close Encounters with Buildings" in special issue of *Arkitekten* no. 9 (2004).

25. Ibid., 6-21.

26. Jan Gehl, op. cit., *Life Between Buildings*: 139-145.

27. Pictures and text from the latest version of façade assessment tools in Jan Gehl, op. cit., *Cities for People*: 250-251.

28. Jan Gehl, *Stadsrum og Stadsliv i Stockholms City* (*Public Space and Public Life in the City of Stockholm*. In Swedish) (Stockholm: Stockholms Fastighetskontor og Stockholms Stadsbyggnadskontor, 1990).

29. The reduced version of the quality criteria with 12 points was later published in Jan Gehl et al., *New City Life* (Copenhagen: The Danish Architectural Press, 2006): 106-107. The 12 points were used in that book to assess numerous public spaces in Copenhagen. The latest published version in book format is in Jan Gehl, op. cit., *Cities for People*: 238-239.

30. Jan Gehl et al., op. cit., *New City Life*: 106-107.

31. For human senses and needs related to public space, see Jan Gehl, op. cit., *Life Between Buildings*, inspired by, among others, Robert Sommer, *Personal Space: The Behavioral Basis of Design* (Englewood Cliffs N.J.: Prentice-Hall, 1969) and anthropologist Edward T. Hall, *The Hidden Dimension* (Garden City, New York: Doubleday, 1990 (1966)).

32. See the latest published version in Jan Gehl, op. cit., Cities for People: 238-239.

33. Ibid., 50 (diagram). Found in earlier versions: published initially in the first English edition of Jan Gehl's seminal work: *Life Between Buildings* (New York: Van Nostrand Reinhold, 1987, reprinted by Island Press, 2011).

34. See among others: Robert Sommer, op. cit., *Personal Space*; Edward T. Hall, *The Silent Language* (Garden City, N.Y. : Doubleday, 1959); Edward T. Hall, op. cit., *The Hidden Dimension*.

35. Jan Gehl, op. cit., *Cities for People*: 50.

36. William H. Whyte, *The Social Life of Small Urban Spaces* (New York: Project for Public Spaces 2001 (1980)): 72-73

37. Camilla Richter-Friis van Deurs from Gehl Architects conducted the experiment with workshop participants from Vest- and Aust-Agder County in Arendal, Norway, January 23, 2012.

38. Jan Gehl, op. cit., *Cities for People*: 27.

39. William H. Whyte, op. cit., *The Social Life of Small Urban Spaces*: 28.

40. Gehl Architects, *Byrum og Byliv. Aker Brygge, Oslo 1998* (*Public Space and Public Life. Aker Brygge, Oslo 1998.* In Norwegian) (Oslo: Linstow ASA, 1998).

41. Jan Gehl, op. cit., *Cities for People*: 27.

42. Donald Appleyard and Mark Lintell, "The Environmental Quality of City Streets: The Residents' Viewpoint." Journal of the American Institute of Planners, no. 8 (March 1972): 84-101. Later published in Donald Appleyard, M. Sue Gerson and Mark Lintell, *Livable Streets* (Berkeley, CA: University of California Press, 1981).

43. Donald Appleyard and Mark Lintell, *The Environmental Quality of City Streets: The Residents' Viewpoint* (Berkeley CA: Department of City and Regional Planning, University of California: year unknown): 11-21.

44. Illustration from Jan Gehl, op. cit., *Life Between Buildings*: 32.

45. Peter Bosselmann, *Representation of Places. Reality and Realism in City Design* (California: University of California Press, 1998): 62-89.

46. Ibid., 78.

47. William H. Whyte, op. cit., *The Social Life of Small Urban Spaces*: 36-37; 54-55.

48. Ibid., 55.

49. Ibid., 110.

50. Ibid., 36.

51. Ibid., 54.

52. Stefan van der Spek, "Tracking Pedestrians in Historic City Centres Using GPS." In *Street-level Desires. Discovering the City on Foot*, ed. F. D. van der Hoeven, M. G. J. Smit and S. C. van der Spek, 2008: 86-111.

53. Ibid.

Chapter 6

1. When Allan Jacobs received a Kevin Lynch Award in 1999, it was largely in response to his work for San Francisco, where he incorporated urban design into the city's planning documents: "As director of the City Planning Commission of San Francisco, Allan Jacobs pioneered the integration of urban design into local government planning, producing a plan that has given San Francisco some of its best places and, two decades later, still stands as a model of its kind." (http://www.pps.org/reference/ajacobs 04.04.2013). Peter Bosselmann has also recieved awards for his work with San Francisco and other American cities: See http://ced.berkeley.edu/ced/faculty-staff/peter-bosselmann (04-04-2013).

2. Jan Gehl, Karin Bergdahl and Aase Steensen, "Byliv 1986. Brugs-mønstre og Udviklingstendenser 1968-1986." ("Public life 1986. Consumer Patterns and Development Trends 1968-1986."), in *Arkitekten* no. 12 (1987): 285-300. Observation studies are often supplemented by interviews in public space-public life studies. While interviews are outside the scope of this book, naturally they are another of the methods relevant as supplements for observation studies.

3. Gehl Architects, *Towards a Fine City for People* (London: City of London, June 2004); Gehl Architects, *Public Spaces Public Life* (Sydney: City of Sydney, 2007).

4. Gehl Architects, op. cit., *Towards a Fine City for People*; New York City Department of Transportation, *World Class Streets: Remaking New York City's Public Realm* (New York: New York City Department of Transportation, 2008); Gehl Architects, *Moscow, Towards a Great City for People: Public Space, Public Life* (Moscow: City of Moscow, 2013), in press.

5. Anne Matan, *Rediscovering urban design through walkability: an assessment of the contribution of Jan Gehl*, Ph.D. thesis (Perth: Curtin University, Curtin University Sustainability Policy (CUSP) Institute, 2011).

6. Ibid., 278.

7. 1968: Car-free area: 20,000 m². Area per stationary activity: 12.4 m². 1986: Car-free area: 55,000 m². Area per stationary activity: 14.2 m². 1995: Car-free area: 71,000 m². Area per staionary activity: 13.9 m². Jan Gehl and Lars Gemzøe, *Public Spaces – Public Life* (Copenhagen: The Danish Architectural Press and The Royal Danish Academy of Fine Arts, School of Architecture Publishers, 1996): 59.

8. City of Melbourne and Gehl Architects, *Places for People* (Melbourne: City of Melbourne, 2004): 12-13; 32-33. The figures were collected for the study on the basis of the City of Melbourne's data.

9. Ibid., 30, 50.

10. Anne Matan, op. cit., *Rediscovering urban design through walkability: an assessment of the contribution of Jan Gehl*: 288.
11. Ibid.
12. The City of New York and Mayor Michael R. Bloomberg, *PlaNYC. A Greener, Greater New York* (New York: The City of New York and Mayor Michael R. Bloomberg, 2007).
13. The results of the study are incorporated in the document prepared by New York City Department of Transportation, *World Class Streets: Remaking New York City's Public Realm* (New York: New York City Department of Transportation, 2008).
14. The New York City Department of Transportation, *Green Light for Midtown Evaluation Report* (New York: New York City Department of Transportation, 2010): 1.
15. Article: Lisa Taddeo, "The Brightest: 16 Geniuses Who Give Us Hope: Sadik-Khan: Urban Reengineer." *Esquire*, Hearst Digital Media: http://www.esquire.com/features/brightest-2010/janette-sadik-khan-1210. Accessed on November 26, 2010 by Anne Matan and quoted in: Anne Matan, op. cit., *Rediscovering urban design through walkability: an assessment of the contribution of Jan Gehl*: 293.
16. Anne Matan, op. cit., *Rediscovering Urban Design Through Walkability: An Assessment of the Contribution of Jan Gehl*: 294.
17. The New York City Department of Transportation, op. cit., *Green Light for Midtown Evaluation Report*: 1.
18. Gehl Architects, op. cit., *Public Spaces Public Life Sydney*: 74-76.
19. Gehl Architects, op. cit., *Towards a Fine City for People: London*.
20. Chief Executive of Central London Partnership Patricia Brown in a letter to Jan Gehl, Gehl Architects, dated June 29, 2004.
21. Gehl Architects, op. cit., *Towards a Fine City for People: London*: 34-35.
22. Ibid., 35.
23. Atkins, *Delivering the New Oxford Circus* (London: Atkins August, 2010): 11.
24. About people's penchant for choosing the shortest route: Jan Gehl, *Cities for People* (Washington D.C.: Island Press, 2010): 135-137.
25. Gehl Architects, *Cape Town – a City for All 2005* (Gehl Architects and Cape Town Partnership, 2005).
26. Jan Gehl and Lars Gemzøe, op. cit., *Public Spaces - Public Life*: 34-37.
27. Jan Gehl, *Cities for People* (Washington D.C.: Island Press, 2010).
28. Ibid., 8-9.

Chapter 7

1. Jan Gehl and Lars Gemzøe, *Public Spaces - Public Life* (Copenhagen: The Danish Architectural Press and The Royal Danish Academy of Fine Arts School of Architecture Publishers, 2004 (1996)): 11.
2. Ibid., 12.
3. Jan Gehl and Ingrid Gehl, "Torve og Pladser." ("Urban Squares." In Danish), in *Arkitekten* (1966, no. 16): 317-329; Jan Gehl and Ingrid Gehl, "Mennesker i Byer." ("People in Cities." In Danish), in *Arkitekten* (1966, no. 21): 425-443; Jan Gehl and Ingrid Gehl, "Fire Italienske Torve" ("Four Italian Piazzas." In Danish), in *Arkitekten* (1966, no. 23): 474-485.
4. Jan Gehl, *Life Between Buildings* (Copenhagen: The Danish Architectural Press, 1971, distributed by Island Press).
5. Jan Gehl, Karin Bergdahl and Aase Steensen, "Byliv 1986. Brugsmønstre og Udviklingstendenser 1968-1986." ("Public Life 1986. Consumer Patterns and Development Trends 1968-1986". In Danish), in *Arkitekten* no. 12 1987: 285-300.
6. Jan Gehl and Lars Gemzøe, op. cit., *Public Spaces - Public Life*.
7. Jan Gehl, Lars Gemzøe, Sia Kirknæs, Britt Sternhagen, *New City Life* (Copenhagen: The Danish Architectural Press, 2006).
8. City of Copenhagen, *A Metropolis for People* (Copenhagen: City of Copenhagen, 2009).
9. Bente Frost in a conversation with Jan Gehl in 1996 in conjunction with the launch of a public space study, quoted freely from memory.
10. "Quality of Life. Top 25 Cities: Map and Rankings." in *Monocle* no. 55 (July-August 2012): 34-56.

BIBLIOGRAPHY

Alexander, Christopher. *A Pattern Language: Towns, Buildings, Construction*. New York: Oxford University Press, 1977.

Alexander, Christopher. *A Timeless Way of Building*. Oxford: Oxford University Press, 1979.

Alexiou, Alice Sparberg. *Jane Jacobs – Urban Visionary*. New Jersey: Rutgers University Press, 2006.

Appleyard, Donald, Lynch, Kevin og Myer, John R. *A View from the Road*. Cambridge MA: MIT Press, 1965.

Appleyard, Donald. *Livable Streets*, Berkeley: University of California Press, 1981.

Appleyard, Donald. "Livable Streets: Protected Neighborhoods?" in *Annals*, AAPSS, 451, (September, 1980)

Appleyard, Donald and Lintell, Mark. *The Environmental Quality of City Streets: The Residents' Viewpoint*. Berkeley CA: Department of City and Regional Planning, University of California: year unknown, p. 11-2-1.

Atkins. *Delivering the New Oxford Circus*. London: Atkins August, 2010.

Barton, Hugh og Tsourou, Catherine. *Healthy Urban Planning*, London: Taylor & Francis, 2000.

Beck, Ulrich. *Risk Society: Towards a New Modernity* (1986). London: Sage, 1992.

Beyond Zucotti Park. *Freedom of Assembly and the Occupation of Public Space*. ed. Shiffman et al. Oakland, CA: New Village Press, 2012.

Bosselmann, Peter. *Representation of Places – Reality and Realism in City Design*. Berkeley, CA: University of California Press, 1998.

Bosselmann, Peter et al. *Sun, Wind, and Comfort. A Study of Open Spaces and Sidewalks in Four Downtown Areas*. Environmental Simulation Laboratory, Institute of Urban and Regional Development, College of Environmental Design, University of California, Berkeley, 1984.

Bosselmann, Peter. *Urban Transformation*. Washington DC: Island Press, 2008.

Bronner, Ethan. "Bahrain Tears Down Monument as Protesters Seethe" in *the New York Times*, March 18, 2011, see: www.nytimes.com/2011/03/19/world/middleeast/19bahrain.html?_r=2& (04-08-2013).

Castells, Manuel. *The Rise of the Network Society. The Information Age: Economy, Society and Culture Vol. I*. Cambridge, MA; Oxford, UK: Blackwell, 1996.

Charter of new urbanism: www.cnu.org

City of Copenhagen, *Copenhagen City of Cyclists. Bicycle Account 2010*, Copenhagen: City of Copenhagen, 2011.

City of Copenhagen, *A Metropolis for People*. Copenhagen: City of Copenhagen, 2009.

City of Melbourne and Gehl Architects. *Places for People*. Melbourne: City of Melbourne, 2004.

The City of New York and Mayor Michael R. Bloomberg. *PlaNYC. A Greener, Greater New York*. New York: The City of New York and Mayor Michael R. Bloomberg, 2007.

Le Corbusier. *Vers une Architecture* (1923). Paris: Editions Flammarion, 2008.

Le Corbusier. *Towards a New Architecture*. London: The Architectural Press, 1927.

Cullen, Gordon. *The Concise Townscape*. London: The Architectural Press, 1961.

Dahl, Torben. Gehl, Jan et al., *SPAS 4. Konstruktionen i Høje Gladsaxe* (Building in Høje Gladsaxe. In Danish), Copenhagen: Akademisk Forlag, 1969.

Danish dictionary: www.ordnet.dk

Danish encyclopedia: www.denstoredanske.dk

Danish Union of Journalists, The. *Fotografering og Privatlivets Fred*. (*Photographing and Privacy*. In Danish), Copenhagen: Dansk Journalistforbund, March 1999.

Davis, Mike. *City of Quartz. Excavating the Future in Los Angeles*. New York: Verso Books, 1990.

Edra 42 Chicago, Conference Proceedings, ed. Daniel Mittleman og Deborah A. Middleton. The Environmental Design Research Association, 2011.

The Endless City: The Urban Age Project by the London School of Economics and Deutsche Bank's Alfred Herrhausen Society. ed. Ricky Burdett og Deyan Sudjic, London: Phaidon, 2007.

Gaardmand, Arne. *Dansk byplanlægning 1938-1992*. (*Danish Urban Planning*. In Danish), Copenhagen: Arkitektens Forlag, 1993.

Gehl Architects. *Byrum og Byliv. Aker Brygge, Oslo 1998*. (*Public Space and Public Life. Aker Brygge, Oslo 1998*. In Norwegian.) Oslo: Linstow ASA, 1998.

Gehl Architects. *Cape Town – a City for All 2005*, Gehl Architects and Cape Town Partnership, 2005.

Gehl Architects. *Chongqing. Public Space Public Life*. Chongqing: The Energy Foundation and The City of Chongqing, 2010.

Gehl Architects. *Moscow – Towards a Great City for People. Public Space, Public Life*. Moskva: City of Moscow, 2013.

Gehl Architects, *Odense Byrum og Byliv. (Odense Public Life and Public Space*. In Danish) Odense: Odense Kommune, 2008.

Gehl Architects. *Perth 2009. Public Spaces & Public Life*. Perth: City of Perth, 2009.

Gehl Architects. *Public Spaces, Public Life. Sydney 2007*. Sydney: City of Sydney, 2007.

Gehl Architects. *Stockholmsförsöket och Stadslivet i Stockholms Innerstad*. (*Stockholm Study and Public Life in the Inner City*. In Swedish), Stockholm: Stockholm Stad, 2006.

Gehl Architects. *Towards a Fine City for People. Public Spaces and Public Life – London 2004*. London: Transport for London, 2004.

Gehl, Ingrid. *Bo-miljø.* (*Housing Environment.* In Danish), København: SBi-report 71, 1971.

Gehl, Jan. *Cities for People,* Washington D.C.: Island Press, 2010.

Gehl, Jan. "Close Encounters with Buildings.", in *Urban Design International*, no. 1 (2006) p. 29-47.

Gehl, Jan. "En gennemgang af Albertslund." ("Walking through Albertslund." In Danish), in *Landskab* no. 2, (1969), p. 33-39.

Gehl, Jan. "For You, Jane" in Stephen A. Goldsmith and Lynne Elizabeth (ed.): *What We See – Advancing the Observations of Jane Jacobs.* Oakland, California: New Village Press, 2010.

Gehl, Jan. *Life Between Buildings.* New York: Van Nostrand Reinhold, 1987, reprinted by Island Press, 2011.

Gehl, Jan. "Mennesker til fods." ("People on Foot." In Danish), in *Arkitekten*, no. 20 (1968), p. 429-446.

Gehl, Jan Gehl. *Public Spaces and Public Life in Central Stockholm.* Stockholm: Stockholm Stad, 1990.

Gehl, Jan. *Public Spaces and Public Life in Perth*, Perth: State of Western Australia, 1994.

Gehl, Jan. "Soft Edges in Residential Streets", in *Scandinavian Housing and Planning Research* 3 (1986), p. 89-102.

Gehl, Jan. *Stadsrum & Stadsliv i Stockholms city.* (*Public Space and Public Life in the City of Stockholm.* In Swedish),

Stockholm: Stockholms Fastighetskontor and Stockholms Stadsbyggnadskontor, 1990.

Gehl, Jan. *The Interface Between Public and Private Territories in Residential Areas.* Melbourne: Department of Architecture and Building, 1977.

Gehl, Jan. "Vore fædre i det høje!" ("Our Fathers on High!" In Danish), in *Havekunst*, no. 48 (1967), p. 136-143.

Gehl, Jan, K. Bergdahl, and Aa. Steensen. "Byliv 1986. Bylivet i Københavns indre by brugsmønstre og udviklingsmønstre 1968-1986". ("Public Life 1986. Consumer Patterns and Development Trends 1968-1986." In Danish), in *Arkitekten*, no. 12 (1987).

Gehl, Jan; A. Bundgaard; E. Skoven. "Bløde kanter. Hvor bygning og byrum mødes." ("Soft Edges. The Interface Between Buildings and Public Space." In Danish), in *Arkitekten*, no. 21 (1982), p. 421-438.

Gehl, Jan; L. Gemzøe, S.; Kirknæs, B. Sternhagen. *New City Life.* Copenhagen: The Danish Architectural Press, 2006.

Gehl, Jan and Ingrid. "Fire Italienske Torve" ("Four Italian Piazzas." In Danish), in *Arkitekten,* no. 23 (1966).

Gehl, Jan and Ingrid. "Mennesker i byer." ("People in Cities." In Danish), in *Arkitekten* no. 21 (1966), p. 425-443.

Gehl, Jan and Ingrid. "Torve og pladser." ("Urban Squares." In Danish), in *Arkitekten* no. 16 (1966), p. 317-329.

Gehl, Jan; L. J. Kaefer; S. Reigstad. "Close Encounters with Buildings," in *Arkitekten*, no. 9 (2004), p. 6-21.

Gehl, Jan and L. Gemzøe. *Public Spaces Public Life*. Copenhagen: The Danish Architectural Press and The Royal Danish Architecture School 1996.

Gehl, Jan and L. Gemzøe. *New City Spaces*. Copenhagen: The Danish Architectural Press 2001.

Guinchard, Claes Göran. *Bilden av förorten*. (*Playground Studies*. In Swedish). Stockholm: Kungl. Tekniska Högskolan, 1965.

Hall, Edward T. *The Silent Language* (1959). New York: Anchor Books/Doubleday, 1990.

Hall, Edward T. *The Hidden Dimension*. Garden City, New York: Doubleday, 1966.

Harder, Henrik. *Diverse Urban Spaces*. Ålborg Universitet: www.detmangfoldigebyrum.dk.

Hillier, Bill. *Space as the Machine. A Configuration Theory of Architecture*. (Cambridge: Press Syndicate of the University of Cambridge 1996) London: Space Syntax, 2007.

Hillier, Bill. Hanson, Julienne. *The Social Logic of Space*. Cambridge, UK: Cambridge University Press, 1984.

Howard, Ebenezer. *Garden Cities of To-Morrow* (1898 or 1902), Cambridge, MA: MIT Press, 1965.

Jacobs, Allan. *Great Streets*. Cambridge Mass.: MIT Press, 1993.

Jacobs, Allan. *Looking at Cities*. Cambridge, MA: Harvard University Press, 1985.

Jacobs, Allan and Appleyard, Donald. "Toward an Urban Design Manifesto" in *The Urban Design Reader*. New York: Routledge (2007), ed. Michael Larice and Elizabeth Macdonald, 2010

Jacobs, Jane. "Downtown is for People.", *Fortune* classic, reprinted in *Fortune* (September 8, 2011)

Jacobs, Jane. *The Death and Life of Great American Cities* (1961). New York: Random House, 1993.

Jameson, Frederic. Postmodernism: *The Cultural Logic of Late Capitalism,* Durham, NC: Duke University Press, 1991.

Jensen, Thomas Bo. *Exner*. Risskov: Ikaros Academic Press, 2012.

de Jonge, Derk. "Seating Preferences in Restaurants and Cafés." Delft, 1968.

de Jonge, Derk. "Applied Hodology". *Landscape* 17 no. 2 (1967-68).

Lynch, Kevin. *The Image of the City*. Cambridge MA: MIT Press, 1960.

Marcus, Clare Cooper and Barnes, Marni. *Healing Gardens, Therapeutic Benefits and Design Recommendations*. New York: Wiley, 1999.

Marcus, Clare Cooper and Sarkissian, Wendy. *Housing as if People Mattered: Site Design Guidelines for Medium-Density Family Housing*. Berkeley: University of California Press, 1986.

Marcus, Clare Cooper and Francis, Carolyn. *People Places: Design Guidelines for Urban Open Spaces*. New York: Van Nostrand Reinhold, 1990.

Matan, Anne. *Rediscovering urban design through walk-ability: an assessment of the contribution of Jan Gehl*, PhD Dissertation, Perth: Curtin University: Curtin University Sustainability Policy (CUSP) Institute, 2011.

Monheim, Rolf. "Methodological Aspects of Surveying the Volume, Structure, Activities and Perceptions of City Centre Visitors" in *GeoJournal* 46 (1998) p. 273-287.

National Institute of Public Health, *Folkesundhedsrapporten* (*Public Health Report*. In Danish), ed. Mette Kjøller, Knud Juel and Finn Kamper-Jørgensen. Copenhagen: National Institute of Public Health, University of Southern Denmark, 2007.

Newman, Oscar. *Defensible Space: Crime Prevention through Urban Design*. New York: Macmillan, 1972.

New York City Department of Transportation. *Green Light for Midtown Evaluation Report*. New York: New York City Department of Transportation, 2010.

New York City Department of Transportation. *World Class Streets: Remaking New York City's Public Realm*. New York: New York City Department of Transportation, 2008.

Perec, Georges. *An Attempt at Exhausting a Place in Paris*. Cambridge, MA: Wakefield Press, 2010.

Perec, Georges. *Life A User's Manual*. London: Vintage, 2003.

Perec, Georges. *Species of Spaces and Other Pieces*. London: Penguin, 1997.

Perec, Georges. *Tentative d'Épuisement d'un Lieu Parisien*. Paris: Christian Bourgois, 1975.

Perec, Georges. *Things: A Story of the Sixties*. London: Vintage, 1999.

Project for Public Spaces, Inc. *How to Turn a Place Around: A Handbook for Creating Successful Public Spaces*, New York: Project for Public Spaces, Inc., 2000.

Realdania: www.realdania.dk.

Rogers, Richard and Gumuchdjian, Philip. *Cities for a Small Planet,* London: Faber and Faber, 1997.

Rossi, Aldo. *L'Architettura della città*. Padova: Marsilio 1966; reprinted Macerata: Edizione Quodlibet, 2011.

Rossi, Aldo. *The Architecture of the City*. Cambridge, MA: MIT Press, 1984.

Sitte, Camillo. *The Art of Building Cities* (Westport, Connecticut: Hyperion Press reprint 1979 of 1945 version). Originally published in German: Camillo Sitte, *Städtebau nach seinen Künstlerischen Grundsätzen*. Vienna: Verlag von Carl Graeser, 1889.

Shoval, Noam. "The GPS revolution in spatial research" in *Urbanism on Track. Application of Tracking Technologies in Urbanism*. ed. Jeroen van Schaick og Stefan van der Spek, Delft: Delft University Press 2008, p. 17-23.

Soja, Edward. *Thirdspace: Journeys to Los Angeles and Other Real-and-Imagined Places*. Oxford: Basil Blackwell, 1996.

Sommer, Robert. *Personal Space: The Behavioral Basis of Design*. Englewood Cliffs N.J.: Prentice-Hall, 1969.

Southworth, Michael and Ben Joseph, Eran. *Streets and the Shaping of Towns and Cities*, Washington DC: Island Press, 1997.

Space Syntax: www.spacesyntax.com.

van der Spek, Stefan. "Tracking Pedestrians in Historic City Centres Using GPS" in *Street-Level Desires: Discovering the City on Foot*. Ed. F. D. van der Hoeven, M. G. J. Smit og S. C. van der Spek 2008.

Statistics Denmark. *Befolkningen i 150 år* (*The Population over 150 Years*. In Danish), Copenhagen: Danmarks Statistik, 2000.

Statistiks Denmark. *Danmark i tal 2012* (*Statistics Yearbook 2012*. In Danish), Copenhagen: Danmarks Statistik, 2012.

Statistics Denmark. *Nyt fra Danmarks Statistik* (*Latest Release*. In Danish), no. 168 March, 2012.

Taddeo, Lisa. "The Brightest: 16 Geniuses Who Give Us Hope: Sadik-Khan: Urban Reengineer". *Esquire*, Hearst Digital Media: www.esquire.com/features/brightest-2010/janette-sadik-khan-1210 (04-11-2013).

The Essential William H. Whyte. ed. Albert LaFarge with a preface by Paul Goldberger, New York City: Fordham University Press, 2000.

"The Most Livable City Index." *Monocle* (issues 5 (2007), 15 (2008), 25 (2009), 35 (2010), 45 (2011), 55 (2012) and 65 (2013). London: Winkontent Limited, Southern Print Ltd., 2007-2013.

The Urban Design Reader, ed. Michael Larice og Elizabeth Macdonald. New York: Routledge, 2007.

United Nations. *Our Common Future*. Oxford: Oxford University Press, 1987.

ILLUSTRATION AND PHOTO CREDITS

Shaw and Shaw, p. 22 top and bottom
Gordon Cullen, *The Concise Townscape* (1961), p. 48
Michael Varming, p. 54 bottom
Project for Public Space, pp. 62, 77
Peter Bosselmann, p. 64 top, pp. 67, 128-129.
Ahlam Oun, p. 82 bottom
Allan Jacobs, p. 68
Allan Jacobs, *Great Streets, with permission of the author and The MIT Press, p. 69*
Andrew Boraine, Cape Town Partnership, p. 154
Atkins London, Westminster City Council, Transport for London, The Crown Estate, p. 153
City of Melbourne, p. 145 left and right
City of Sydney, p. 150
Donald Appleyard og Mark Lintell, p. 126
JW Foto, p. 124
Leon Krier, p. 78 top and bottom
New York City, Department of Transportation, p. 148-149
Stefan van der Spek, TU Delft, pp. 84, 132, 133
Space Syntax, pp. 86, 87
Stadsarkivet, City of Copenhagen, p. 164 top, p. 168 top
Ursula Bach, photo of Tina Saaby Madsen, p. 158
William H. Whyte, Project for Public Spaces, p. 130-131

Jan Gehl, Lars Gemzøe and **Gehl Architects**
all other photos.

Camilla Richter-Friis van Deurs and **Janne Bjørsted**
all other illustrations.